Fundamentals of
ActionScript 3.0
DEVELOP AND DESIGN

Doug Winnie

Peachpit
Press

Fundamentals of ActionScript 3.0: Develop and Design
Doug Winnie

Peachpit Press

1249 Eighth Street
Berkeley, CA 94710
510/524-2178
510/524-2221 (fax)

Find us on the Web at: www.peachpit.com
To report errors, please send a note to errata@peachpit.com
Peachpit Press is a division of Pearson Education
Copyright © 2012 by R. Douglas Winnie

Editor: Nancy Peterson
Production editor: Myrna Vladic
Development editor: Robyn G. Thomas
Copyeditor: Liz Merfeld
Technical Editor: Christopher Coudron
Cover design: Aren Straiger
Cover production: Mimi Heft
Interior design: Mimi Heft
Compositor: Danielle Foster
Indexer: Jack Lewis

ISBN 13: 978-0-321-77702-7
ISBN 10:   0-321-77702-6

9 8 7 6 5 4 3 2 1

Printed and bound in the United States of America

This book is dedicated to Hoover. Hoover was a big part of my life,

and was always by my side while doing "tech-no" things. I miss you Hoover!

This book is also dedicated to my husband, Mike.

While not always into my "tech-no" things, he is my inspiration for doing

great things—"tech-no" or not. Thanks, Groovy Dude!

ACKNOWLEDGEMENTS

With too many people to mention individually, I'm going to do a group acknowledgement of all of the members of the Adobe Flash Professional, Flash Player, AIR, and Flex teams that have inspired me to create great things, and to a platform that overcomes amazing obstacles to give creative and web professionals the ability to express themselves wherever they go.

I also want to acknowledge Chris Coudron, my tech reviewer and friend, for his effort to make me look good in code and for reminding me that there is not a NOR operator in ActionScript. D'oh!

CONTENTS

Introduction xiii

Welcome to ActionScript 3.0 xvi

PART 1 GETTING THE FUNDAMENTALS

CHAPTER 1 ACCESSING AND MANIPULATING OBJECTS **2**

Creating a New Project for ActionScript 3.0 4

Accessing Objects on the Stage 5

Sending Messages to the Output Panel 8

Working with Object Parameters 12

Wrapping Up 19

CHAPTER 2 DYNAMICALLY ADDING OBJECTS TO THE STAGE **20**

Creating Named Library Assets 22

Introducing the Display Stack 25

Creating New Objects on the Stage *25*

Messing with the Display Stack *29*

Assigning Properties to Dynamically Created Instances ... *30*

Working with Comments 31

Creating Comments *31*

Working with Spaces *32*

Wrapping Up 33

CHAPTER 3 WORKING WITH FUNCTIONS **34**

Fundamentals of Functions 36

Accepting Values in Functions 39

Possible Errors when Working with Functions *42*

Required Parameter Error *42*

Type Mismatch Error *43*

Returning Values from Functions 44

More about Parentheses (and Curly Braces) *46*

Wrapping Up 47

CHAPTER 4 ACTIONSCRIPT AND MATH **48**

Mathematical Operators 50

Addition and Subtraction *50*

Addition or Concatenation? *51*

Multiplication and Division *53*

*Modulo, the Operator Formerly Known as Long Division
with Remainders* *53*

Variables and Combined Assignment Operators 55

Variables *56*

Combined Assignment Operators *57*

Increment and Decrement Operators 58

Order of Operations 60

Using Parentheses to Force Order 62

Summing up Math Operations 64

Wrapping Up 65

CHAPTER 5   **CREATING EVENTS** **66**

Events: Explained 68

Creating a Mouse Event Handler 70

Adding Other Events 74

Wrapping Up 76

CHAPTER 6   **USING TIMELINE SCRIPTING WITH MOUSE EVENTS** **78**

Explaining the Project 80

Controlling Timeline Playback 81

Stopping Playback *81*

Seeking to a Specific Frame *83*

Working with MovieClip Timelines 85

Using the Event Callback Object and Handling Scope 87

The Event Callback Object *87*

Using the Event Callback Object *89*

Shortcuts for gotoAndStop( ) *92*

The Finished Example *92*

Another e *Example* *94*

Working with Simple Callback Functions 96

Wrapping Up 97

CHAPTER 7   **CREATING TIMER AND FRAME EVENTS** **98**

Using the Timer Event 100

Stopping the Timer *102*

Using the Enter Frame Event 104

Removing Event Listeners 106

When to Use Frame vs. Timer Events 108

Wrapping Up 111

PROJECT 1   **COUNTDOWN CLOCK** **112**

Project Specification: Countdown Clock 114

Visual Design Review 115

Kick-Off Meeting Notes: Countdown Clock 116

Solution and Walkthrough: Countdown Clock 117

Project Setup in Flash Professional *117*

ActionScript Setup *119*

Auto-Generated Imports *121*

Display Objects *122*

Event Listener for the Start Button *123*

Timer and Timer Event Listeners *124*

Callback Function for Starting the Timer *124*

Callback Functions for Timer Events *125*

Wrapping Up 127

PART 2 EXPLORING THE BASICS OF CLASSES

CHAPTER 8   **WHAT IS A CLASS?** **130**

Overview of a Class 132

Variables Revealed 133

Creating a Class 134

Wrapping Up 138

CHAPTER 9   **BUILDING OUT THE CLASS** **140**

Parts of a Class 142

Package *Statement* *142*

Import *Statement* *142*

Class *Statement* *143*

Class Constructor *143*

Creating a Class Instance 144

Adding Constructor Parameters 146
Customizing the Button Label *146*
Customizing Multiple Properties *148*
Making Constructor Parameters Optional *150*
Creating Methods 152
Accessing Methods from Outside the Class 153
Wrapping Up 154

CHAPTER 10   **DOING MORE WITH CLASSES** **156**
What is the public Keyword for? 158
Restricting Access with private 161
Using Best Practices for Naming Private Members 163
Getters and Setters: Keeping Things Polite 164
Creating Getter and Setter Methods *165*
Using the get and set Statements *166*
Going Frame-Script-Free: Creating a Document Class 169
Creating an Initialization Method *171*
Wrapping Up 173

CHAPTER 11   **ORGANIZING YOUR CLASSES** **174**
Your Package Has Been Delivered 176
Creating a Package Folder *176*
Referring to All Classes in a Package *180*
Creating Nested Packages *182*
Changing the Source Path *183*
Wrapping Up 187

PART 3   **RESPONDING TO CONDITIONS AND WORKING WITH LOGIC**

CHAPTER 12   **CONDITIONALS** **190**
Boolean Variables and Equality 192
Testing for Equality *194*
Testing for Inequality *195*
Demonstrating Equality and Inequality *196*

Building Drag and Drop for the Mouse *198*

Adding Feedback *200*

Testing Conditions 202

The if *Statement* *204*

The if...else *Statement* *206*

The if...else *if statement* *209*

Wrapping Up 213

CHAPTER 13 **ADVANCED BOOLEAN LOGIC AND RANDOM NUMBERS** **214**

Using Logic Operators 216

The AND *Operator* *217*

The OR *Operator* *218*

The NOT *Operator* *218*

Building Complex Conditionals 219

Generating Random Numbers 221

Wrapping Up 225

CHAPTER 14 **WORKING WITH TEXT AND THE KEYBOARD** **226**

Working with Text Fields 228

Customizing the Text Style 231

Making Changes to Style Later on *233*

Creating Your Own ActionScript Fonts *234*

Creating the Quiz Layout 238

Working with Escape Sequences *241*

Creating the KeyboardEvent Handler 246

Differences between Code Types: Key Codes versus
Character Codes *250*

Recognizing Special Keys *251*

Wrapping Up 254

CHAPTER 15 **CREATING GROUPS OF OBJECTS AND REPEATING**
ACTIONS USING LOOPS **256**

What Are Loops? 258

Using the for *Loop* *258*

Controlling the Flow of Loops with break *and* continue *261*

Nesting Loops *262*

Another Style of Loops, the do *Loop* *264*

Creating Groups of Items with Arrays 265
Modifying an Array 266
Using Loops to Create Arrays 269
Looping through an Array 274
Wrapping Up 277

PROJECT 2   **DICEOUT!** **278**
Project Specification: DiceOut 280
Visual Design Review: DiceOut 281
Kick-Off Meeting Notes: DiceOut 283
Solution and Walkthrough: DiceOut 284
Overview of the Document Class 284
Walkthrough of the Document Class 288
Wrapping Up 297

PART 4   GETTING CREATIVE WITH ACTIONSCRIPT

CHAPTER 16   **DRAWING WITH ACTIONSCRIPT** **300**
Drawing and Code 302
Sprites: MovieClips without Timelines 302
Your First Shape 303
Extending the Sprite *Class* 305
Drawing Lines and Working with Strokes 307
Drawing Ahead of the Curve 312
Drawing Shapes 315
Using Fills 318
Building Gradients 321
Looping with the Drawing API 326
Wrapping Up 330

CHAPTER 17   **ANIMATION USING ACTIONSCRIPT** **332**
ActionScript Animation = Location + Time 334
Moving an Object Using a Timer 336
Creating Random Animations 338
Animating Multiple Objects with Loops 343

Fine-Tuning Animations 348

Wrapping Up 366

CHAPTER 18 **WORKING WITH EXTERNAL MEDIA** 368

Using Images 370

Playing Audio from the Web 373

Playing Video from the Web 376

Altering the Playback of Video 379

Pausing Video 382

Rewind and Seek 384

Wrapping Up 389

PART 5 CREATING MULTI-SCREEN PROJECTS

CHAPTER 19 **DESKTOP APPLICATIONS WITH ADOBE AIR** 392

Getting Started 394

Working with Desktop Events 397

Minimize 397

Maximize 398

Drag 401

Close 404

Resize 406

Creating a Resizable Layout 411

Configuring Your AIR Project 419

Icons 419

Certificate 420

Publish and Install 422

Wrapping Up 425

CHAPTER 20 **MOBILE APPLICATIONS WITH ADOBE AIR** 426

Getting Started 428

Setting Up Your Testing Devices 429

Creating a Mobile Project 431

Your First Android Application 431

Your First iOS Application 434

Creating Interactions for Devices 439
Tip, Tap—Basic Touch Interactions 439
Simple Dragging with Touch 442
Taking Your Time with Long Touches 445
Working with Gesture Events 450
Pinch to Zoom 450
Rotate 455
Debugging over USB 458
Debugging on Android 458
Debugging on iOS 460
Optimizing Content 463
Wrapping Up 465

PROJECT 3   **FLIPR** **466**
Project Specification: Flipr 468
Visual Design Review: Flipr 469
Kick-Off Meeting Notes: Flipr 470
Solution and Walkthrough: Flipr 471
Review of the Flash Professional Project 471
Review of the Document Class 475
Display the Splash Screen 479
Display the Main Controls 480
Create the Game Logic 482
Create the Game Board 491
Set Up the Score and Timer Displays 493
Set Up the Player Controls and Game Rules 494
Wrapping Up 501

APPENDIX A   **CONFIGURING YOUR MOBILE ENVIRONMENT** **502**
Setting Up an Android Device for Testing 504
Setting Up an iOS Device for Testing 506

Index 512

INTRODUCTION

Welcome to ActionScript. Over the next several chapters, you'll be introduced to one of the most versatile programming languages to create web applications for the browser, desktop applications, and mobile apps for multiple platforms. For years the Flash Platform has provided people with the most powerful set of technologies to creatively express themselves across multiple screens and platforms with its combination of the Flash Player and AIR runtimes, tools like Flash Professional CS5.5 and Flash Builder 4.5, and languages and frameworks like ActionScript 3.0 and Flex 4.5.

Over the last several years, I have taught people how to make their projects interactive and how to captivate and engage users. During that time at San Francisco State University, my series on Adobe TV, and conference appearances, I have appreciated the difficulty of learning scripting and coding. Learning programming is a steep task, and there are many ways to teach it. What I have found is that combining programming basics, simple examples, problem solving, and real-world projects has been very effective, and it is what you have in your hands (or on your screen) now.

WHO THIS BOOK IS FOR

This book is crafted for people who are familiar with Flash Professional, the animation and interactive design tool from Adobe Systems that is part of Creative Suite. The lessons and projects here assume that you have a basic understanding of the Flash Professional product. This book is designed for people who are new to coding or are struggling with the migration from ActionScript 2.0 to 3.0. Here are some examples of what you should know and be able to do before attempting to start with this book:

- Import graphical assets from Creative Suite design tools

- Create timeline animations using tweens using keyframes

- Create symbols using the Library panel

- Organize and rename timelines in the Timeline panel and symbols in the Library panel

- Publish and build animations for the web browser

With these basic skills, you can create very interesting web animations; however, without ActionScript, the animations lacked any interaction with the user, and there is no way to bring them to other platforms including mobile devices. That is exactly what this book will teach you—how to make these projects interactive and take them further.

The latest edition, Flash Professional CS5.5, has added a significant number of new features to support mobile app creation that are covered at the end of the book.

WHO THIS BOOK IS NOT FOR

If you are already an intermediate or advanced coder, this book may be too basic for your needs. There are a significant number of books that focus on advanced ActionScript 3.0 concepts, including the adoption of best practices and code design patterns that will make you a better and more proficient coder.

In addition, if you have never worked with Flash Professional, I recommend you learn how to use the basic product before tackling the contents here. There are excellent books available to help you learn how to get started with Flash Professional to create animations and how to master design workflows when working with Creative Suite design applications like Photoshop, Illustrator, and Fireworks.

HOW YOU WILL LEARN

This book has a specific methodology for how the concepts are introduced. First are the fundamentals of how to interact and work with objects that are on the Stage. The examples that are in the book are simple—and this is intentional, to help you understand how ActionScript works without getting into the weeds of your project's design or assets. You can adapt and expand these simple examples for your own projects.

After you gather a sizable amount of new ActionScript know-how, it is time to put it to work. There are three major projects in the book that pose real-world situations for you to solve using the skills you have learned. The projects present you with a programming challenge and ask you to solve it. You can compare your finished projects with the examples in the book to discover how your approach matches or differs.

WHAT YOU WILL LEARN

This book is divided into five major parts.

PART 1: GETTING THE FUNDAMENTALS

You'll learn general ActionScript concepts that you can use to make ActionScript interact with objects on the Stage and in the Library of your project. You'll build on this, understanding how to flow your code through reusable modules called functions, and then how to respond to user interaction with event handlers.

PART 2: EXPLORING THE BASICS OF CLASSES

You'll jump into the basics of what is called object-oriented programming (OOP), which is what separates the coders from the scripters. Through OOP you can unlock a lot of flexibility in how you create projects, learning how to make reusable objects and containers that can extend the sophistication of your projects.

PART 3: RESPONDING TO CONDITIONALS AND WORKING WITH LOGIC

Adapting your project based on certain conditions then is the focus of the next section, where through the use of conditionals, your project can adapt to different interactions from the user or even to random events to begin introducing gaming concepts to your project.

PART 4: GETTING CREATIVE WITH ACTIONSCRIPT

Although ActionScript is a programming language, it has its creative side. This is covered in the fourth section, where you will learn how to draw, animate, and work with external assets in your projects.

PART 5: CREATING MULTI-SCREEN PROJECTS

After you have mastered all the previous topics, it is time to take your projects out of the browser and take advantage of the Flash Platform to create desktop applications for Windows and Mac OS X operating systems and mobile apps for the popular Android and iOS platforms.

You'll cover a lot, but at the end, you'll have a solid foundation on how Action-Script works and the power that you have at your fingertips to express yourself across screens and platforms.

So let's get started!

WELCOME TO ACTIONSCRIPT 3.0

ActionScript 3.0 is the programming language of the Adobe Flash Platform, a multi-screen and mutli-device development platform for creating interactive and expressive content. With the latest generation of the Adobe runtimes, Flash Player and AIR, you can take your ideas and creative vision to the browser, desktop, mobile phones, tablets, and Internet-enabled televisions. Let's review some of the tools that you'll be working with.

THE TOOLS AND RUNTIMES

In the course of this book, there are three main tools and runtimes that you'll be working with:

FLASH
PROFESSIONAL CS5.5

The latest generation of the Flash authoring tool combines powerful animation capabilities, library management, and an integrated coding environment designed for ActionScript 3.0 coding. Part of Creative Suite 5.5, Flash Professional CS5.5 adds new support to work with the latest generation of Adobe AIR and Flash Player 10.2 to create content and applications for the popular Android and iOS mobile platforms.

FLASH PLAYER 10.2

Flash Player is what brings the web to life. It is the Internet plug-in for your desktop or mobile phone that allows you to play interactive content, video, and games. The latest version includes enhanced support for hardware acceleration, better video playback, and memory and processor performance optimization.

ADOBE AIR 2.6

The Adobe AIR runtime is what allows interactive designers and developers to take their applications outside the browser and bring them to the Windows and Mac OS X operating systems as desktop applications, or to the Android and iOS platforms as installable mobile applications.

OTHER HELPFUL TOOLS

Although not part of this book, there are other tools that are helpful for working with the Flash Platform, including:

ADOBE FLASH BUILDER 4.5

Flash Builder is the professional coding IDE for the Flash Platform. It includes advanced programming functionality to optimize projects, and it makes working with larger projects and coordinating projects with teams easier. Flash Builder also supports working with Flash Professional projects and using the Adobe Flex framework.

ADOBE FLEX 4.5

The Flex framework is used specifically to create data-driven applications for the browser, desktop, and mobile devices. Incorporating skinnable components, declarative layout, ActionScript logic, and support for a growing set of platforms, it is the fastest way to create a robust application for multiple screens and devices.

ADOBE FLASH CATALYST CS5.5

Flash Catalyst is designed to work in a team environment when a designer and a developer are building an Internet application using the Flex framework. Interaction designers can create skins for Flex components and craft the overall user interface of a Flex application as a wireframe, prototype, or a finished application. Flash Catalyst CS5.5 introduces round-trip functionality with Flash Builder 4.5 to allow designers and developers to work collaboratively.

PART 1

GETTING THE FUNDAMENTALS

1

ACCESSING AND MANIPULATING OBJECTS

ActionScript gives everyone the ability to add interactivity to graphics, video, and other items that are placed on the Stage. In order to add this functionality, ActionScript needs a way to access the various objects that are on the Stage. In this opening section, you'll learn how to access these objects so you can later add basic interactivity.

In this chapter, you'll learn how to change the visual properties of objects that you place on the Stage. To do this, you'll discover more about the importance of converting objects to symbols and giving objects names, called *instance names*. You'll create your first ActionScript code to change how things look on the screen. Along the way, you'll learn some powerful tools to help Flash communicate back to you through the Output panel with messages that can help you see how your code is working.

CREATING A NEW PROJECT
FOR ACTIONSCRIPT 3.0

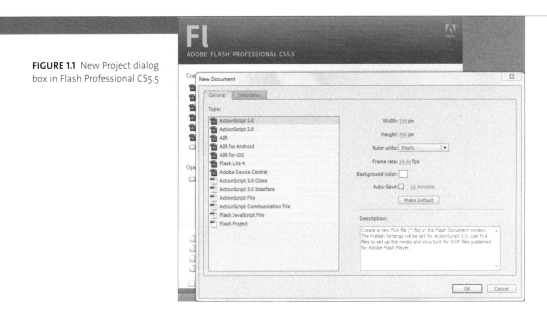

FIGURE 1.1 New Project dialog box in Flash Professional CS5.5

When you create a new file in Flash, you need to define which version of Action-Script you're going to work with. In addition, if you're creating an application for a mobile device, like a phone or tablet using the new AIR for Android or iOS feature, you need to specify that when you start your project. You can alter your settings later on, but knowing the ActionScript version and the deployment device ahead of time will help your workflow when working with Flash Professional CS5.5.

1. Launch Flash Professional CS5.5.

2. Select New from the File menu.

   You'll then be prompted with the New Project dialog box (**Figure 1.1**), where you can define the new project type.

3. Choose ActionScript 3.0 as the Type.

   The projects in this book use the ActionScript 3.0 language. You should also choose ActionScript 3.0 if you are building a basic project for a web browser.

ACCESSING OBJECTS
ON THE **STAGE**

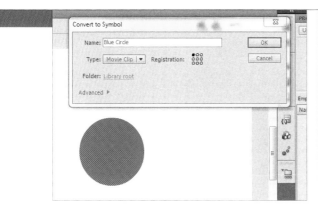

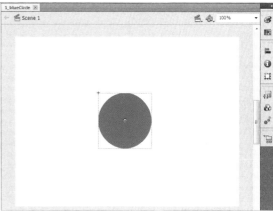

When you create a new file in Flash, you create objects, place them on the Stage, and animate them using the timeline. You can access each of these items through ActionScript if you follow a couple of general rules.

FIGURE 1.2 Convert to Symbol dialog box

FIGURE 1.3 Blue Circle MovieClip

- You must convert the visual objects you want to access using ActionScript to a MovieClip. This is a special type of object in Flash that can be connected to ActionScript commands.

- You must give each instance a unique name.

Let's start with a simple example using a generic circle.

1. Draw a circle on the Stage using the Flash drawing tools.

   To work with the circle on the timeline, or with ActionScript, you need to convert it to a MovieClip.

2. Right-click the circle and select Convert to Symbol to convert it to a MovieClip.

   All MovieClips must have a name, which you can define in the Convert to Symbol dialog box (**Figure 1.2**).

3. Name the MovieClip **Blue Circle**. It will be listed as Blue Circle in the Library (**Figure 1.3**).

FIGURE 1.4 Sticky note "stacks" as Library objects versus individual notes as instances

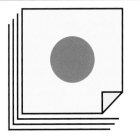
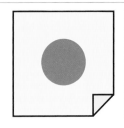
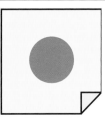

Stack of "Blue Circle" MovieClips

Instance of "Blue Circle"

Another instance of "Blue Circle"

A good way to think of this is to imagine that the Blue Circle in the Library is an infinite stack of sticky notes, each looking exactly the same; in this case a moderately large blue circle. When you want to put one of these circles on the Stage, you peel off one of the sticky notes and place it on the Stage. This is called an *instance* of the symbol. No matter how many sticky notes you put on the Stage, they are all from the same sticky pad, looking exactly the same (**Figure 1.4**).

When you place the sticky note on the Stage, you need to have some way of referring to it. The name Blue Circle refers to the stack of sticky notes, not the individual instances. To refer to each instance discretely, you need to give it a unique instance name. The instance name is a special name that refers to only that specific instance.

4. Select the instance on the Stage, and open the Properties panel. The field at the top of the panel is where you enter the unique name for this instance of the circle. Name it **circle_1** (**Figure 1.5**).

Instance names can contain letters, numbers, and underscores, but no other punctuation marks. They can never start with numbers. In addition, instance names generally are not capitalized; capitalized words in ActionScript refer to a different type of object that we'll cover a bit later.

Now the instance of your circle (MovieClip) has a name, and you're ready to access it using ActionScript.

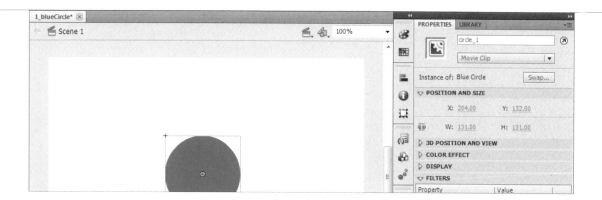

RULES FOR NAMING INSTANCES USING CAMEL CASE

FIGURE 1.5 Instance name defined as circle_1 in the Properties panel

There is a best practice for naming instances. It is called *camel case*, and it involves combining multiple words together in a format that is easy to read but is also a legal name that ActionScript will accept.

Camel case rules specify that the first letter of the instance name is lower-case, and then separate words are combined together without spaces, but each word is capitalized.

For instance, if you have "red box", camel case rules would make that "redBox". The first word, "red", is not capitalized, and the second word, "box", is capitalized, and is added after "red" without a space.

You can use this for multiple words, and it is an established best practice with developers that works in ActionScript and other languages.

SENDING MESSAGES TO
THE OUTPUT PANEL

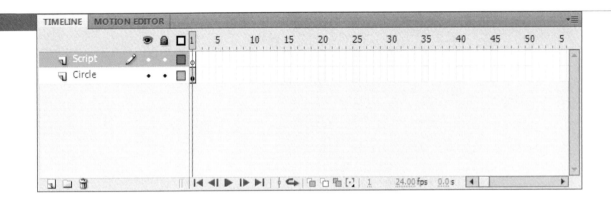

FIGURE 1.6 Timeline layers created and named

Before you create any ActionScript, I want to point out that there is more than one way to create ActionScript in Flash Professional CS5.5. The type you are going to use initially is a *frame script*, where you create some code that you place on the timeline itself. The other method is a *class-based script*, which you'll learn about in a future chapter and will use for the rest of the book.

A frame script exists in the timeline on the keyframe of your choosing. Usually, frame scripts exist on Frame 1, with other scripts on other frames for when you want to stop or branch your animation or content. Frame scripts are usually on their own timeline *layer*. These layers refer to the various rows of timelines you can create in your project in the Timeline panel. Before you continue, name the current layer and then create a new one.

1. Double-click the current layer name and rename it **Circle**.

2. Create a new layer by clicking the new layer button at the bottom of the Timeline panel ▯.

3. Label the new layer **Script**.

   The new layer will have a blank keyframe denoted by a hollow circle on the first keyframe; the layer containing the Blue Circle MovieClip has a filled circle (**Figure 1.6**).

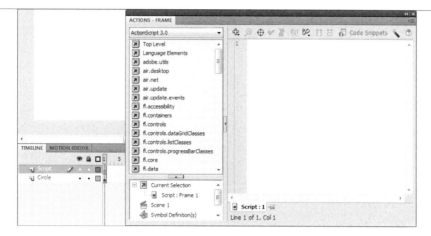

FIGURE 1.7 Frame 1 selected and the Actions panel open

Now that you have created a layer for the scripts, you need to begin writing ActionScript using the Actions panel in Flash Professional CS5.5. The Actions panel allows you to add ActionScript to frames on the timeline. Before opening the Actions panel, you need to select where you want to place the script before writing your code.

4. Select Frame 1 in the Script layer on the timeline.

5. Open the Actions panel from the Window menu (**Figure 1.7**).

You're going to enter some code in the Actions panel that won't make much sense yet, but just follow along and everything will be explained fully in a bit.

NOTE: You won't be using the left side of the Actions panel. To collapse it, click the disclosure icon to the right of the left column.

6. Enter the following in the Actions panel (**Figure 1.8**):

```
trace("Hello ActionScript!");
```

You might see some tool tips pop up while you type. Don't worry, you can ignore them for now; just make sure that the line of code is typed and spelled correctly. In code, spelling and capitalization count, and frequently the most frustrating errors are caused by a typo, so make sure you pay attention to your spelling and capitalization.

7. Open the Control menu and select Test Movie > Test, making sure that Flash Professional is selected (**Figure 1.9**). You can also use the keyboard shortcut Control-Enter (Windows) or Command-Enter (Mac).

8. Test the project. You will see a preview of the movie, with the circle, and the Output panel will open (**Figure 1.10**).

The Output panel displays the message "Hello ActionScript." The ActionScript trace statement takes what's in the parentheses and sends it to the Output panel. In this case, it is the contents inside the quotation marks. Note that the quotation marks aren't displayed. The quotes let ActionScript know when a piece of text begins and ends. Text is also known as a *string* in ActionScript.

The trace statement is helpful to send yourself messages that may help you debug issues or monitor what is going on in your application. Statements sent to the Output panel using trace do not appear when you publish to Flash Player or AIR; they are used only when you're working within Flash and are testing your project.

Congratulations, you have successfully written and executed your first ActionScript command! Now, if only everything were that easy, right?

FIGURE 1.8 ActionScript code added to the Actions panel

FIGURE 1.9 Menu command to test movie

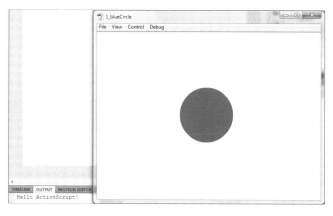

FIGURE 1.10 Publish preview with Output panel opened

WORKING WITH OBJECT PARAMETERS

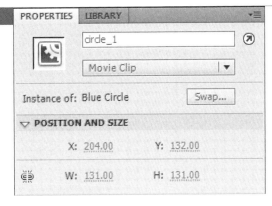

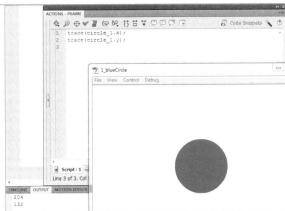

FIGURE 1.11 Properties of the circle_1 instance

FIGURE 1.12 Output panel with x and y coordinate locations

Now that you have the basics down, you'll start writing some ActionScript that will manipulate the blue circle that you have on the Stage.

Every object, symbol, graphic, and animation has properties, or attributes, that define certain parts or values. For example, the circle on the Stage has a few obvious properties right off the bat.

Based on the Properties panel, you know that the circle has a value for its width, height, and its position on the x and y axes (**Figure 1.11**).

You can access these properties using ActionScript to read their current value or to send new values that overwrite the existing ones.

To access these, you need to identify the object you are working with, which is why you need to give all the instances unique instance names.

1. With Frame 1 selected in the Script layer, delete the trace statement that you placed earlier and enter in the following:

```
trace(circle_1.x);
trace(circle_1.y);
```

2. Run the movie from the Control menu again. You'll see the same movie, but you'll see two numbers appear in the Output panel (**Figure 1.12**).

These two lines are accessing the circle_1 instance on the Stage, accessing the location of the object on the x axis, and sending that to the trace statement, which sends the value to the Output panel. It repeats the process again but for the location of the instance on the y axis.

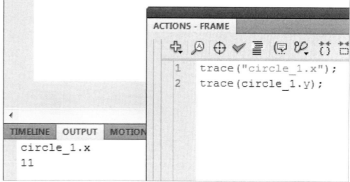

So you have successfully accessed the x and y properties of the instance of the circle on the Stage.

FIGURE 1.13 Output panel with x- and y-coordinate locations after moving on the Stage

FIGURE 1.14 Output panel with string and y coordinate

3. Move the location of the circle on the Stage and run the movie again. You'll see that the values sent to the Output panel change to reflect the x and y properties of the new location (**Figure 1.13**).

   Notice that unlike the first time you used the `trace` statement, there are no quotation marks before or after the contents in the parentheses. If you remember, the quotation marks indicate the begin and end points of a sequence of text. Instead of a discrete set of text, or string, you are accessing a stored value for the x and y coordinates. These are also called *variables*.

   Variables are containers that store data. They can be accessed or modified through ActionScript. When you refer to variables, or variable properties of instances, you don't use quotation marks. Change the first line to illustrate this.

4. Insert quotation marks before and after the contents of the parentheses so your code looks like this:

   ```
   trace("circle_1.x");
   trace(circle_1.y);
   ```

5. Run the movie. Notice that the first line of the Output panel contains the text "circle_1" and then the next line contains a number (**Figure 1.14**). That is because you told the `trace` statement to use the string identified with the

FIGURE 1.15 Circle repositioned at the 0,0 coordinate

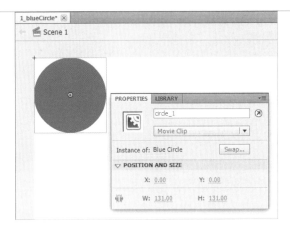

quotation marks instead of accessing the x coordinate variable property of the circle_1 instance.

So now that you are able to access the instance's properties, you can change them using ActionScript. Before continuing though, move the object to the upper-left corner of the Stage.

6. Using the Properties panel, enter **0** for the x coordinate and **0** for the y coordinate (**Figure 1.15**).

Next, you'll overwrite the values that are stored in the Properties panel with values you'll define in ActionScript. When you run the movie, the ActionScript code will run and immediately replace the x and y values of the circle_1 instance.

When accessing values of objects, you use their names as placeholders, and ActionScript finds the values that they hold and then replaces the names with the actual values. All MovieClips have a set of properties. In this example, you have been working with the x and y properties of the object. These map to the x and y coordinates on the Stage.

When you want to change a value in a variable, you need to assign a value to it by using the assignment operator, which is an equals sign (=).

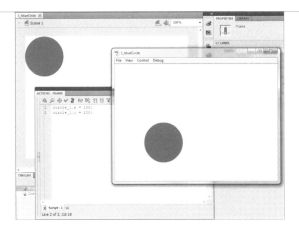

FIGURE 1.16 Circle repositioned at coordinate 100,200 using ActionScript

7. In the Actions panel, replace the contents with the following code:

```
circle_1.x = 100;
circle_1.y = 200;
```

This code accesses the x and y properties of the circle_1 instance and assigns the values on the right side of the assignment operator to them. So for the x coordinate, the x property value is 100, for the y coordinate, the y property value is 200.

The period between `circle_1` and x and y indicates that you are accessing the x and y properties of the instance named before the period, in this case `circle_1`. This is called *dot notation*, where you can select properties of objects by chaining them together using periods.

I should also point out the semicolons at the end of each line. The semicolons at the end of the line tell ActionScript when you have finished with a specific action. Consider them the "periods" of your ActionScript "sentences." They are required, so be sure you include them!

8. Run the movie. Notice that even though the circle was positioned at the upper-left corner of the Stage (at coordinate 0,0), the ActionScript overwrote those settings and placed the object at a new location (**Figure 1.16**).

To prove that ActionScript is overwriting the manual settings for the instance, add some more code to track the values of the coordinates.

FIGURE 1.17 Displaying the before and after positions of the object

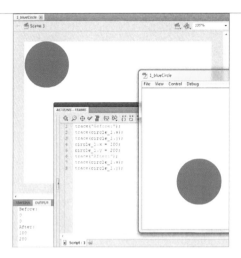

9. Update the Actions panel with the highlighted lines in the following code:

```
trace("Before:");
trace(circle_1.x);
trace(circle_2.y);
circle_1.x = 100;
circle_1.y = 200;
trace("After:");
trace(circle_1.x);
trace(circle_2.y);
```

10. Run the movie. Notice that the Output panel shows the values are still 0 and 0 when the movie starts, but the assignment operator overwrites the initial values with the new coordinates. The Flash runtime then shows them at the desired location (**Figure 1.17**).

You might ask why you didn't see the circle at the first 0,0 coordinate when the project ran. The simplest explanation is that the operation ran so fast that Flash Player didn't have a chance to display it at the first location. As you continue to work with ActionScript, you'll learn how you can time the changes to properties to display them like an animation.

There are a lot of properties that you can modify using ActionScript. Some of the more popular ones are listed in **Table 1.1**.

There are some properties listed in Table 1.1 that use property values that are either "true" or "false." To use these, you need to assign the value true or false to the property. Take a look at the visible property as an example.

TABLE 1.1 Common MovieClip properties

PROPERTY	DESCRIPTION	VALUES
.alpha	Sets the transparency level of an object. A low value makes the object more transparent, a high value makes it more opaque.	0 (Invisible) through 1 (fully opaque)
.width	Defines the width of an object in pixels.	Decimal number greater than 0
.height	Defines the height of an object in pixels.	Decimal number greater than 0
.x	Defines the x coordinate of an object, based on its registration point, in pixels.	Decimal number, positive or negative
.y	Defines the y coordinate of an object, based on its registration point, in pixels.	Decimal number, positive or negative
.scaleX	Widens an object based on a percentage value. A value of 1 (100%) keeps an object at its natural size. A value of .5 (50%) scales the width down 50%. To double the width, use a value of 2 (200%).	Decimal number greater than 0
.scaleY	Changes the height of an object based on a percentage value. A value of 1 (100%) keeps an object at its natural size. A value of .5 (50%) scales the height down 50%. To double the height, use a value of 2 (200%).	Decimal number greater than 0
.rotation	Rotates the object, in degrees, in a clockwise direction.	Decimal number, positive or negative
.visible	Determines if an object is visible or not.	true (visible), false (not visible)

FIGURE 1.18 Visibility set to false

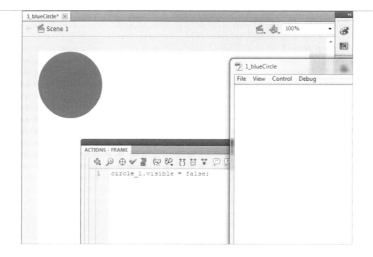

11. Add the following code to the end of your ActionScript:

```
circle_1.visible = false;
```

Notice that the value false isn't placed in quotation marks. This is a special value type called *Boolean* that you'll learn about in a future chapter.

12. Run the movie. Notice that the object is no longer visible. The instance is still there, but you told Flash Player to hide it by changing the visible property to be false (**Figure 1.18**).

WRAPPING **UP**

Using basic ActionScript commands, you can get and set common properties of MovieClips that you have on the Stage. To do this successfully you need to keep the following in mind:

- Give your object an instance name using the Properties panel while the object is selected on the Stage.

- Refer to the instance name when getting or assigning a property value.

- Use dot notation to work with properties that are part of instances.

- Use the assignment operator (=) when you want to assign a value to a property of an object.

- Place semicolons at the end of each ActionScript statement to signal the end of an action to ActionScript.

- Remember to use quotation marks when displaying text, or strings, but not around instance names.

With these general rules, you can start playing with the properties for objects you have on the Stage. In the next chapter, you'll learn how to add objects to the Stage exclusively with ActionScript.

2

DYNAMICALLY **ADDING OBJECTS** TO THE **STAGE**

Now that you know how to access and manipulate objects that are already on the Stage, you'll learn how to add objects dynamically from the Library using ActionScript.

The difference with this method is that the objects you are going to manipulate are not placed on the Stage in the Flash application, also called at *authortime*. Instead, you'll use objects that are in the Library, and after the application is compiled into a SWF, you'll dynamically update the Stage using ActionScript with objects in the Library.

CREATING NAMED LIBRARY ASSETS

If you remember, in order to access the properties or attributes of items on the Stage, you needed to have an instance name that ActionScript could reference. When you place objects on the Stage from the Library, you need unique instance names as well. You need to give a name to the "stack of sticky notes" in the Library to let ActionScript take an instance of the stack and place it on the Stage.

1. Create a new ActionScript 3.0 project in Flash Professional CS5.5.

2. On the Stage, create a simple circle and convert it to a symbol.

3. Name the symbol **Blue Circle** and make sure MovieClip is selected as the symbol type.

   Generally in Flash, objects that you dynamically place on the Stage need to be MovieClips. Before you click OK though, you need to give ActionScript a name it can use to place an instance of the circle on the Stage.

WHAT IS THE **DIFFERENCE** BETWEEN A **MOVIECLIP** AND A **GRAPHIC?**

When you create a symbol, you'll notice that you have a choice of three symbol types: MovieClip, Graphic, and Button. When working with Action-Script, only MovieClips can be targeted using ActionScript. When you use the Graphic type, you cannot control it with ActionScript. Graphic symbols are for use in animations or designs that need to be encapsulated in a reusable symbol format, but aren't intended to be controlled with ActionScript.

Button is an object type as well, but it is a pared down version of a MovieClip that was commonly used in earlier versions of ActionScript. You can continue to use it, but it is far less flexible than a MovieClip, and as a best practice you should use MovieClips instead of Buttons.

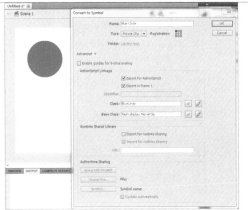

BlueCircle Class

circle_1 instance   circle_2 instance
of BlueCircle class   of BlueCircle class

4. Access the Advanced portion of the window.

    With this view open, you'll see an ActionScript Linkage section in the middle. This section is used to give the object a name that you can use to place it on the Stage.

5. Select the Export for ActionScript check box.

    The Class and Base Class fields will auto fill with **BlueCircle** and **flash.display.MovieClip**.

    When you're finished, your Convert to Symbol dialog box should look like the one in **Figure 2.1**.

    Unlike names given to objects in the Library, names used for ActionScript cannot contain spaces. That is why the Class field doesn't have a space. A Class is the way that ActionScript represents the "stack." The "stack" of blue circles is called the BlueCircle class. You can see this analogy if you look again at the diagram from Chapter 1 (**Figure 2.2**).

    In order for Flash to know what type of object it is, it needs to have a base class defined; in this case it's flash.display.MovieClip. You can ignore the items before "MovieClip" for now; you'll learn about those in future chapters. Just know that the stack of blue circles is now referred to as the BlueCircle class.

FIGURE 2.1 Convert to Symbol dialog box, Advanced mode section

FIGURE 2.2 Another look at the stack and instances with ActionScript names

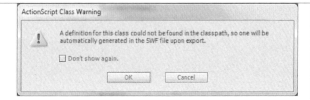

ActionScript Class Warning

⚠ A definition for this class could not be found in the classpath, so one will be automatically generated in the SWF file upon export.

☐ Don't show again.

OK   Cancel

PROPERTIES   LIBRARY

Untitled-1

1 item

Name   ▲ | AS Linkage
🖼 Blue Circle   BlueCircle

FIGURE 2.3 Error message that can be ignored, for now

FIGURE 2.4 Library panel displaying the Blue Circle object, linked to the BlueCircle class

6. Click OK. You'll get an error message (**Figure 2.3**).

    You can ignore this error message for now. In the future, you'll be creating a special ActionScript file that will define how the BlueCircle class works and behaves.

    In the Linkage column of the Library, you'll see that the Blue Circle item is linked to BlueCircle, the class name you'll be using in ActionScript to create instances of the Blue Circle (**Figure 2.4**).

NOTE: The error message that displays is notifying you that a special ActionScript file called a Class hasn't been defined for this object. Later in the book, you'll learn how to create these files.

INTRODUCING THE DISPLAY STACK

In Flash, there are some rules that define how items are displayed in the window. All displayed items are part of a special group called the *display stack*. The display stack is a list from which you can remove or add objects. As you create instances of objects using ActionScript, they won't be displayed until you add them to this special group.

So why have the display stack? At times, you may want to create an object and be able to modify it, but not actually display it for the user. It could be an item that isn't ready for use quite yet, or something that needs to be hidden from time to time. The object is still there, but just can't be seen.

In the past, Flash users would set the `.visible` property to `false` to hide an item, or they would set the `.alpha` value to zero. Either property setting has the same effect, but if you have a significant number of items, it can slow down playback.

CREATING NEW OBJECTS ON THE STAGE

So now that you know about the display stack, it's time to write some code. Creating objects in ActionScript from the Library is pretty straightforward now that you know about classes and the display stack.

Since you are going to place the circle using just code, you need to remove any objects you have on the Stage.

1. Select the circle on the Stage in Flash and delete it.

2. Create a new timeline for your ActionScript code in your now-empty ActionScript 3.0 project.

3. Name the timeline **scripts.**

4. Select the empty frame in the new scripts timeline.

5. Open the Actions panel.

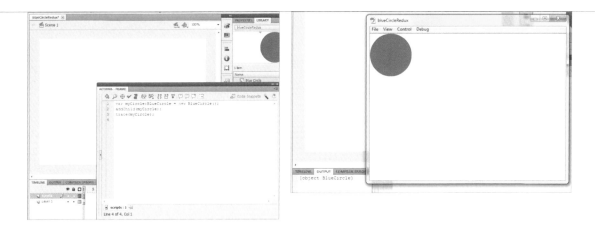

FIGURE 2.5 Actions and
Timeline panels with new
code added

FIGURE 2.6 Dynamically
placed BlueCircle object

6. In the Actions panel, type in the following code:

   ```
   var myCircle:BlueCircle = new BlueCircle();
   addChild(myCircle);
   trace(myCircle);
   ```

   When you're finished, your project should look like the one shown in
   Figure 2.5:

7. Run the code.

   You'll see that part of your blue circle is in the upper-left corner of the
   display (**Figure 2.6**). This is because the registration point for the circle is
   in the upper-right corner, and the Flash runtime positions the circle based
   on the coordinate 0,0, which is the default location for objects when you
   create them.

   So let's step through the code to see how it all works. The first line

   ```
   var myCircle:BlueCircle = new BlueCircle();
   ```

   can be read like this: A new object named myCircle has been created, which is
   an instance of the BlueCircle class. That object is assigned a new instance of the
   BlueCircle class. The process is shown in **Figure 2.7**.

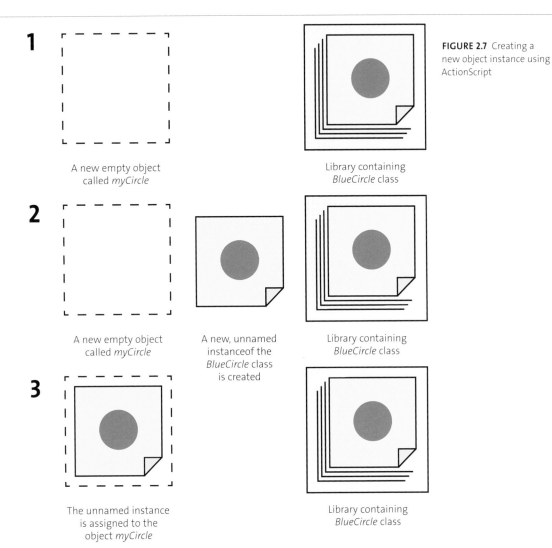

1 A new empty object called *myCircle*

Library containing *BlueCircle* class

FIGURE 2.7 Creating a new object instance using ActionScript

2 A new empty object called *myCircle*

A new, unnamed instanceof the *BlueCircle* class is created

Library containing *BlueCircle* class

3 The unnamed instance is assigned to the object *myCircle*

Library containing *BlueCircle* class

In this illustration, the first row shows that you are creating a new named object called myCircle. You'll learn more about the var statement in an upcoming chapter, but just remember that the name of the new instance you created is called myCircle. You also have the BlueCircle "stack of sticky notes," or class, available in the Library to use.

The second step says that you are "tearing off a sticky note" from the stack using the new statement, creating a new instance of the BlueCircle class. At this point, the instance doesn't have a name, but it exists in your program.

The third step takes that unnamed instance of the BlueCircle class and assigns it to the named object myCircle. You need to do this in order to send any actions or make property changes on the object since it requires an instance name before you can work with it.

This process is the same as dragging an object from the Library, placing it on the Stage, and giving it an instance name of myCircle.

Take a look at the second line of code:

```
addChild(myCircle);
```

This line of code adds the shiny new blue circle to the display stack so it can be visible to the user. The addChild statement takes the item referenced in the parentheses, and adds it to the list of items that are displayed.

When the Flash runtime plays, it continually checks the contents of the display stack and renders the objects within it on the screen. Now that the blue circle is in the display stack, you can see it on the screen.

Take a look at the last line and the unusual text that appears in the Output panel:

```
trace(myCircle);
```

The last line traces the entire object to the Output panel. Notice that the panel displays the following:

```
[object BlueCircle]
```

Since the object itself doesn't have any meaningful textual or numerical value, this line of code is sending a statement that the object being referenced is an object of the BlueCircle class. The trace statement then sends that to the Output panel.

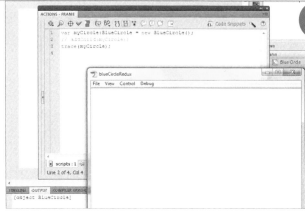

MESSING WITH THE DISPLAY STACK

Now, you'll update the code to show what the display stack does.

1. Change the code to read like this:

```
var myCircle:BlueCircle = new BlueCircle();
// addChild(myCircle);
trace(myCircle);
```

When you add the two slashes before the second line, you are doing what programmers call "commenting out." You'll learn more about using comments in the next section, but for now just know that the two forward slashes hide the code from Flash, so it skips it, ignoring any commands or actions on that line. Notice that the code in Flash turns grey. That is the default color for showing comments (**Figure 2.8**).

Without the addChild statement, the myCircle object is not added to the display stack.

2. Run this code. You'll see an empty page.

Check the Output panel. You'll see that the trace statement still works as expected because the object is still there; it just isn't part of the display stack (**Figure 2.9**).

FIGURE 2.8 Showing comment coloring in the Actions panel

FIGURE 2.9 Result when removing addChild from the code

FIGURE 2.10 Change of location after modifying the x and y properties

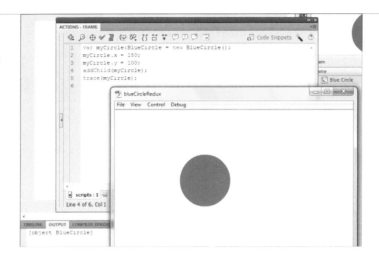

This is a common mistake that a lot of new coders make: creating an instance of an object and forgetting to add it to the display stack. You'll see that you get no errors when you run the project, because the object is there, but you haven't specifically told Flash to render it on the screen.

3. Add the addChild statement back in by removing the leading double slashes.

4. Run the program again. You'll see that you restored the object.

ASSIGNING PROPERTIES TO DYNAMICALLY CREATED INSTANCES

If you want to position the object at a certain location when you place it, you can assign values to the instance properties x and y after the object is created.

1. Update the code to assign values to these properties after the line that creates the initial instance with the new statement:

```
var myCircle:BlueCircle = new BlueCircle();
myCircle.x = 150;
myCircle.y = 100;
addChild(myCircle);
trace(myCircle);
```

2. Display the object. Its location will be at the coordinate 150,100 (**Figure 2.10**).

WORKING WITH COMMENTS

Comments are a huge part of your programming, and are critical for you and your team members to understand the code that you are writing. Comments allow programmers to add notes, hints, and explanations within their code, so they or others can understand it.

Even if you are working alone, comments are extremely important to help you understand your code after you stop working on a project for a while and need to get back to it. Many developers wrestle with confusing code that made perfect sense when they originally wrote it, but can't remember how it worked when they went back to it months later.

CREATING COMMENTS

You have two basic ways to comment in Flash. The first is a single-line comment. To create one, start the line of code with a double forward slash, //. Any contents after these, on that line only, are hidden by Flash and aren't executed. For example:

```
// This code creates a blue circle on the screen
var myCircle:BlueCircle = new BlueCircle();
addChild(myCircle);
trace(myCircle);
```

In this example, the first line is a comment, and is ignored by Flash when it runs the code.

The second type of comment is a multi-line comment. To create this type, you need to mark the beginning and ending of the comment using two special two-character sequences: /* and */. You'll wrap the text you want to hide from Flash using these two sequences. Here is an example:

```
/* This code creates a blue circle
    on the screen at 150,100 */
var myCircle:BlueCircle = new BlueCircle();
myCircle.x = 150;
myCircle.y = 100;
addChild(myCircle);
trace(myCircle);
```

The contents inside the opening /* and the closing */ are hidden from Flash, and the contents between them can be as long as you want. You might see some code use these opening and closing symbols in various ways, but they always do the same thing: start and end a multi-line comment.

WORKING WITH SPACES

Generally, you can add whitespace characters (spaces, tabs, and carriage returns) in your code. Sometimes these are helpful to segment related pieces of code together, usually with a comment above the segment to identify what the code does. There are some best practice rules for using tabs in your ActionScript, which you'll learn later in the book.

The blue circle example could be expanded to make the code's function very clear and explicit:

```
/* This code creates a blue circle
    on the screen at 150,100 */
// Create a new instance of the BlueCircle class
var myCircle:BlueCircle = new BlueCircle();
// Position the myCircle on the screen
myCircle.x = 150;
myCircle.y = 100
// Add myCircle to the display stack
addChild(myCircle);
// Send myCircle to the Output panel to confirm it is there
trace(myCircle);
```

WRAPPING **UP**

Using a few new ActionScript commands, you are able to dynamically add objects to the Stage. When working with object instances using ActionScript, make sure you do the following:

- Make sure that the object in your Library is named and has been configured for "Export to ActionScript" using the Advanced mode section of the Convert to Symbol dialog box.

- Create a named object to hold your new instance using the var statement.

- Generate a new instance of the object from the Library using the new statement, assigning the object to the named object using the = assignment operator.

- Add the object to the Flash display stack using addChild to render the object on the screen.

- Remember to add comments using single-line or multi-line comments to document what your code does for others to understand, or for you to understand when you return to your project later.

3

WORKING WITH FUNCTIONS

When you work with ActionScript, there are sequences of code that you may want to execute multiple times. To do this, you need a way to group the code into a logical block and give it a name that will tell the Flash run-time to execute the code.

Functions are the way to do exactly that. Using functions, you can group commonly used commands for repetitive use throughout your application. In this chapter, you'll learn the commands and syntax to create a basic function, and then learn how you can extend the use of your functions to send and receive data in and out of them.

FUNDAMENTALS OF FUNCTIONS

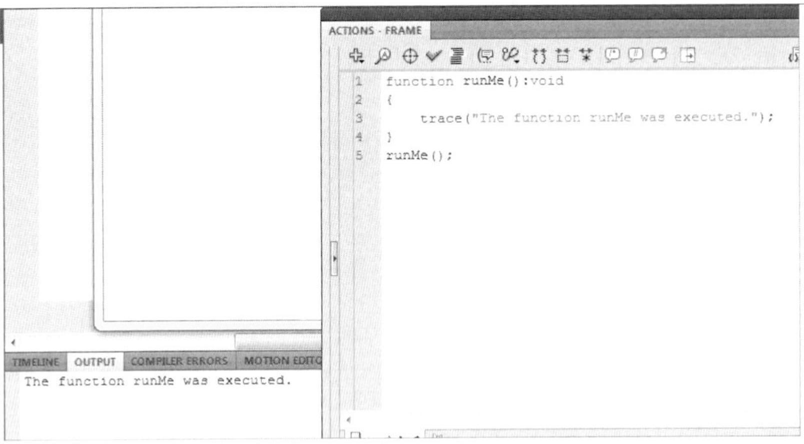

FIGURE 3.1 Results from your first function

To get started with functions, let's look at the following example.

1. Create a new ActionScript 3.0 Flash file and enter the following code into the frame script on the timeline:

```
function runMe():void
{
    trace("The function runMe was executed.");
}
runMe();
```

2. Run the code. The phrase "The function runMe was executed" appears in the Output panel in Flash (**Figure 3.1**).

```
function runMe():void
  {
     trace("The function runMe was executed.");
  }
runMe();
```

FIGURE 3.2 An example function with callouts

Let's walk through the code and explain how it works, referring to the numbered elements in **Figure 3.2**.

First, the `function` statement ❶ tells Flash that you are starting a new named function that will contain a number of commands or statements. After the `function` statement, you need to provide a name for this group of commands so you can access them later. In this case, you are using the name `runMe` ❷. You finish the function definition with a pair of parentheses ❸ and with the text `:void` that you'll learn about in a bit ❹.

The statements that are part of the function need to be wrapped with a matching set of curly braces ❺. Inside these braces are the statements that are part of the function. Notice that Flash indents these lines of code for you automatically. Using tabs to indent code that is placed within curly braces is a best practice. This makes the code easier to read and makes identifying code that is part of code blocks quicker. The tabs are called white-space characters.

The last line is the function call ❻. To tell Flash to run the contents of a function code block, you need to refer to the function name followed by a pair of parentheses. Since this is a single line of code, you need to end it with a semicolon.

Notice that the function line and each of the curly braces do not have semicolons at the end. They are not required on these lines. In fact, they would cause an error. Only the lines within the curly braces that define the code block should end in semicolons.

As you work with other programmers, you may see the curly brace locations shift from time to time. Their exact position is not critical, but they need to be in the correct order. For example, the following two functions are identical to the previous example, but are formatted just a bit differently:

```
// Example 1 - Opening curly brace on function line
function runMe():void {
    trace("The function runMe was executed.");
}
// Example 2 - Opening curly brace on line below function
function runMe():void
{
trace("The function runMe was executed.");
}
// Example 3 - All white space removed
function runMe():void { trace("The function runMe was executed."); }
```

This is an example of how white-space characters (spaces, tabs, or line breaks) don't affect the function of the code, but can be used to make code look cleaner; all three examples will run the same way.

ACCEPTING VALUES
IN FUNCTIONS

In the previous example, the function did not request or submit any information back to the program, it simply executed a sequence of commands. By adding a few options to the function, you can have it change its functionality based on values that are submitted to it.

In this example, you'll start by creating an object in the Library that you can access using ActionScript:

1. Create a new ActionScript 3.0 project.

2. Create a blue circle on the Stage and convert it to a MovieClip symbol, activating the Export for ActionScript option in the ActionScript Linkage section. Call the object Blue Circle, which will automatically output as BlueCircle.

3. Remove the symbol that was just converted on the stage. You won't need it..

4. Open the Actions panel and add the following code to your timeline:

```
// Create new BlueCirle instance
var circle:BlueCircle = new BlueCircle();
circle.x = 50;
circle.y = 50;
addChild(circle);
// Reposition function
function reposition(newX:Number):void
{
    circle.x = newX;
}
// Reposition circle
reposition(100);
```

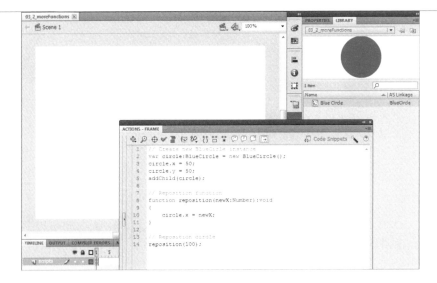

FIGURE 3.3 Library with the BlueCircle linked object and the Actions panel

In this example, you are placing an object on the Stage and are accessing the function reposition(). To change the behavior of the function, you are passing a value to the function.

For a function to accept a value, the function declaration needs to have the required parameters expressed inside the parentheses, and it needs to have a name it can give the parameter for the duration of the function. The function also needs to know what type of object the parameter is. In this example, the new name for the parameter is newX and is defined as a number by adding :Number after the name. This temporary value will be thrown away when you're finished with the function. It exists only while the function is running.

You might be asking yourself what the :Number and :void mean in your Action-Script. When working with functions, ActionScript needs to know the type of data that is going in and out of it. In this case, you are defining that newX will be a number, which is a data type in ActionScript. There are a lot of data types that ActionScript can use. The Number type includes any number that is a decimal value that is either positive, like 123.45, or negative, like -234.56. The :void statement indicates that there isn't any data being used, meaning it is "void" of data. You'll learn more about data types in the future, but that sums up the types in this example.

```
// Create new BlueCirle instance
var circle:BlueCircle = new BlueCircle();
circle.x = 50;
circle.y = 50;
addChild(circle);


// Reposition function
❶ function reposition(newX:Number):void
   {                              ❸
      circle.x = newX; ❹
   }


// Reposition circle
❷ reposition(100);
```

FIGURE 3.4 Example function that accepts a parameter with callouts

Now, in order to pass this value to the function when it is run, you need to specify the parameter value within the parentheses when you call the function.

Refer to the numbered elements in **Figure 3.4** while walking through this in more detail.

You have defined a function that requires a number parameter called newX for the duration of the function ❶.

You call the function reposition() and pass in the value of 100 ❷.

The function gets that value, verifies it is a number, and assigns it to the name newX ❸.

The function runs, overwriting the x attribute of the circle object with the value of newX, and then ends the function since there are no other statements before the closing curly brace ❹.

FIGURE 3.5 Result of the code using the `reposition()` function.

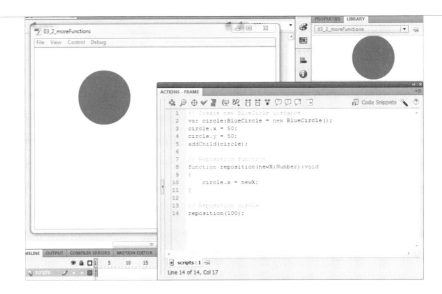

The result when you run the project looks like **Figure 3.5**.

POSSIBLE ERRORS WHEN WORKING WITH FUNCTIONS

When running a function, there are a couple of ways that you could inadvertently get an error: failing to send a required parameter and sending the wrong value type.

REQUIRED PARAMETER ERROR

When you define a parameter, the parameter is required by default, but there are ways to make a value optional. If you fail to pass in a value to the function, you'll get an error.

The following example shows how the missing parameter error occurs:

1. Modify your code to remove the 100 within the `reposition()` function call on the last line. It should read like this:

```
// Reposition circle
reposition();
```

2. Run your project again.

3. Look at the Compiler Errors panel that will display. You'll see the following error display:

```
1136: Incorrect number of arguments.  Expected 1.
```

This error is indicating that you are executing a function that requires a parameter or argument, but in this case you failed to send one.

TYPE MISMATCH ERROR

Another type of error occurs if you pass in a value of the wrong type. Remember that the :Number statement indicates that newX is of the Number data type. If you pass in a string to the function, you'll get a type mismatch error.

The following example shows how the type mismatch error occurs:

1. Modify the reposition() function and add a string within the parentheses. It should read like this:

```
// Reposition circle
reposition("100");
```

2. Run your project again.

3. Look at the Compiler Errors panel that will display. You'll see the following error:

```
1067: Implicit coercion of a value of type String to an
unrelated type Number.
```

To correct this, check your code and make sure you are using the right format for your function parameter value. You can adjust either the value you are passing in or the type of value that the function is expecting.

RETURNING VALUES FROM FUNCTIONS

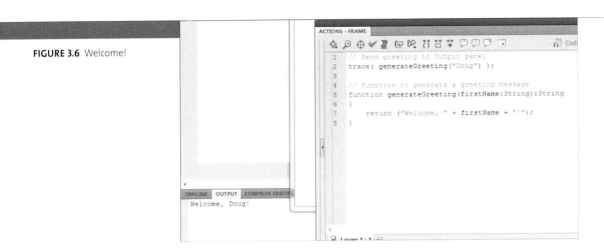

FIGURE 3.6 Welcome!

In this last example, you'll look at how to make the function return a value to the location from which it was called. Let's look at a new example. Here is some example code for a new project:

```
// Send greeting to Output panel
trace( generateGreeting("Doug") );
// Function to generate a greeting message
function generateGreeting(firstName:String):String
{
    return ("Welcome, " + firstName + "!");
}
```

In this code is a trace statement that is calling a function instead of providing a variable name or a string that would be sent to the Output panel. When you use a function name in this way, you are asking the function to run and replace the function name with the value it returns.

The function itself is similar to the previous examples; however, it is requiring a string value as its required parameter. After the parameter definition and at the end of the function declaration, you have :String. In previous examples, you used :void at the end to signify that the function didn't return any value when it was finished. That is no longer true; this time the function will return a string when it is finished.

```
// Send greeting to Output panel
trace( generateGreeting("Doug") );
  ①              ④
```

FIGURE 3.7 Example function with a **return** statement

```
// Function to generate a greeting message
function generateGreeting(firstName:String):String
{                                    ②
    return ("Welcome, " + firstName + "!");
}                            ③
```

Inside the function is a new command, the return statement. The sole purpose of the return statement is to send a value back to the calling location of the function; in this case, inside the trace statement.

The return statement is followed by an expression, where you are combining strings together. This is also called *concatenation*. You can combine strings together by using the plus sign (+) to link them together. You are also using the variable firstName, which is a temporary container for the value sent to the function, in this case the word "Doug." The return statement sends the concatenated string back to the calling location and ends the function. The return statement ends the function, regardless of whether there are commands after it.

Figure 3.6 shows the result.

Refer to the numbered elements in **Figure 3.7** while running through this example.

Inside the parentheses for the trace statement, you run the function generateGreeting() instead of providing a string or variable ❶.

That function runs and accepts the value "Doug" as its parameter value and assigns it to the firstName variable for the duration of the function ❷.

Inside the return statement, you combine three strings together to form a single string "Welcome, Doug!" using the + operator to concatenate the strings, and then exit out of the function with the return statement sending the single string back to the original call ❸.

Back in the trace statement, with the function returning a value, the function call itself is replaced by the contents from the function. The trace statement executes, sending the string to the Output console ❹.

If you failed to use the `return` statement, you would get the following error:

```
1170: Function does not return a value.
```

When you define a return type, in this case `String`, you must return this type of value from the function. Otherwise, you will get the 1170 error above. If you have a function that doesn't return a value, make sure you always define its return type as void.

MORE ABOUT PARENTHESES (AND CURLY BRACES)

You'll notice that the previous code example uses a lot of use of parentheses. For example, this line:

```
trace( generateGreeting("Doug") );
```

Parentheses, and also curly braces, are important for grouping things that you want to evaluate together. In this case, you have the phrase "Doug" being evaluated with the `generateGreeting()` function. This is the evaluation within the `trace` statement that sends the returned value to the Output panel.

What can sometimes trip up coders when they first start in ActionScript is to forget to have matching parentheses pairs, as in the following example:

```
trace( generateGreeting("Doug");
```

If you attempt to run this code, you'll get the following error in the Output panel:

```
1084: Syntax error: expecting rightparen before semicolon.
```

This error indicates that you are missing a parenthesis. The parentheses around "Doug" are correct, but you have failed to add a closing parentheisis for the `trace` statement.

Wrestling with parentheses and curly braces is something that every coder needs to deal with. Make sure you double-check your opening and closing parentheses and curly braces to ensure that they are all matched correctly.

WRAPPING **UP**

Functions are one of the most commonly used features of ActionScript, and you'll be using them over and over again. All functions share the same basic rules, regardless of their function or use in your application. Here are some general rules to keep in mind when working with functions:

- All functions begin with the `function` statement and have a name associated with them.

- All code that is part of a function is enclosed within a code block, denoted by opening and closing curly braces.

- Any values that you can send into a function must be declared within the function definition, inside the parentheses. All values must have a name that will be used to represent the values during the function, and the values must have a type.

- Every function must either define what type of value it will return or define that it will return nothing by using a return type of `void`.

- When working with parentheses, make sure they are all properly closed (matched) to avoid any errors.

4

ACTIONSCRIPT
AND MATH

ActionScript has tons of mathematical operators built in to the language to help you evaluate mathematical equations. Now, I wouldn't throw away your handheld calculator just yet. ActionScript has a lot of power, but it's designed to help with your applications, not for general use. In addition to these mathematical operators, there are some functions that can help with common mathematical tasks like rounding numbers.

In this section, you'll learn all the basic arithmetic operators that you'll use in ActionScript. Also, there are some convenient shortcuts to make working with math easier that you'll cover as well.

MATHEMATICAL **OPERATORS**

In ActionScript, you can use simple math operators to perform arithmetic functions with your numbers or variables. The math functions that are part of ActionScript are nearly identical to basic math functions that you already know. Some of the symbols and names are different, but the principles are the same.

ADDITION AND SUBTRACTION

Let's get started with adding and subtracting numbers.

1. Create a new ActionScript 3.0 project in Flash Professional CS5.5 and enter the following code into the timeline:

    ```
    // Math operators: addition and subtraction
    trace ( 2 + 3 );
    trace ( 3 - 2 );
    ```

2. Run the project and look at the Output panel; you'll see the following:

    ```
    5
    1
    ```

    This shouldn't be surprising, since you are adding and subtracting the numbers. You use the + and - operators to indicate that you are adding or subtracting. One thing to note is the white-space characters used in the example. Notice the spaces between the operators and the numbers. This is for readability and doesn't affect the execution of the code. You can remove the spaces if you want, for example:

    ```
    trace ( 2 + 3 );
    trace (2+3);
    ```

    These two lines perform exactly the same function and will generate the same result.

ADDITION OR CONCATENATION?

In the previous chapter, you used the + sign, but it wasn't a mathematical operator. You can use the + operator to do two things. When working with strings, the + operator is called the concatenation operator and takes two strings and combines them together, in essence gluing the end of one string to the beginning of the next. When working with numbers, the + operator is the addition mathematical operator, adding two numeric values together and generating a new numeric result.

Look at the following example.

1. Remove the existing code and enter the following code:

```
// Addition vs. Concatenation
trace ( 2 + 2 ); // addition
trace ( "two" + "two" ); // concatenation
trace ( "2" + "2" ); // concatenation
```

2. Run this code; you'll see the following displayed in the Output panel:

```
4
twotwo
22
```

The first line of code in the example is pretty simple; you are adding the numbers 2 and 2 using the addition operator, resulting in a value of 4.

The second line of code has two strings, denoted by quotation marks, that are being "glued" together, creating a single string using the string concatenation operator. The result is "twotwo."

The last line uses the number 2 on both sides of the operator. Notice that the numbers are surrounded by quotation marks, which means that it is no longer a number value, but instead the character 2. When you force the number 2 to be a string using quotation marks, the + operator concatenates the strings, "gluing" them together forming the string, 22.

What makes this confusing is that the Output panel doesn't distinguish between strings and numbers. So, when you see 22 in the Output panel, is it a number or a string? There is a way to find out the type of a value and display it: by using the typeof statement.

3. To see how typeof works, update the previous example as follows:

```
// Addition vs. Concatenation
trace ( typeof(2 + 2) ); // addition
trace ( typeof("two" + "two") ); // concatenation
trace ( typeof("2" + "2") ); // concatenation
```

4. Run this updated example; you'll see the following in the Output panel:

```
number
string
string
```

What is happening is that the operation (either addition or concatenation) is taking place, and the typeof statement is determining the type of the result and then sending that to the Output panel via the trace statement.

Now for one final twist. If you mix up the number and string types, what happens?

5. Replace the existing code with the following:

```
trace ( 2 + "2" );
```

Wow. Now you have a number on the left side, and a string on the right side. Who wins?

6. Run the project.

The answer is that the string wins. The result is the string, "22". In this case the operator converts the number 2 to the string "2" and then "glues" it to the right "2" creating the string "22". It seems confusing at first, but after you work with it a while, it will become second nature to you—promise!

MULTIPLICATION AND DIVISION

Now, look at the * and / operators for multiplication and division.

1. Replace the code in the timeline with the following:

```
// Math operators: Multiplication and Division
trace ( 2 * 3 );
trace ( 5 / 2 );
```

$$
\begin{array}{r}
2 \ \ r1 \\
2\overline{)5} \\
-4 \\
\hline
1
\end{array}
$$

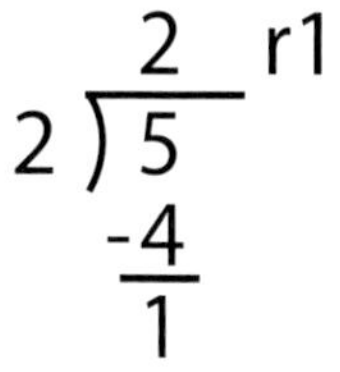

FIGURE 4.1 5 divided by 2 written in long division format, showing the remainder, or modulo.

The first statement uses the multiplication operator, which is an asterisk, *. The division operator is a forward slash, /, and the order of the division is that it divides the value on the left by the value on the right.

2. Run the project; you'll see the following in the Output panel:

```
6
2.5
```

Again, pretty simple stuff—but the next one will probably be new to you.

MODULO, THE OPERATOR FORMERLY KNOWN AS LONG DIVISION WITH REMAINDERS

The *modulo* operator finds the remainder after a division operation. The modulo is quite helpful in many situations, including determining if a number is odd or even. Take a look at how it works.

1. Replace the code you have with the following, and take a look at the output:

```
// Math operators: Modulo
trace ( 5 % 2 );
```

2. Run the project; you'll see the following displayed in the Output panel:

```
1
```

The % symbol invokes the modulo operator, finding the remainder after attempting a division of the value on the left with the value on the right. In this example, it divides 5 by 2, resulting in 2 and a remainder of 1. To see this written out in long division format, check out **Figure 4.1**.

WHAT ON EARTH IS MODULO USED FOR?

That is a great question, and one that has a great answer as well. One of the most common uses is to determine if a value is a multiple of another. For example, to find out if a value is an even multiple of 3, you can use something like this:

myValue % 3;

If the result is 0, that means there are no remainders, and the number is an even multiple of 3.

Another common use is to determine if a number is even or odd. Even numbers are evenly divisible by 2, so by that definition you could use this:

myValue % 2;

If the result is 0, the number is evenly divisible by 2, making it even. If it isn't, then the number is odd.

VARIABLES AND COMBINED ASSIGNMENT OPERATORS

You'll commonly want to complete a math function and assign the resulting value back to some named object, called a *variable*. ActionScript makes this easier by letting you combine arithmetic and assignment operators together. Take a look at an assignment operator example:

1. Create a new ActionScript 3.0 project and enter in the following code for the project:

```
// Assignment Operators
var myValue:Number = 2;
myValue = myValue + 2;
trace(myValue);
var myOtherValue:Number = 2;
myOtherValue += 2;
trace(myOtherValue);
```

2. Run the project. You'll get the following in the Output panel:

```
4
4
```

Let's walk through the code and explain how you get this result and what role variables and combined assignment operators play.

VARIABLES

You haven't really seen much about the var statement yet, so let's reveal a little bit more about it. You have used it in the past to create named object containers that you have then assigned MovieClip symbols to using the new statement. You can also use var to create variables; in fact, variables is what var stands for. Variables are named objects that can contain variable values.

Take a look at the second line of the assignment operators example:

```
var myValue:Number = 2;
```

The var statement is creating a variable called myValue. See that :Number after the variable name? You have to tell ActionScript what type of data your variable can hold, similar to how you did when using the function statement. In this case, you are saying that myValue will contain a number. When you create the variable, it is empty, but when you assign the numeric value 2 to it, you can refer to that value using the name myValue.

```
myValue = myValue + 2;
trace(myValue);
```

On the second line above, you are accessing the myValue object and are assigning a new value to it. Notice that you are not using the var statement here, because var is only used to create a new variable. You don't need to use it again if you are referring to a variable that has already been created. Before you assign the value, you need to complete the evaluation on the right side of the assignment operator. In this case, you are taking the existing value of myValue, 2, and adding the value 2 to it. This value is then assigned back to myValue, overwriting the existing value. In the last line of the first block, you send that value to the Output panel using the trace statement, which displays 4.

This completes the analysis of the first part of the code.

COMBINED ASSIGNMENT OPERATORS

Take a look at the second block of code. This section of code works identically to the first block, with two exceptions. In this section, you are creating a new variable called myOtherValue:

```
var myOtherValue:Number = 2;
myOtherValue += 2;
trace(myOtherValue);
```

In the first line, you need to use the var statement since you have not created that variable before. You then assign the numeric value 2 to it.

On the next line, you come across the first combined assignment operator, +=. This operator is combining addition with assignment. In this case it is taking the existing value of myOtherValue and is adding 2 to it and automatically assigning it back to the myOtherValue variable. Always put the arithmetic operator before the assignment operator. You can use this shortcut with any of the basic arithmetic operators:

```
// All combined assignment operators
var myValue:Number = 100;
myValue += 50; // 100+50 = 150
myValue -= 125 // 150-125 = 25
myValue *= 3    // 25*3 = 75
myValue /= 5    // 75/5 = 15
myValue %= 4    // 15%4 = 3
trace (myValue);
```

Programmers often use these combined assignment operators as shortcuts since they are nice time savers. Hopefully, you'll find they are too!

INCREMENT AND DECREMENT OPERATORS

When you work with ActionScript a lot, you'll commonly be adding or removing 1 from variables and properties.

To make this process easier, there is a shortcut called the *increment* and *decrement* operators. Take a look at the following code.

1. Create a new ActionScript 3.0 project and enter in the following code for the project:

```
// Increment and Decrement
var myValue:Number = 5;
trace(myValue);
myValue++;
trace(myValue);
myValue--;
trace(myValue);
```

2. Run this project. You'll see the following in the Output panel:

```
5
6
5
```

In the increment and decrement example, the value of myValue is initially set at 5 and is sent to the Output panel. The number is then increased by 1 and sent again, resulting in 6.

When you add a double minus, --, to the end, it decrements the value by 1. The value of myValue is already 6 based on the previous function, and is then decremented to be 5 again.

When you add a double plus, ++, to the end of a variable name, you increment it by 1. As a result, the following three lines of code do the exact same thing:

```
myValue = myValue + 1;

myValue += 1;

myValue++;
```

The following three lines of code do the same thing, similarly to the example earlier for the increment operator:

```
myValue = myValue - 1;

myValue -= 1;

myValue--;
```

ORDER OF OPERATIONS

FIGURE 4.2 Incorrect left-to-right order of operations

LEFT TO RIGHT EVALUATION

$$2 + 3 * 2 / 4 - 1$$
$$5 * 2 / 4 - 1$$
$$10 / 4 - 1$$
$$2.5 - 1$$
$$1.5$$

By default, mathematical functions do not run from left to right, but follow a specific *order of operations*. You may recall from math classes that certain mathematical functions are calculated before others, regardless of their left-to-right order.

1. Create a new ActionScript 3.0 project and enter in the following code for the project:

```
// Order of Operations
var answer:Number = 2 + 3 * 2 / 4 - 1;
trace(answer);
```

In this example, you have a number of math functions that are running from left to right. If you don't follow the order of operations and evaluate it from left to right, you get 1.5, as shown in **Figure 4.2**.

2. Run the code. You'll see what might seem unexpected: 2.5. Why? Because certain math functions are executed before others. In fact, this is the order:

   1. Multiplication, Division, and Modulo

   2. Addition and Subtraction

ORDER OF OPERATIONS EVALUATION

$$2 + 3 * 2 / 4 - 1 \quad ①$$
$$2 + 6 / 4 - 1 \quad ②$$
$$2 + 1.5 - 1 \quad ③$$
$$3.5 - 1 \quad ④$$
$$2.5 \quad ⑤$$

FIGURE 4.3 Correct order of operations for the evaluation

All the multiplication, division,and modulo operations are processed from left to right to the end. Then calculation starts again from the left and processes addition and subtraction. Look at **Figure 4.3** to see how this works.

When the Flash runtime looks at the ActionScript, it starts from the left, evaluating the expression:

- It ignores the 2 + 3, since the rules dictate processing only multiplication, division, and modulo at this point.

- $3 \times 2 = 6$ ❶

- $6 / 4 = 1.5$ ❷

Since there are no more multiplication, division, or modulo operations, it returns to the beginning and processes addition and subtraction.

- $2 + 1.5 = 3.5$ ❸

- $3.5 - 1 = 2.5$ ❹

You have the final result, 2.5 ❺, which is then sent to the Output panel.

You can alter the order of operation by using parentheses. This will force Flash to adopt a specific path of calculating the results. You'll learn about overriding the order of operation rules in the next section.

USING PARENTHESES
TO **FORCE ORDER**

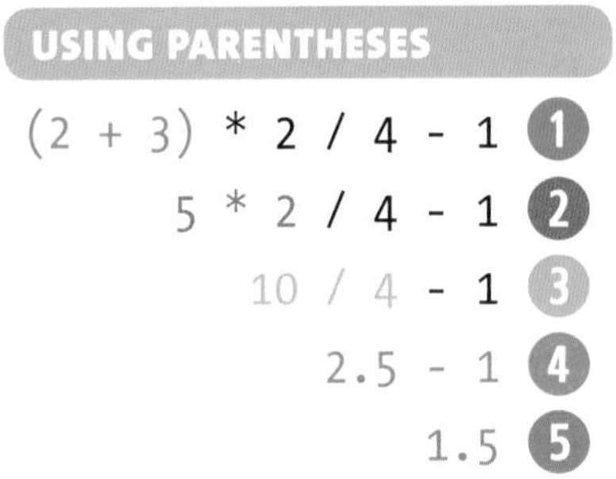

FIGURE 4.4 Forcing the order
with parentheses using order
of operations

USING PARENTHESES

```
(2 + 3) * 2 / 4 - 1   ①
      5 * 2 / 4 - 1   ②
         10 / 4 - 1   ③
            2.5 - 1   ④
                1.5   ⑤
```

You can force the earlier example to follow the order of operation that results in the value of 1.5. You can use parentheses to group calculations together. In the order of operations, math operations that are grouped within a pair of parentheses are always calculated first.

You can adjust the example to get the 1.5 that you originally calculated by performing the calculations from left to right:

```
// Order of Operations
var answer:Number = (2 + 3) * 2 / 4 - 1;
trace(answer);
```

Now instead of skipping the first addition action, the Flash runtime calculates what is inside the parentheses first and then continues across, as shown in **Figure 4.4**.

When the Flash runtime looks at the ActionScript, it starts with the first set of parentheses it finds:

- 2 + 3 = 5, which is the only set of parentheses ❶

It then starts back at the beginning with multiplication, division, and modulo:

- 5 × 2 = 10 ❷
- 10 / 4 = 2.5 ❸

Now that it is finished with multiplication, division, and modulo, it starts back on the left and evaluates addition and subtraction:

- 2.5 - 1 = 1.5 ❹

You end up with 1.5 ❺, which is then sent to the Output panel.

You can nest parentheses within each other, but just make sure that every opening parenthesis has a matching closing parenthesis. This is one of the most common bugs you'll find in your programs, unmatched parentheses and braces.

SUMMING UP MATH OPERATIONS

You have covered a lot of math in this chapter, but more importantly, you were able to expand your knowledge of working with numbers and variables and start doing some calculations with them. **Table 4.1** will serve as a handy reference for the operations that were covered in this chapter:

TABLE 4.1 Mathematical Operators

OPERATOR	DEFINITION	EXAMPLE
+	Addition	4 + 5 results in 9
−	Subtraction	5 − 4 results in 1
*	Multiplication	2 * 3 results in 6
/	Division	5 / 2 results in 2.5
%	Modulo	5 / 2 results in 1
+=	Addition assignment	if x is 5, x += 3 changes x to 8
-=	Subtraction assignment	if x is 5, x -= 2 changes x to 3
*=	Multiplication assignment	if x is 5, x *= 3 changes x to 15
/=	Division assignment	if x is 5, x /= 2 changes x to 2.5
%=	Modulo assignment	if x is 5, x %= 2 changes x to 1
++	Increment	if x is 5, x++ changes x to 6
--	Decrement	if x is 5, x-- changes x to 4

WRAPPING **UP**

In this chapter, you learned the basics of working with variables and how to change numeric values using arithmetic operators in ActionScript. You also learned some of the common shortcuts advanced programmers use to save time when working with math operators, including working with combined assignment operators and the increment and decrement operators.

When working with operators in ActionScript, keep the following in mind to avoid common pitfalls and errors:

- When creating a variable and referring to it the first time, you need to use the var statement to create it. You can then refer to it without the var statement afterwards.

- When using the + operator, be sure to not inadvertently mix up strings and numbers, as strings will concatenate and ignore the numeric values.

- The modulo operator calculates the remainder after attempting to complete an even division.

- If you are working with a combination of multiplicative (multiplication, division, or modulo) functions and summation (addition or subtraction) functions, remember that ActionScript will evaluate your equation using mathematical order of operations.

- To quickly modify an existing value based on a function, you can use combined assignment operators to save time.

- If you are adding or subtracting 1 to or from a value, you can use increment or decrement operators, using ++ or -- as a quick shortcut.

- To force the order of operations to do something specific, you can use parentheses to group evaluations you want to process first.

5
CREATING EVENTS

So far, none of your projects has been interactive. In fact, they haven't required any user interaction at all to work. When you want to build in the ability for someone to control a project, you are building an interface for it. Interfaces are powered by events. When you need to respond to mouse clicks, keyboard presses, or anything that the user is doing, you'll use events in ActionScript. Events are Flash's way of letting objects know that something is happening. In this chapter, you'll learn how events work and how to create a couple of basic event types.

EVENTS: EXPLAINED

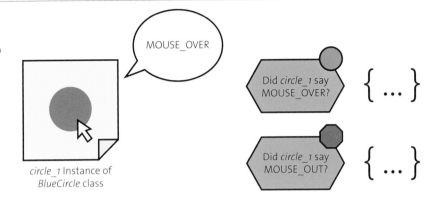

FIGURE 5.1 Event Relationship

circle_1 Instance of
BlueCircle class

Events in ActionScript have two parts, just like a two-way conversation. In a conversation, there is a speaker and a listener. The speaker says something, and the listener is ready to hear what is being said.

Did you ever play the game "Simon Says"? The rules are simple. A group of children listens to the leader, who tells the group to do various things like step forward, jump, sit down, and so on. The trick is that they do these things only if the leader says, "Simon says," before the requested action. If the children don't hear it, they ignore the instruction and do nothing.

In ActionScript, the same relationship between the speaker and listener exists. In Flash, instead of a speaker, or leader, there is a broadcaster that sends out notifications that events, or actions, are happening. There are then listeners that listen for these notifications and then take action when they hear an event they are listening for.

Look at the relationship a bit more using the diagram in **Figure 5.1**.

In Figure 5.1, there is an object that broadcasts a message, in this case the circle_1 instance of BlueCircle. When the user performs an interaction with a MovieClip, the circle_1 instance sends a message describing the event. In the example, the user moved their pointer over circle_1, so the instance broadcasts that the MOUSE_OVER event occurred.

Events include many different types of actions, such as hovering the pointer over an object, clicking an object, using a keyboard to interact with the project, or using a multi-touch screen.

An application has objects called *listeners* that keep their "ears" open for specific types of events. The listener at the top is listening specifically for the MOUSE_OVER event. When it hears this event from the broadcaster, it springs into action and executes a function called a *callback* function.

The second listener is looking for the MOUSE_OUT message, which the broadcaster is not sending in this example, and it ignores the MOUSE_OVER message.

To demonstrate this partnership, let's create a simple *event handler* that will respond to the click of a mouse. An event handler is a function that will execute based on a specific event taking place.

CREATING A MOUSE EVENT HANDLER

FIGURE 5.2 Click!

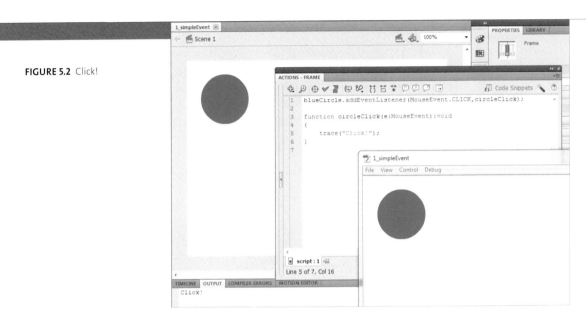

When you create interactive applications, you want to know when the user clicks the mouse on buttons or other elements. You need to create an event handler that will monitor how the mouse interacts with these objects.

For instance, if you want a button to display a message when it is clicked, you need to tell Flash to listen for when the mouse clicks the button. Not all buttons care if they are clicked. Some might be more interested in whether the pointer is hovering over it instead of clicking it. For that reason, you need to specify exactly what you want to track for each item in your Flash project (**Figure 5.2**).

Only certain types of objects have events associated with them. Drawing objects and other similar elements cannot react to the mouse, so you won't be able to track interactions with them. The most common object that supports interaction in Flash is the MovieClip object.

1. Create a new project in Flash Professional CS5.5.

2. Create a blue circle on the Stage and convert it to a MovieClip.

3. Give it an instance name of **blueCircle**. Now you have an object on the Stage, and since it is a MovieClip, you can monitor how the mouse interacts with it using events.

4. Create a new timeline layer for your script and name it as you wish.

5. Go into the Actions panel and make sure the blueCircle MovieClip isn't selected. You want to add your ActionScript to the frame and not on the object itself, since that isn't allowed in ActionScript 3.0.

6. Type the following lines in the frame:

```
blueCircle.addEventListener(MouseEvent.CLICK,circleClick);
function circleClick(e:MouseEvent):void
{
    trace("Click!");
}
```

7. Run the project.

8. Click the blue circle. You'll see the phrase "Click!" display in the Output panel.

Let's review what exactly is going on with the first line of code that you typed:

```
blueCircle.addEventListener(MouseEvent.CLICK,circleClick);
```

You are accessing the blueCircle object and adding an event listener to the object with the addEventListener command. When you add an event listener to an object, you are telling Flash to listen for a specific event broadcasted from the object and then do something if that event is heard.

Inside the parentheses that follow the addEventListener command are two required items, separated by a comma. The first is the type of event you want to track. There are many types of events; you can even create your own! Some of the most common are mouse events, keyboard events, touch events, and timer events. Since you want to watch for a mouse event, you specify MouseEvent type.

There are several actions you can perform with a mouse: move it, hover over an object, move away from an object, click, double-click, and others. In this example, you want to track if the mouse clicks the blueCircle object. So you append a period and the phrase CLICK in all caps to MouseEvent. You just told the event listener that you want it to listen for a mouse click on the blueCircle object.

FIGURE 5.3 A basic CLICK event example

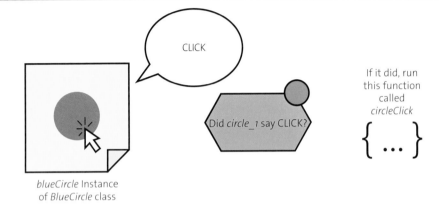

blueCircle Instance of *BlueCircle* class

When the event listener hears a mouse click, you want it to do *something*. The second item in the parentheses is that *something*. In the code example, you are telling the Flash file to run a function with the name `circleClick`. You'll notice that you don't need a set of parentheses after the function name here. In fact, you would get an error if you included them.

If you click outside the blue circle, you'll notice that the Output panel doesn't say anything. That is because the mouse isn't interacting with the MovieClip, which is what the event listener is tracking.

However, when the mouse is clicked over the blue circle, the event is broadcasted, the listener picks it up, determines if it is a click event (which it is), and tells Flash to run the code in the `circleClick` function. The `circleClick` executes the `trace` command, sending the phrase "Click!" to the Output panel.

Figure 5.3 illustrates the simple event you just created.

Take a closer look at the `circleClick` callback function:

```
function circleClick(e:MouseEvent):void
{
    trace("Click!");
}
```

Notice that the `circleClick` function has a parameter called e. When an event handler accesses a function in the listener, the handler sends an event object, in this case it is a `MouseEvent` type of event object. The event object contains information about the event that was broadcasted that you can use in your function. In this case, you aren't doing anything with it, but you need to include it in your function parameter definition since the broadcaster is sending it. It is a general practice to call this e, evt, or event in your function parameter declaration.

You aren't going to work with the event object in this chapter, but later you will work more with the various properties of the object to have greater flexibility in working with events.

WHAT IS A MOUSEEVENT TYPE?

You might be asking yourself why you use MouseEvent instead of String or Number like you have in previous function parameter examples. ActionScript strings and numbers are objects that contain letters or numeric values. ActionScript supports many more complex or custom types of objects, such as the MouseEvent that is sent by the broadcaster when the event is sent. You'll be working with more complex events later in the book, and even create your own custom events.

FIGURE 5.4 Hover! and Click!

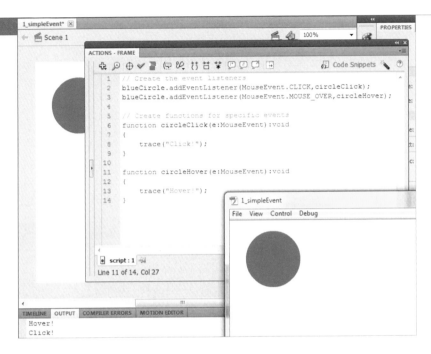

You can add more ActionScript to your code to track other actions, such as a mouse hover. You should also add comments to make your code easier to understand:

1. Update the code to contain the following:

```
// Create the event listeners
blueCircle.addEventListener(MouseEvent.CLICK,circleClick);
blueCircle.addEventListener(MouseEvent.MOUSE_OVER,circleHover);
// Create functions for specific events
function circleClick(e:MouseEvent):void
{
    trace("Click!");
}
function circleHover(e:MouseEvent):void
{
    trace("Hover!");
}
```

You have added a second event listener. This one is listening for the MOUSE_OVER event, which happens when the pointer moves over a specific object.

2. Run the project.

3. Move the pointer over the blue circle. You'll see "Hover!" in the Output panel.

4. Click the blue circle. You'll still see the "Click!" message (**Figure 5.4**).

There are several mouse actions that you can track, and you can track them in the same exact way you did with the click and hover examples. **Table 5.1** lists some common mouse events you can use in your applications:

TABLE 5.1 Common Mouse Events

EVENT	TYPE OF EVENT
MouseEvent.CLICK	Broadcasted when the mouse single-clicks the object
MouseEvent.DOUBLE_CLICK	Broadcasted when the mouse double-clicks the object
MouseEvent.MOUSE_DOWN	Broadcasted when the pointer is over the object and the mouse button is pressed
MouseEvent.MOUSE_MOVE	Broadcasted when the mouse is moved
MouseEvent.MOUSE_OUT	Broadcasted when the mouse moves off the object
MouseEvent.MOUSE_OVER	Broadcasted when the pointer is over the object
MouseEvent.MOUSE_UP	Broadcasted when the pointer is over the object and the mouse button is released
MouseEvent.MOUSE_WHEEL	Broadcasted when the mouse wheel is scrolled up or down
MouseEvent.ROLL_OUT	Broadcasted when the mouse moves off the object
MouseEvent.ROLL_OVER	Broadcasted when the pointer is over the object

WRAPPING **UP**

In this chapter, you learned the basics of working with events, specifically responding to mouse interactions. Events are at the core of building interactivity into your projects. When working with events, here are a set of guidelines to help you avoid errors:

- To create an event, you need to create an event listener by attaching the addEventListener statement to the object you want to listen to.

- To respond to specific events, the addEventListener needs to have two parameters: the event type you are listening to and the name of a function that will run if the listener hears the event.

- Event types have two parts: the type of event, like MouseEvent, followed by a period; and then an all-caps phrase to define the specific event, like CLICK.

- In your event listener, you are naming the callback function, not creating it, so don't use parentheses after the callback function name.

- When you create the callback function, you need to accept a specific object called a MouseEvent object, typically called e in the function definition.

6

USING **TIMELINE SCRIPTING** WITH **MOUSE EVENTS**

Everything you have done so far has used ActionScript and for the most part, ignored the timeline. I want to reassure you that you don't need to choose one over the other, the timeline and ActionScript can peacefully coexist. In fact, they work very well together, and you'll be able to create some amazing projects using both.

There are certain ActionScript commands that can alter the playback of the timeline. In this chapter, you'll learn about all of these timeline controls. Some of these might be familiar to you already, but in this chapter you'll use these controls in combination with mouse events to create an interactive project.

EXPLAINING THE PROJECT

FIGURE 6.1 Example project before starting to create code

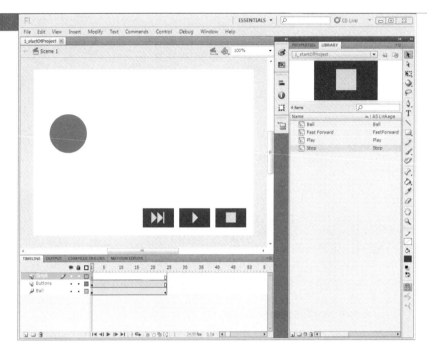

The project in this chapter has a ball that moves across the screen. Let's check out the project and see how you can add mouse events to the existing timeline scripts (**Figure 6.1**).

This starting project is available on the book's website (www.peachpit.com/ actionscript3dd) as the 1_startOfProject.fla file. Download the file to your computer and open the FLA file in Flash Professional CS5.5.

The ball on the stage is an instance of the Ball Library object with the instance name of myBall. This instance is tweened on the Ball timeline layer from frame 1 to 24. The tween animates the ball from the left side of the stage to the right.

The Stage also has single instances of the Fast Forward, Stop, and Play Library objects on the stage. These have the instance names of forwardButton, stopButton, and playButton respectively and are on the Buttons layer.

If you run the project now, the ball will move across the screen the project will repeat, because Flash automatically repeats the main timeline unless you specifi-cally tell it to stop at a certain point.

Now you are ready to start adding some ActionScript to control the button actions.

CONTROLLING TIMELINE PLAYBACK

Let's start looking at ways you can let the user modify the playback of the project. Controlling playback will require that you combine playback commands with the mouse events that you learned in the last chapter. You'll start with adding a playback control to stop the movie when you click the stop button.

STOPPING PLAYBACK

On the Script timeline layer, you can stop playback of the overall project and link that action to a mouse event broadcasted from the stopButton instance.

1. Add the following code to the Script layer:

```
/*
Demonstrate how to combine frame controls with ActionScript code
*/
// Add event listener and callback function for the STOP button
stopButton.addEventListener(MouseEvent.CLICK, stopBall);
function stopBall(e:MouseEvent):void
{
    trace("Stop playback");
    stop();
}
```

FIGURE 6.2 Stopping playback using an event listener

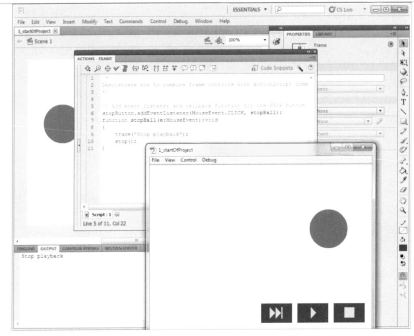

2. Save and run the project. When you click the stop button, you'll stop the playback of the project.

What you are doing here is adding an event listener to the stopButton object. This listener will listen for the CLICK mouse event. When it hears this event, it will execute the stopBall function. The stopBall function accepts the event from the listener, sends a message to the Output panel, and executes the stop() function that halts the playback of the main timeline. **Figure 6.2** shows an example of how this looks.

I should point out that while the script is on frame 1, it still works when the project is playing a different frame. When the project starts, the code that is in frame 1 is processed and remains resident in the application. It is one reason why when working with tweens and timelines that your ActionScript should be on frame 1, unless you are doing something very specific at a particular frame.

As you type in Flash Professional CS5.5, you may notice that there are some additional lines of code that are added to the top of your ActionScript. It might look something like this:

```
import flash.events.MouseEvent;
```

These will be covered in more depth later in the book, but the simple explanation is that this allows the functionality and information that is part of the MouseEvent inside your code, allowing you to refer to it and use it inside your project.

For now, make sure you keep the line in place; otherwise your project won't work.

SEEKING TO A SPECIFIC FRAME

In addition to stopping playback, you can also *seek* (go to) a specific numbered frame in the project and stop playback at that point. You can do that by adding a new event listener to the forwardButton instance, and create a new callback function.

1. Add the following code to the bottom of your existing project:

```
// Add event listener and callback function for the FAST
// FORWARD button
forwardButton.addEventListener(MouseEvent.CLICK, jumpBall);
function jumpBall(e:MouseEvent):void
{
    trace("Seek and stop to frame 24");
    gotoAndStop(24);
}
```

FIGURE 6.3 Seeking to a specific frame and stopping playback

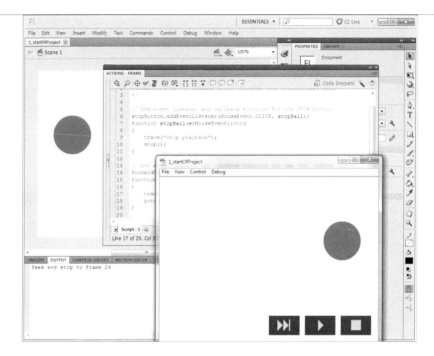

2. Save and run your project.

3. Click the fast forward button to activate the new event handler.

    In this code, you are adding an event listener to the jump button. The callback function in this case is executing the gotoAndStop() function, which moves the playback to a specific frame and then stops the playback at that point. An example is shown in **Figure 6.3**.

    If you didn't want to stop playback after seeking to the specified frame, but instead continue playback, you could replace the gotoAndStop() function with the gotoAndPlay() command.

WORKING WITH MOVIECLIP TIMELINES

All these examples have been working with the main timeline. However, each of the MovieClips in the Library have their own timeline that you can work with and build motion and animations with and then control from the main timeline.

The buttons in this project are pretty flat. They don't highlight when you mouse over them, or show any other visual effects. You can use their internal timelines to create special effects to make them more interesting.

To edit these timelines, you can either double-click the object in the Library, or double-click the instance on the Stage. Double-clicking the instance on the Stage will show you the edits in context of the instance, which is often helpful. This technique is called *editing-in-place*.

1. Double-click the playButton instance on the Stage to edit-in-place.

    You'll see that you now have access to the internal timeline of the object and you can make modifications inside. When you make changes in this way, you'll apply the changes to all instances of the object since you are editing an instance of an object in the Library. In this case, you have only one instance, but this is important to remember.

    Also note the breadcrumb trail at the top of the window; it shows that you are within the Play object in the Library.

2. Add a new frame by selecting frame 2, right-clicking, and selecting Insert Keyframe.

    This will create a duplicate of the previous keyframe in the project, in which you can modify the design of the object to be unique from the object in the keyframe before it.

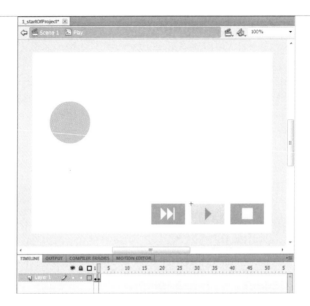

FIGURE 6.4 Editing a MovieClip's internal timeline

3. Change the color of the background and play icon using the Paint Bucket tool, or through the color picker.

   You should have something that looks like **Figure 6.4**.

4. Run the project.

   You'll instantly see there is a problem. The playButton instance is flipping between the two frames you created. As you learned earlier, Flash automatically repeats timelines unless you specifically stop them. So to avoid this, you need to stop playback on the first frame.

5. While inside the stop button, create a new timeline layer and name it **Script**. If you are on the main timeline, double-click the stop button to enter it.

6. Select frame 1 of the new Script timeline layer, right-click, and select Actions.

7. Enter stop(); in the Actions panel.

8. Run the project again.

   Now the button won't oscillate when you run the project.

   Repeat this process for the other two buttons in the project.

USING THE EVENT CALLBACK OBJECT AND HANDLING SCOPE

Since you started learning about events, you've accepted an event object named e in the callback function. While you haven't used the object yet, it contains valuable information about the event that you can use in your code. Let's put this valuable information to work. But first, you need to see how the scope of this information affects your project.

THE EVENT CALLBACK OBJECT

Often when you hover over a button, there will be some sort of action that takes place. For instance, the button might change color, or it might move slightly. You created these effects in the last section, but now you need to hook them up to the mouse events of the button for them to work.

There are a couple of ways you can link this effect with events. You have not been doing much with the event callback object. Let's introduce how that can be used, and why.

Let's first start with a basic event listener for the play button.

1. Add the following code to the bottom of the code that is already in the project:

    ```
    // Create rollovers for the playback control buttons
    playButton.addEventListener(MouseEvent.MOUSE_OVER, hoverButton);
    function hoverButton(e:MouseEvent):void
    {
        gotoAndStop(2);
    }
    ```

2. Run the project. You won't get something you expect.

3. Hover over the play button.

    The entire movie stops playing back and goes to frame 2. That is because when you hover, you execute the hoverButton callback function and the *scope* of the code is taking place on the main timeline. You need some way to tell the hoverButton function that you are focusing on the playButton instance. You can do that by defining the instance before the gotoAndStop() statement using dot notation.

4. Prepend `playButton.` to the `gotoAndStop(2)` statement inside the `hoverButton()` function:

```
// Create rollovers for the playback control buttons
playButton.addEventListener(MouseEvent.MOUSE_OVER, hoverButton);
function hoverButton(e:MouseEvent):void
{
    playButton.gotoAndStop(2);
}
```

5. Run the project. You'll see that you have the desired roll on effect for the `MOUSE_OVER` event.

Let's finish the button by adding an effect to the `MOUSE_OUT` event.

6. Update the code like this:

```
// Create rollovers for the playback control buttons
playButton.addEventListener(MouseEvent.MOUSE_OVER, hoverButton);
playButton.addEventListener(MouseEvent.MOUSE_OUT, hoverOffButton);
function hoverButton(e:MouseEvent):void
{
    playButton.gotoAndStop(2);
}
function hoverOffButton(e:MouseEvent):void
{
    playButton.gotoAndStop(1);
}
```

7. Run the project. You now have everything working for the play button.

But you have two more buttons to do. Does that mean you have to repeat *all* of this to get the buttons working?

No. You don't—and this is when you use the event callback object.

USING THE EVENT CALLBACK OBJECT

You have been accepting an event callback object, named e. Now you'll start using its valuable information.

The e object contains a number of properties that you can use in your projects. One of these is a property called target, which is the name of the object that triggered the event. Let's take the previous example and add a trace statement to see how this works.

1. Modify the hoverButton() function to add this trace statement:

    ```
    function hoverButton(e:MouseEvent):void
    {
        trace(e.target);
    playButton.gotoAndStop(2);
    }
    ```

2. Run the project.

3. Move your mouse over the play button. You'll see the phrase [object Play] appear in the Output panel, indicating that it is taking an object of the Play class and is sending it to the Output panel. This indicates that e.target is a reference to the object that sent the event, in this case the Play object.

    You can now use e.target as a substitution for explicitly calling playButton() in the callback function.

When using the gotoAndStop and gotoAndPlay statements, you can also use frame labels as substitutes for frame numbers. These labels can be created in the main timeline by selecting a keyframe and adding a label in the Properties panel. You can then refer to it using quotation marks, for example:

```
function ballOver(e:MouseEvent)
{
    myBall.gotoAndStop("glow");
}
```

4. Change the code to swap e.target for the playButton instance:

```
// Create rollovers for the playback control buttons
playButton.addEventListener(MouseEvent.MOUSE_OVER, hoverButton);
playButton.addEventListener(MouseEvent.MOUSE_OUT, hoverOffButton);
function hoverButton(e:MouseEvent):void
{
    e.target.gotoAndStop(2);
}
function hoverOffButton(e:MouseEvent):void
{
    e.target.gotoAndStop(1);
}
```

5. Run the project. You'll see that the program works just as it did before.

Now, here is where you will really maximize the benefits of all that information available in that little e. All the examples you have worked on so far using events have had a matching callback function; but you can also use the same callback function multiple times for different event listeners. You don't need to have a one-to-one matching of them in your project.

In this case, you need to create new event listeners for the other objects that will use the same callback functions. Since the callback functions now know to look for the e.target object as its reference, you can use this callback function for different event listeners.

The next step to get this all working, is to finish creating the event listeners for the other objects.

6. Add the following MOUSE_OVER and MOUSE_OUT event code for the forwardButton and stopButton instances:

```
// Create rollovers for the playback control buttons
playButton.addEventListener(MouseEvent.MOUSE_OVER, hoverButton);
playButton.addEventListener(MouseEvent.MOUSE_OUT, hoverOffButton);
forwardButton.addEventListener(MouseEvent.MOUSE_OVER,
    hoverButton);
forwardButton.addEventListener(MouseEvent.MOUSE_OUT,
    hoverOffButton);
stopButton.addEventListener(MouseEvent.MOUSE_OVER, hoverButton);
stopButton.addEventListener(MouseEvent.MOUSE_OUT, hoverOffButton);
function hoverButton(e:MouseEvent):void
{
    e.target.gotoAndStop(2);
}
function hoverOffButton(e:MouseEvent):void
{
    e.target.gotoAndStop(1);
}
```

7. Run the project. The buttons behave the same as they did before the changes.

SHORTCUTS FOR gotoAndStop()

In this example, when you hover or move off the buttons, you are moving the playhead of the button movie clips up or back one frame. There are two commands that make this more explicit and don't force you to remember and specify frame numbers: nextFrame() and prevFrame().

1. Substitute the gotoAndStop statements with the nextFrame() and prevFrame() functions:

```
function hoverButton(e:MouseEvent):void
{
    e.target.nextFrame();
}
function hoverOffButton(e:MouseEvent):void
{
    e.target.prevFrame();
}
```

2. Run the project. The buttons behave the same as they did before the changes.

THE FINISHED EXAMPLE

Now your code is dynamic and more flexible. Your project should look like the following code. The completed project is named 2_internalTimelines.fla and is available on the book website (www.peachpit.com/actionscript3dd).

```
import flash.events.MouseEvent;
/*
Demonstrate how to combine frame controls with ActionScript code
*/
// Add event listener and callback function for the STOP button
stopButton.addEventListener(MouseEvent.CLICK, stopBall);
function stopBall(e:MouseEvent):void
```

```
{
    trace("Stop playback");
    stop();
}
// Add event listener and callback function for the FAST FORWARD button
forwardButton.addEventListener(MouseEvent.CLICK, jumpBall);
function jumpBall(e:MouseEvent):void
{
    trace("Seek and stop to frame 24");
    gotoAndStop(24);
}
// Add event listener and callback function for the PLAY button
playButton.addEventListener(MouseEvent.CLICK, playBall);
function playBall(e:MouseEvent):void
{
    trace("Play");
    play();
}
// Create rollovers for the playback control buttons
playButton.addEventListener(MouseEvent.MOUSE_OVER, hoverButton);
playButton.addEventListener(MouseEvent.MOUSE_OUT, hoverOffButton);
forwardButton.addEventListener(MouseEvent.MOUSE_OVER, hoverButton);
forwardButton.addEventListener(MouseEvent.MOUSE_OUT, hoverOffButton);
stopButton.addEventListener(MouseEvent.MOUSE_OVER, hoverButton);
stopButton.addEventListener(MouseEvent.MOUSE_OUT, hoverOffButton);
function hoverButton(e:MouseEvent):void
{
    e.target.nextFrame();
```

FIGURE 6.5 Another event
callback object example

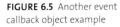
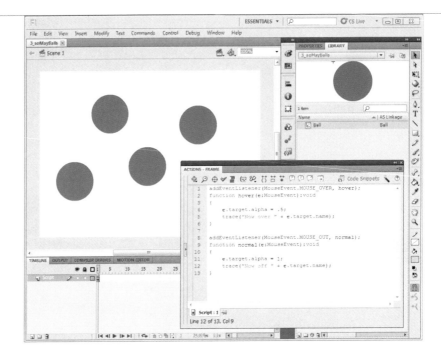

```
}
function hoverOffButton(e:MouseEvent):void
{
    e.target.prevFrame();
}
```

ANOTHER e EXAMPLE

Using the event target data is one way to make your event handlers dynamic. Let's look at another example that will illustrate this. The project is available on the book website (www.peachpit.com/actionscript3dd) as the file named 3_soManyBalls.fla and is shown in **Figure 6.5**.

In this example, you have the same Ball object in the library with multiple instances on the stage called ball1, ball2, ball3, ball4, and ball5. On the Scripts layer of the main timeline is the following code.

```
addEventListener(MouseEvent.MOUSE_OVER, hover);
function hover(e:MouseEvent):void
{
    e.target.alpha = .5;
    trace("Now over " + e.target.name);
}
addEventListener(MouseEvent.MOUSE_OUT, normal);
function normal(e:MouseEvent):void
{
    e.target.alpha = 1;
    trace("Now off " + e.target.name);
}
```

Instead of placing the event listener on a specific object, it has been placed at the current scope of the main timeline. The event handlers capture the event object and manipulate the alpha level of the event target. To help illustrate the event target, a trace statement is used to output the name of the event object target. The name attribute is used to display the instance name that has been applied to the object in Flash once the file is running.

When you run this, if the mouse moves over any of the balls, its transparency value is affected, and the Output panel displays a message.

Even though this code uses only a single event handler, it is still dynamic because it uses the event object's data values. When you learn about conditionals, you can apply greater amounts of control over what happens in the callback function based on the type of event broadcasted or the event target.

WORKING WITH SIMPLE
CALLBACK FUNCTIONS

The last callback function is pretty simple. It contains only a single line of Action-Script code. You could understandably wonder why you would need to create four lines of code just to do a single action.

Luckily, you can put all of this on a single line by using a generic unnamed function in the event listener itself. This function cannot be called in any other area of the code because it is fully encapsulated within the event listener; but if your callback is doing only one thing, it can make your code more concise:

```
// Add event listener and callback function for roll out of the
// PAUSE button
myBall.addEventListener(MouseEvent.MOUSE_OUT,
    function (e:MouseEvent) {myBall.gotoAndStop('normal'); });
```

This code replaced the callback function name in the event handler with a specific function definition. This function doesn't have a name, but does contain the other basic parts, the `function` statement, the parameter definition, and the code block.

Notice that this example introduces a new item: single quotes. You have used double quotes to denote strings, but it is just as legal to use matching single quotes for strings as well, and can be helpful and even preferable for some situations.

While completely optional, this approach can make your simple callback functions more concise. The limitations are that you can't execute this function outside the callback function, and adding multiple commands can make this approach cumbersome.

NOTE: Some code blocks in this book contain a single line of Action-Script code; however, it cannot fit on the printed page. Therefore, the line indention is an indication of a continued line and not a new line.

WRAPPING **UP**

In this chapter, you learned how you can combine timelines with mouse events. There are lots of ways to combine main and encapsulated timelines with your projects using mouse events. When working with events and timelines, try to keep in mind the following to avoid issues or errors:

- Use basic playback commands like `stop()`, `play()`, `gotoAndStop()`, `gotoAndPlay()`, `nextFrame()`, and `prevFrame()` to control playback of your main timeline.

- To control items in encapsulated timelines from the main timeline, prefix your playback commands with the instance name containing the timeline.

- Remember that timelines automatically loop unless you say to do otherwise using `stop()` in your timeline.

- Use the callback event object e to access the name of the object using the `target` property that triggered the event for use in your callback function.

7

CREATING TIMER
AND FRAME **EVENTS**

In addition to mouse events, there are two types of events that will be helpful for you in your applications. The first is the timer event, which is an internal stopwatch in ActionScript that you can use to trigger events after a specific amount of time. The second is the frame event, which is triggered every time a new frame in the Flash runtime is displayed.

This chapter will introduce both types of events and will show you when to use them appropriately.

USING THE TIMER EVENT

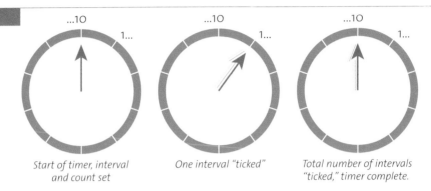

FIGURE 7.1 Anatomy of
a TimerEvent

*Start of timer, interval
and count set*

One interval "ticked"

*Total number of intervals
"ticked," timer complete.*

When you need to create events based on time, you need to use a timer, known in ActionScript as *Timer*. A timer and its related event type, TimerEvent, is like a countdown clock. You define how long you want a timer to run, and it will broadcast a special event when the allotted time expires. You can customize the timer to repeat indefinitely or for a set number of times.

Some of the attributes that define a time are shown in **Figure 7.1**. You will work with these attributes to learn how to create a timer event.

A timer has a few properties that define how it works, the events it broadcasts, and how it completes. A timer is first created and defined with two parameters. The first, the *interval*, is the amount of time that passes each time before the timer sends an event, similar to when you hear a tick on a stopwatch. The second defines the number of intervals that the timer will have, or if it will run forever, or infinitely. When the last interval "ticks," the timer indicates that it is finished and stops running.

Figure 7.1 shows a timer that has been configured with a 1-second interval, meaning that each "tick" of the timer will last 1 second. It has also been configured to have a total number of ten intervals, so after the tenth interval the timer will be complete.

Each of these two parameters define the events that are fired by the timer. When the timer is started, and the first "tick" takes place after a second, the TimerEvent.TIMER event is broadcasted from the timer. When the last interval "ticks," the timer then broadcasts a TimerEvent.TIMER_COMPLETE event, signifying that the timer has completed its operation.

Let's start with a basic example.

1. Create a new ActionScript 3.0 file and enter the following code as a frame script:

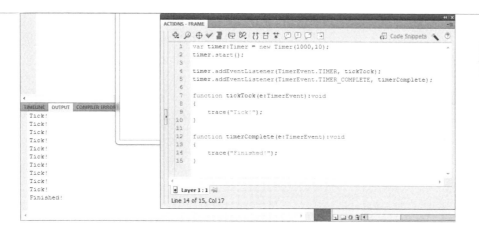

FIGURE 7.2
An example timer
in ActionScript

```
var timer:Timer = new Timer(1000,10);

timer.start();

timer.addEventListener(TimerEvent.TIMER, tickTock);

timer.addEventListener(TimerEvent.TIMER_COMPLETE,
timerComplete);

function tickTock(e:TimerEvent):void

{

    trace("Tick!");

}

function timerComplete(e:TimerEvent):void

{

    trace("Finished!");

}
```

2. Run the project.

The Output panel (**Figure 7.2**) adds a "Tick!" to the display at regular intervals. After ten "Tick!" displays, the Output panel displays "Finished!" What you are doing is creating a timer that will broadcast an event every second after it is started and when the final interval runs. Then when each event is broadcasted, you are adding a line to the Output console.

Let's step through the code to see how it works. The first line creates the timer itself and then customizes its parameters. In this case, you are creating a timer that will last for 1 second. The values for these parameters are defined in milliseconds, and since there are 1000 milliseconds in a second, you set this as 1000. You want the timer to have ten intervals, which is defined by the second parameter. If you wanted the timer to run infinitely, you would omit this parameter.

A timer doesn't start running until you tell it to start. You do that on the second line using the start() function that is part of the timer instance.

You then create the event listeners. In this case, you are listening for a timer event instead of a mouse event, so you use the TimerEvent type inside the listener parameters. The TimerEvent event type has an event called TIMER that is what is broadcasted with each interval of time—in this case, after the timer has run for 1000 milliseconds, or a single second. Just like with the previous examples, you also provide a callback function, which in this example is called tickTock().

You then create the second listener for when all the timer intervals end, using the TIMER_COMPLETE event type of the TimerEvent event. This triggers a different callback function called timerComplete().

The callback function accepts an event object parameter, in this case a TimerEvent object instead of a MouseEvent, which then sends "Tick!" to the Output panel using the trace statement in the first callback function, or "Finished!" in the second.

STOPPING THE TIMER

If for some reason you need to stop the timer, you can add the stop() function, which will end the timer. The following is an example:

```
var timer:Timer = new Timer(1000,10);

timer.start();

timer.addEventListener(TimerEvent.TIMER, tickTock);

timer.addEventListener(TimerEvent.TIMER_COMPLETE, timerComplete);

function tickTock(e:TimerEvent):void

{
```

```
    trace("Tick!");

    timer.stop();

}

function timerComplete(e:TimerEvent):void

{

    trace("Finished!");

}
```

In this example, the code contains a stop() function that targets the timer object. When this code runs, it produces only one "Tick!" in the Output panel. Notice also that the timerComplete() callback function isn't executed. Although the timer stopped, the code doesn't broadcast the TIMER_COMPLETE event, because this event broadcasts only when the timer completes naturally—without interruption using stop().

USING THE ENTER FRAME EVENT

Another type of event that you will use in your project is the ENTER_FRAME event. This event takes place each time your project plays another frame in the Flash runtime.

One precaution about this event is to not overload or over use it. Putting too much processing power into the ENTER_FRAME event can affect performance in your project. For basic activities, this event will work fine, but this is good to know as you get to more advanced projects.

The implementation of the ENTER_FRAME event is pretty basic. Let's look at this example.

1. Create a new ActionScript 3.0 project in Flash Professional CS5.5.

2. Create a new MovieClip named **Ball** and add it to the Library, removing it from the Stage.

3. Enter the following into the main timeline as a frame script:

```
// Create a new ball and add to the display stack
var myBall:Ball = new Ball();
myBall.x = 50;
myBall.y = 50;
addChild(myBall);
// Add ENTER_FRAME event
myBall.addEventListener(Event.ENTER_FRAME, moveBall);
// Callback function for ENTER_FRAME event
function moveBall(e:Event):void
{
    myBall.x++;
}
```

4. Run the project. You'll see the ball slowly inch across the screen.

Congratulations! You have created your first ActionScript-only animation! As you become more proficient in ActionScript, you'll find that creating animations in ActionScript will give you extensive control and capabilities that the timeline alone can't offer. But enough congratulations for now—take a look at the code and walk through how it works.

In the opening section, you are creating an instance of the Ball class called myBall, positioning it on the Stage, and adding to the display stack.

The event listener in this case is listening for the ENTER_FRAME event type that is part of the generic Event object. You then indicate that you want to run the moveBall() callback function when the listener hears the event.

The moveBall() callback function then increases the x property by 1, changing the location on the Stage. You'll find that the object will move off the Stage but continue to run. This is because the location is now beyond the width of the project.

REMOVING EVENT LISTENERS

Now that you can add event listeners, you should also remove them when you no longer need them. In fact, removing unwanted listeners is a best practice for enhancing performance, especially when you start working with larger applications and projects.

Removing event listeners uses the exact same format as adding them, except you use the removeEventListener() function to disable and remove the listener, stating the specific event and callback function that you no longer want to listen for and trigger.

Let's take the previous example, where you were animating a simple ball across the stage using the ENTER_FRAME event, and add a mouse event to remove the listener to stop the animation.

1. Modify the existing code as follows:

```
// Create a new ball and add to the display stack
var myBall:Ball = new Ball();
myBall.x = 50;
myBall.y = 50;
addChild(myBall);
// Add ENTER_FRAME event
myBall.addEventListener(Event.ENTER_FRAME, moveBall);
// Add CLICK event
myBall.addEventListener(MouseEvent.CLICK, stopEvents);
// Callback function for ENTER_FRAME event
function moveBall(e:Event):void
{
    myBall.x++;
    trace("Ball is at " + myBall.x);
}
// Callback function for CLICK event
```

```
function stopEvents(e:MouseEvent):void
{
    myBall.removeEventListener(Event.ENTER_FRAME, moveBall);
    myBall.removeEventListener(MouseEvent.CLICK, stopEvents);
}
```

2. Run the project.

The first section of new code adds a new event handler for the mouse click on the ball. Next, the original callback function for the ENTER_FRAME event is now displaying the current x property location in the Output panel.

The next section of code is the new callback function for the CLICK event. By using removeEventListener(), you are indicating what event type and what callback you are removing as a listener. In this case, you are no longer listening for the ENTER_FRAME event from myBall, and will then remove the reference to the callback function, moveBall(). You know this is working because when you run the project and click on the ball, the ball no longer moves, and the trace statement doesn't execute anymore, meaning that the moveBall() callback function is not running any longer.

Since this action would happen only once in the project, you are also being diligent and removing the CLICK event as well, since there is now no reason to keep listening for that event.

WHEN TO USE FRAME VS. TIMER EVENTS

FIGURE 7.3 Frame rate property (FPS) in the Properties panel

A common question for people new to ActionScript is when to use timers or enter frame events. The answer isn't a clear-cut one, but here is an example to help you understand the differences.

Let's modify the example used earlier.

1. Replace the code in the project with the following to help illustrate the point:

```
// Create a new ball and add to the display stack
var myBall:Ball = new Ball();
myBall.x = 50;
myBall.y = 50;
addChild(myBall);
// Add ENTER_FRAME event listener
myBall.addEventListener(Event.ENTER_FRAME, moveBall);
// Callback function for ENTER_FRAME
function moveBall(e:Event):void
{
    myBall.x++;
}
```

2. Run the project. The project runs exactly as before, with the ball slowly creeping across the screen.

Flash Professional projects have something called a frame rate. This value defines the number of frames that pass in a second. By default, the frame rate is 24 frames per second. Based on this, you can say with reasonable accuracy that using the code moves the ball 24 pixels to the right in a second.

What happens if you change the frame rate?

In Flash Professional CS5.5, your project properties allow you to change your frame rate, or FPS. Let's modify that now.

3. Deselect any objects and open the Properties panel (**Figure 7.3**).

4. Set the frame rate (FPS) to **5**.

5. Run the project again. You'll notice that the animation runs much slower. This is because it is now firing the ENTER_FRAME only 5 times per second instead of the 24 that it was doing earlier.

ENTER_FRAME is directly connected to your frame rate. If you modify your frame rate, any animation you create using ENTER_FRAME will be affected.

Let's change the code to use a timer and see what the difference is.

6. Change the ActionScript code to match the following, but keep the frame rate at 5:

```
// Create a new ball and add to the display stack
var myBall:Ball = new Ball();
myBall.x = 50;
myBall.y = 50;
addChild(myBall);
// Create a animation timer
var myTimer:Timer = new Timer(100);
// Add TIMER event listener
myTimer.addEventListener(TimerEvent.TIMER, moveBall);
// Start timer
myTimer.start();
// Callback function for ENTER_FRAME
function moveBall(e:TimerEvent):void
{
    myBall.x++;
}
```

7. Run the project. You'll see that the ball continues to creep across the stage. In fact, you are setting the timer to broadcast the TIMER event every tenth of a second (100 milliseconds).

Now, let's mess with the frame rate a bit more.

8. Access the FPS property again and change it to **100**.

Setting the frame rate to 100 is really high, but it will illustrate a point.

9. Run the project and you'll see what I mean.

Notice that the rate of motion of the ball doesn't change. The only thing you may notice is that the animation is a little smoother than it was before. Here's why: The FPS is indicating how many frames per second are being rendered, which directly affects the ENTER_FRAME event. The timer is based on time, and is independent of the FPS value, so you can set the value high, low, or whatever—the animation will always run at the same rate. The difference is that the fluidity of the movement may be better using high FPS since there are more frames being rendered each second to show your timer animation. If you want this timer-based animation to run faster, you would need to modify the interval of the timer, perhaps lowering it to 50 milliseconds to make it run twice as fast, or increasing it to 200 milliseconds to make it run twice as slow.

WRAPPING **UP**

In this chapter, you learned how to use timers and frames to control actions using the `TIMER`, `TIMER_COMPLETE`, and `ENTER_FRAME` events. You also covered the differences in how they work and how they relate to your project's frame rate, or FPS. Here are some tips to help you work with these new capabilities in ActionScript:

- To use a timer, create a new timer using the new statement and define the timer properties: interval duration in milliseconds and, optionally, the number of intervals in the timer.

- To create an infinitely running timer, omit the number of intervals in the timer.

- When using a timer, remember to use the `start()` function to start it "ticking."

- Listen for the `TimerEvent.TIMER` for each "tick" of the timer, and `TimerEvent.TIMER_COMPLETE` for when the last interval runs.

- Use the `stop()` function to interrupt the timer.

- When working with frame events, listen for the `Event.ENTER_FRAME` event.

- Remember that frame rate (FPS) directly affects the rate of an `ENTER_FRAME`-based animation.

- FPS doesn't affect the speed of a timer-based animation, but can affect its fluidity.

- Increase or decrease the interval of a timer-based animation to change the rate of the animation.

- Remember to remove unwanted listeners using the `removeEventListeners()` function.

PROJECT 1

COUNTDOWN CLOCK

You've learned a lot about ActionScript so far, and now it is time to apply these new skills in a project that you try on your own. The projects in this book are divided into two parts. The first defines the requirements of the project, and gives you some hints and things to consider before you launch Flash Professional CS5.5 and start cranking out code. This structure is very similar to how you might use Flash in your job. Your client or company has a set of requirements in a document or some other form that you need to include in your finished project. You also probably have some people that you work with that you can get some advice and guidance from as well.

The second part is a walkthrough of a finished project that meets the project requirements and includes how it was completed. The finished example is also available on the book website (www.peachpit.com/actionscript3dd) for you to download and tinker with. Let's get started.

PROJECT SPECIFICATION:
COUNTDOWN CLOCK

A clock needs to be created for someone to trigger a countdown timer, see an analog representation of the remaining amount of time, and send notification when the clock has completed counting down.

The countdown timer has a fixed duration of 10 seconds, the countdown clock has an analog unit of measurement of 1 second, and it does not show smaller increments of time.

Working like an analog clock or stopwatch, a clock hand starts pointing up at the "12 o'clock" position and rotates clockwise around the analog dial, ending back at the "12 o'clock" position.

The project should have a trigger button that starts the countdown. The button should be removed when the countdown starts, and when the timer is complete.

The user interface design should match the wireframe comps that are part of the design specification for the project. Visual design requirements are not specified and are at the interactive designer's discretion.

VISUAL DESIGN REVIEW: COUNTDOWN CLOCK

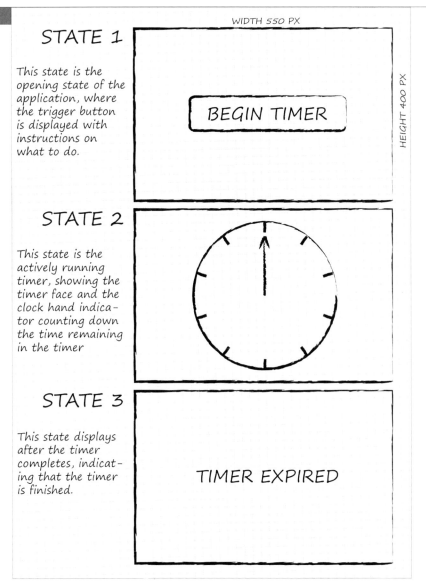

FIGURE P1.1 Clock wireframe

WIDTH 550 PX

HEIGHT 400 PX

STATE 1

This state is the opening state of the application, where the trigger button is displayed with instructions on what to do.

BEGIN TIMER

STATE 2

This state is the actively running timer, showing the timer face and the clock hand indicator counting down the time remaining in the timer

STATE 3

This state displays after the timer completes, indicating that the timer is finished.

TIMER EXPIRED

After reviewing the project spec, the user experience designer created a wireframe (**Figure P1:1**) that outlines the user interface and defines how the user interacts with the clock.

KICK-OFF **MEETING NOTES**:
COUNTDOWN CLOCK

Before starting the project, a number of people on the team hold a quick kick-off meeting. These quick meetings allow team members to bounce ideas off each other on how to create the project and to learn from what has and hasn't worked in previous projects.

A team member suggested that you build the application using three states. Using ActionScript, you can change the visibility and display of objects to create these states. The project will show what is in the wireframe as State 1. When the timer is started, the display changes to show State 2. When the timer expires, the interface changes to State 3.

While discussing the timer, two specific parameters of the timer were covered: The timer has an interval of one second; and the timer will have ten seconds, or ten intervals, each of one second.

A designer reminded you where the second hand rotation point is, and suggested you make sure that the rotation point of the second hand is in the right location to rotate correctly using ActionScript.

SOLUTION AND WALKTHROUGH: COUNTDOWN CLOCK

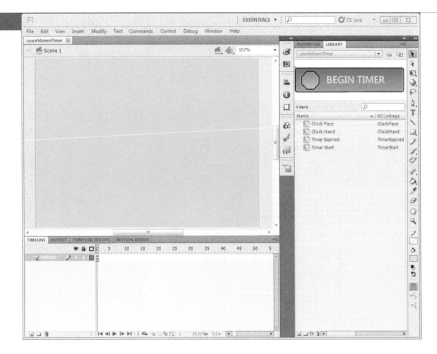

FIGURE P1.2 Project setup in Flash Professional

How did you do?

This project incorporated almost everything you have learned so far in Action-Script. Let's walk through a finished example that I made and see how it works.

Something to consider, and this will apply to all the projects in this book, is that this is just one way to solve this project. There are multiple ways to complete the project using Flash and ActionScript, which is one of the great benefits of Flash. Remember that this is an example, but you might find some techniques that I used that will make doing this project again easier.

PROJECT SETUP IN FLASH PROFESSIONAL

The project file in Flash Professional is pretty simple (**Figure P1.2**). There are no timelines to speak of, with the exception of the single frame with ActionScript code that you will look at more closely later. The Library is populated with four objects, each exported for ActionScript with a class name.

FIGURE P1.3 Setting up the hand of the clock

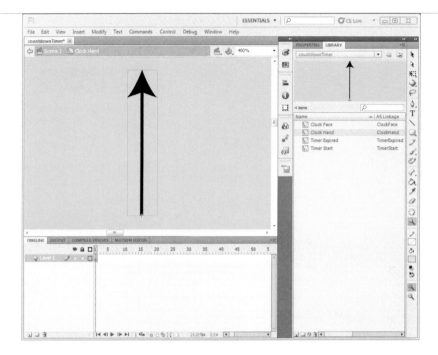

Lookng at Figure P1.2, the first item is the face of the clock (ClockFace) and then the second hand (ClockHand). Then there are two MovieClips that are used to start and end the clock. The start MovieClip (TimerStart) is used as a trigger to start the timer. When the timer ends, the TimerExpired MovieClip is displayed to show the user that time is up.

The project itself is set with a light blue background and has been set with the right dimensions defined in the design spec.

One thing that should be mentioned is the setup for the clock hand. When you create graphics in Flash Professional or import them from another product (like Adobe Illustrator), the registration point defaults to the upper-left corner of the MovieClip. The catch is that this is also where the object rotates from, which is not what you want for the hand of the clock.

The hand of the clock needs to rotate from the bottom of the arm, so the registration point needs to be configured there (**Figure P1.3**).

With the rotation point in the right place, the clock hand will rotate correctly around the clock face.

Pretty simple stuff—but let's take a look at the code next.

ACTIONSCRIPT SETUP

The ActionScript for the project is in a single frame on the timeline. Here are the contents:

```
import flash.events.MouseEvent;
import flash.utils.Timer;
import flash.events.TimerEvent;


// Create objects to display
var beginButton:TimerStart = new TimerStart();
beginButton.x = 40;
beginButton.y = 148;
beginButton.width = 471;
beginButton.height = 100;
addChild(beginButton);


var clockFace:ClockFace = new ClockFace();
clockFace.x = 99;
clockFace.y = 23;
clockFace.width = 350;
clockFace.height = 350;
clockFace.visible = false;
addChild(clockFace);


var clockHand:ClockHand = new ClockHand();
clockHand.x = 275;
clockHand.y = 202;
clockHand.width = 32;
clockHand.height = 150;
clockHand.visible = false;
```

```
addChild(clockHand);

var timerEnd:TimerExpired = new TimerExpired();
timerEnd.x = 40;
timerEnd.y = 148;
timerEnd.width = 471;
timerEnd.height = 100;
timerEnd.visible = false;
addChild(timerEnd);

// Add event listener to start timer
beginButton.addEventListener(MouseEvent.CLICK, startTimer);

// Create the timer object
var clockTimer:Timer = new Timer(1000,10);

// Add event listeners for timer
clockTimer.addEventListener(TimerEvent.TIMER, tickTimer);
clockTimer.addEventListener(TimerEvent.TIMER_COMPLETE,
    timerExpired);

// Start timer
function startTimer(e:MouseEvent):void
{
    beginButton.visible = false;
    clockFace.visible = true;
    clockHand.visible = true;
    beginButton.removeEventListener(MouseEvent.CLICK, startTimer);
```

```
        clockTimer.start();
}


// Timer tick callback
function tickTimer(e:TimerEvent):void
{
        clockHand.rotation += 36;
}


// Timer complete callback
function timerExpired(e:TimerEvent):void
{
        clockFace.visible = false;
        clockHand.visible = false;
        timerEnd.visible = true;
        clockTimer.removeEventListener(TimerEvent.TIMER, tickTimer);
        clockTimer.removeEventListener(TimerEvent.TIMER_COMPLETE,
            timerExpired);
}
```

Ok, to make this easier to work through, let's focus on specific areas, one at a time.

AUTO-GENERATED IMPORTS

As you may recall, Flash Professional will add import statements to the top of your code automatically. These lines need to stay in your project. You'll learn what the import statement does later in the book.

```
import flash.events.MouseEvent;
import flash.utils.Timer;
import flash.events.TimerEvent;
```

DISPLAY OBJECTS

This next section of code creates instances of the objects in the Library, positioning them on the Stage, setting their visibility, and adding them to the display stack.

```
// Create objects to display
var beginButton:TimerStart = new TimerStart();
beginButton.x = 40;
beginButton.y = 148;
beginButton.width = 471;
beginButton.height = 100;
addChild(beginButton);


var clockFace:ClockFace = new ClockFace();
clockFace.x = 99;
clockFace.y = 23;
clockFace.width = 350;
clockFace.height = 350;
clockFace.visible = false;
addChild(clockFace);


var clockHand:ClockHand = new ClockHand();
clockHand.x = 275;
clockHand.y = 202;
clockHand.width = 32;
clockHand.height = 150;
clockHand.visible = false;
addChild(clockHand);


var timerEnd:TimerExpired = new TimerExpired();
timerEnd.x = 40;
```

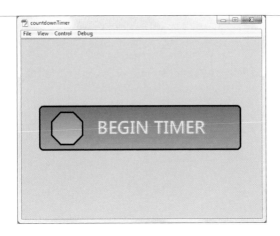

FIGURE P1.4 The clock start button

```
timerEnd.y = 148;
timerEnd.width = 471;
timerEnd.height = 100;
timerEnd.visible = false;
addChild(timerEnd);
```

Something important to notice is that the clock face is created before the clock hand. As you add children to the display stack they are placed on top of the previous objects. If you created the clock hand first and then the clock face, the hand would be obscured by the face and you couldn't see the hand.

Although the design specification defined three states to the application, you are instead using ActionScript to control the objects in the states using the `visible` property. You can toggle this property when you need to restructure the objects that are displayed in each state of the application.

EVENT LISTENER FOR THE START BUTTON

The next segment of code detects when the user clicks the start button:

```
// Add event listener to start timer
beginButton.addEventListener(MouseEvent.CLICK, startTimer);
```

Using a simple `MouseEvent.CLICK` event, you are attaching a listener to the start button of the project and executing a callback function when the user clicks the button (**Figure P1.4**).

TIMER AND TIMER EVENT LISTENERS

This section creates the timer and listens for when the user clicks the start button:

```
// Create the timer object
var clockTimer:Timer = new Timer(1000,10);


// Add event listeners for timer
clockTimer.addEventListener(TimerEvent.TIMER, tickTimer);
clockTimer.addEventListener(TimerEvent.TIMER_COMPLETE,
   timerExpired);
```

You create an object called clockTimer and define two properties. You set the interval duration to last 1,000 milliseconds, or one second. You also set a total number of ten intervals in the timer before it broadcasts an event that it is finished.

The two event listeners that are attached to the timer instance will execute a callback function when each interval is complete and when the final interval is finished.

CALLBACK FUNCTION FOR STARTING THE TIMER

This section creates the function to start the timer:

```
// Start timer
function startTimer(e:MouseEvent):void
{
    beginButton.visible = false;
    clockFace.visible = true;
    clockHand.visible = true;
    beginButton.removeEventListener(MouseEvent.CLICK, startTimer);
    clockTimer.start();
}
```

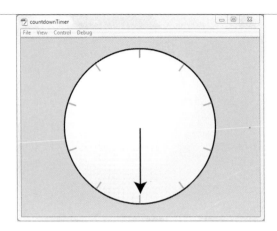

FIGURE P1.5 Showing the clock face

When you click the start button for the project, you need to execute the startTimer callback function. The function disables the visibility of the start button and then displays the clock face and hand. You don't need the button listener anymore, so remove it and then start the timer (**Figure P1.5**).

CALLBACK FUNCTIONS FOR TIMER EVENTS

This section of code handles the rotation of the clock hand:

```
// Timer tick callback
function tickTimer(e:TimerEvent):void
{
    clockHand.rotation += 36;
}


// Timer complete callback
function timerExpired(e:TimerEvent):void
{
    clockFace.visible = false;
    clockHand.visible = false;
    timerEnd.visible = true;
```

FIGURE P1.6 End of the timer

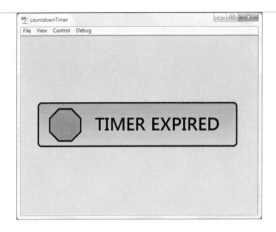

```
clockTimer.removeEventListener(TimerEvent.TIMER, tickTimer);
clockTimer.removeEventListener(TimerEvent.TIMER_COMPLETE,
    timerExpired);
}
```

The first callback function, tickTimer, is for when each interval of the timer executes. In this case, you want to change the location of the clock hand to show the passage of a second of time. Since you set up the object to rotate correctly in the MovieClip definition, you need to rotate it around the center point.

A circle measures 360 degrees around, and this clock contains ten intervals, so therefore, each interval is one-tenth of the circle, or 36 degrees. You can add 36 to the current value of the rotation property of the clock hand instance to show it rotating around the clock face.

The second callback function, timerExpired, executes when the final interval takes place. In it, you are hiding the clock face and hand and are displaying the timer expired MovieClip (Figure P1.6). For good measure, you remove the timer event listeners as well, and the project stops at this point.

This project combines a lot of concepts that were covered in the first chapters of the book. First, objects were dynamically added to the stage, positioned, and added to the display stack. Then, the types of objects that were displayed were manipulated based on user interactions. The first interaction being that of the mouse to start the timer, the second interaction was based on the timer itself.

Although this is a fairly simple example, this project embodies the core basics that you will be building on in future chapters. Having a strong understanding of the event listener model is the basis for any interactions you'll create.

You are well on your way—in the next section you'll learn how to formalize your coding in a method called "object-oriented programming" and then use that to create more complex projects, and eventually learn how to create desktop and mobile applications using Adobe AIR.

PART 2

EXPLORING THE BASICS OF CLASSES

8

WHAT IS A CLASS?

As your projects become more complex, having all your code in a frame script will become cumbersome and difficult to maintain. You need a way to structure your code and link code to the objects themselves. You need classes. The term for using classes to structure your code is *object-oriented programming.*

ActionScript allows you to define the classes, or building blocks, of applications, and give them specific actions and functionality. Let's start by exploring how classes work and dive deeper into the topic of variables. From there we'll discuss how classes are created and how to add functionality to them using *methods.* Finally, you'll learn how to formalize your class structures, making them easier to use and debug.

OVERVIEW OF A **CLASS**

Earlier, you saw objects that are in the Library as "stacks of sticky notes." For objects that you place into the Library, you can create multiple instances on the Stage either in the Flash application, or as you have learned, through ActionScript by giving them a name that the object links to.

These objects in the Library are MovieClips, graphics, or buttons; but they contain no functionality themselves. They are simply graphics. All the functionality and behaviors you apply to an object are coded outside of it in a frame script. Imagine if you could keep all that functional code linked directly with the object itself. That is what a class is.

If you remember, when you created objects and placed them in the Library, you needed to open the Advanced mode of the panel to define a class name to give ActionScript the ability to place the item on the Stage at runtime. Behind the scenes, Flash created an empty ActionScript class file for the object in the Library. What you are going to do is create that file yourself, and add interactivity and behaviors to the object, so all instances of the object will behave in the same way.

Over the course of this review of classes, you'll incrementally learn more things that you can do to classes and add more sophisticated ActionScript over time.

VARIABLES REVEALED

One item that you learned about briefly was the var statement. The var statement allows you to create a named object that can contain various values like numbers or strings. It is also how you create instances of classes; in fact, when you create numbers and strings with the var statement, you are creating instances of the Number and String classes.

Let's look at this example:

```
var myNumber:Number = 5;
```

In this example, you are creating a named object called myNumber that will contain the numeric value of 5. This line is a bit of a shortcut; if you rewrote this using the full code, it would look like this:

```
var myNumber:Number = new Number(5);
```

This format is a little more verbose, and shows more of what is actually happening. The var statement is creating a named object called myNumber, and this object will be an instance of a certain type, or class. In this case, the Number class. You then use the assignment operator to set the value of this named object to a new instance of the Number class, which you define with the value of 5.

This may be a bit confusing because you may be thinking, why would a number be a class? Well, everything in Flash is a class of some kind, even the simplest of objects, like a number or a string.

Let's review another example you used previously:

```
var circle_1:BlueCircle = new BlueCircle();
```

In this example, you use the var statement to create a new named object called circle_1. You state that this object will be an instance of the BlueCircle class. Then, using the assignment operator, you create a new instance of the BlueCircle class and assign it to the named object circle_1.

If you return to the "stack of sticky notes" example, the BlueCircle class is a stack of these notes, each one looking exactly the same. The new statement is the act of peeling a note off of the stack, and the assignment is linking this new class instance to a name you can refer to later on.

The previous example with the Number class is the same; it is just that the sticky notes aren't graphics, but rather containers that can accept numbers.

So whenever you use the var statement, you aren't creating just a variable, but also a named container that can contain instances of various classes.

FIGURE 8.1 Contents of the
Red Button MovieClip

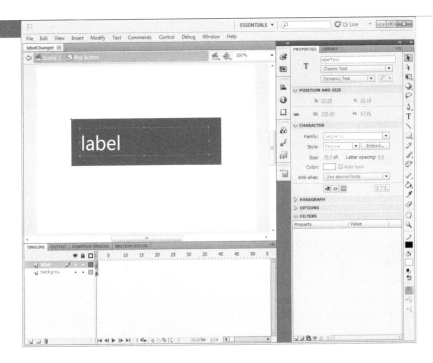

OK, enough talk, let's get down to some code and demonstrate how this works.
First, start with a basic button graphic and Library item definition before you
move forward (**Figure 8.1**).

In a new Flash ActionScript 3.0 project, I have created a MovieClip symbol that
contains two layers. The bottom layer, named "background," contains a red rectangle.
The top layer, named "label," contains a dynamic text field with the instance name
labelText. Make sure it is Dynamic Text. Static text fields cannot be changed with
ActionScript, which you'll want to do later to give the button a custom label name.
As a placeholder, the text field contains the word "label."

You haven't worked with text much in Flash Professional, so here are a few hints
to get you initially through this. When working with text and dynamic content using
ActionScript, you'll need to create ActionScript fonts that are linked to embedded
fonts from your system. This process will be covered in detail in a future chapter.
However, for now, the best way to ensure that you are working with fonts correctly
when interacting with ActionScript is to set the anti-alias setting to "Use device
fonts" as shown in Figure 8.1.

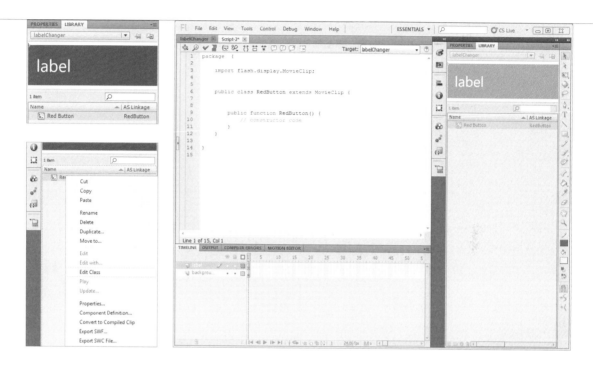

In the Library panel the symbol is named Red Button, and in the Symbol Properties window the object has been exported for ActionScript with the class name RedButton filled in (**Figure 8.2**).

In the previous examples, you would end here, but in this case you want to customize the class. In Flash, classes are created by creating a separate file called an ActionScript file. To create this file, right-click the Red Button object in the Library and select Edit Class (**Figure 8.3**).

When you work with an ActionScript file, you are working exclusively in code, so panels such as the Library, Timeline, and Properties aren't needed. You'll also notice that the Actions panel is disabled, and instead the code takes the place that the Stage usually occupies (**Figure 8.4**).

FIGURE 8.2 Symbol Properties window for Red Button

FIGURE 8.3 Editing a new class for a Library object

FIGURE 8.4 Creating your first ActionScript class

Because of the different setup, you can create a workspace that is designed for ActionScript development when working with an ActionScript file (**Figure 8.5**).

You'll see the following has been created in this new, untitled ActionScript file:

```
package  {
    import flash.display.MovieClip;
    public class RedButton extends MovieClip {
        public function RedButton() {
            // constructor code
        }
    }
}
```

You'll learn what this code means in the next section, but for now, you want to make sure that you can link this custom ActionScript class to the object in the Library.

In order to save this and have it link with the Red Button object in the Library, you need to save this as a class. To do that, save the file in the same place as the Flash FLA file created earlier and name it exactly as it is listed in the Class field in the Linkage section of the Symbol Properties window. As a reminder, it is listed as RedButton, so save this as RedButton.as.

With the file saved, go back to the Flash FLA file and open the symbol properties for the Red Button object in the Library. When you click the check mark next to the class name in the window, you'll see that it is able to find the file (**Figure 8.6**). If you click the edit button next to it, Flash will open the class file.

The class file has been created and linked successfully to the object in the Library. In the next chapter, you'll dive into the ActionScript and make sense of the code that you put in the ActionScript file.

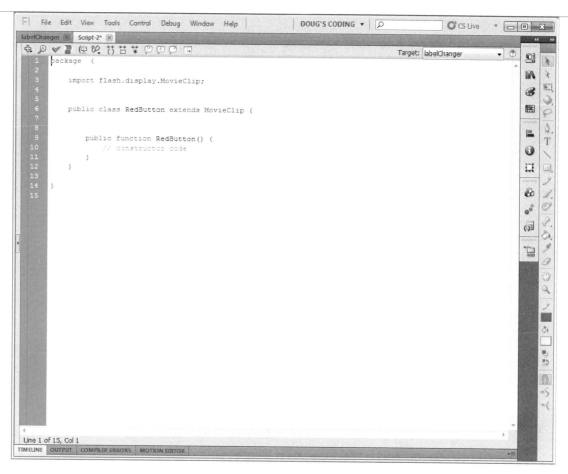

```
package {

    import flash.display.MovieClip;


    public class RedButton extends MovieClip {


        public function RedButton() {
            // constructor code
        }
    }

}
```

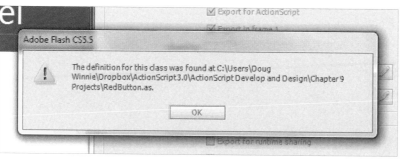

FIGURE 8.5 Custom coding workspace

FIGURE 8.6 Finding the class definition

The definition for this class was found at C:\Users\Doug Winnie\Dropbox\ActionScript 3.0\ActionScript Develop and Design\Chapter 9 Projects\RedButton.as.

OK

WRAPPING **UP**

In this chapter, you took the first steps to learning how to create ActionScript classes to give each of the Library objects unique behaviors that are attached to each instance. Here are some tips to remember as you continue learning about classes in ActionScript:

- Each time you use the new statement, you are creating a named container that will contain data that maps to a class. This can be a number, a string, or a new instance of an object in your project's Library.

- You can start to define behaviors that are associated with the class, and therefore all instances of the class, by right-clicking the object in the Library and selecting Edit Class.

- When creating a new ActionScript class using Edit Class, Flash Professional CS5.5 will create some ActionScript to get you started.

- When you save your class, remember to name it exactly as the Linkage class name reads in the Library panel. Flash Professional will name your class automatically for you when you attempt to save it.

- Although you'll learn more about where to organize and save classes in the future, for now, remember to save your ActionScript class .as file in the same location as your project's FLA file.

- To check if Flash Professional can find your class, open the symbol properties and click the check mark button next to the class name. Flash Professional will say if it can find the file.

9
BUILDING OUT
THE CLASS

In the last chapter, you learned what a class is, created a RedButton class file, and linked it to the Library object; but you didn't step through the code to analyze what it was doing or how it was doing it. So, let's do that now and add to it the code to define how the red button looks and behaves.

PARTS OF A CLASS

All classes have a few basic parts. Take a look at the RedButton class code and dissect what the parts of the code do:

```
package  {
    import flash.display.MovieClip;
    public class RedButton extends MovieClip {
        public function RedButton() {
            // constructor code
        }
    }
}
```

Package STATEMENT

The first part is the package statement. All classes are grouped into categories called *packages*. A package is like a directory, and can have other packages inside of it. Packages are used to organize your classes into categories or different functions. In this example, you are using the default package which is represented by a single package statement. Later, you'll cover how to create custom packages you can use to organize your classes.

Import STATEMENT

The import statement defines the classes that are used within the classes. The compiler understands some of the very basic content types like String, Number, and so on, but some of the more complex types need to be added into the class for the compiler to use them. The stub code includes the following import statement:

```
import flash.display.MovieClip;
```

This import statement is telling the class that you will want to be able to access the functionality within the MovieClip class in this class. Notice that there is a prefix to MovieClip called flash.display. This is an example of how classes are organized in packages. Packages are a way to group and organize your classes in a logical way.

Class STATEMENT

The class statement starts a section of the code that defines the class itself. Ignore the public statement for now, but just know that it needs to be there for your class statement to work properly. After the class statement is the name of the class.

```
public class RedButton extends MovieClip {
```

Classes are always capitalized to make it easier to differentiate variables and class instances from the classes themselves.

When you create classes, you can create them completely from scratch, or you can use another class as the basis for your new class. For instance, when car makers design a new car, they generally don't do it from scratch. They use the chassis, engine, wheels, and other items from an existing car and then improve them. The same exists with classes. In this example, you have a class that you want to "inherit" the properties of the MovieClip class, but you want to add your own improvements to it. The RedButton class is based on MovieClip, but you are going to augment that with some designs and functionality that make it unique. To do this, you need to add the extends keyword and then define the class it is extending, in this case the MovieClip class.

CLASS CONSTRUCTOR

The constructor is a special kind of function that "constructs" each instance of the class. For example, to create an instance of this class that you are defining, you would use a var and new statement to create a new instance:

```
var myButton:RedButton = new RedButton();
```

This line constructs an instance of the RedButton class. You may have wondered why you use new RedButton(), making it seem like a function. That is because it actually is a function, the constructor function.

Every class has a constructor. The constructor function contains everything you need to get an instance up and running. It always has a return type of void, because you can't return anything from a constructor; it is used to create an instance of the class and nothing more. The public statement in the beginning is required—just make sure you include it for now and learn why later.

A constructor function can accept values when created, and you can define the function's parameter values in the same way you would in any other function.

CREATING A CLASS INSTANCE

Now that you understand the basic parts of a class, let's add some simple code to show that everything is running. You'll need the files from the end of the last chapter. This includes the RedButton.as file and the FLA project itself:

1. Update the RedButton.as file from Chapter 8 to read:

```
package  {
    import flash.display.MovieClip;
    public class RedButton extends MovieClip {
        public function RedButton() {
            trace("An instance of the RedButton class has been
                created.");
        }
    }
}
```

2. In the Flash FLA file, remove any instances you have on the Stage and add this code to the timeline in frame 1:

```
var myButton:RedButton = new RedButton();
myButton.x = 150;
myButton.y = 50;
addChild(myButton);
```

3. Run the project. You'll see an instance of the RedButton class display on the screen and the phrase "An instance of the RedButton class has been created" sent to the Output panel (**Figure 9.1**).

FIGURE 9.1 First instance of a custom class

ADDING **CONSTRUCTOR PARAMETERS**

When you create a class instance, you often want to pass information to it that can help configure the unique instance in some way.

In this example, you want to customize the button label, which is defined by a text label with the instance name `labelText`. You need to pass custom text for the label. You can do that using a dynamic text label.

Dynamic text labels are like MovieClips and other objects because they contain properties that you can manipulate with ActionScript. You can alter a text field using the `.text` property, which accepts a string defining the text field label.

CUSTOMIZING THE BUTTON LABEL

To send a custom button label to the instance, you add a constructor parameter and use that to update the `labelText.text` property.

1. Modify the Button class code as follows to define the parameter using the constructor, and then using that parameter to populate the text on the button:

```
package  {
    import flash.display.MovieClip;
    public class RedButton extends MovieClip {
        public function RedButton(newLabel:String) {
            trace("An instance of the RedButton class has been
               created.");
            labelText.text = newLabel;
        }
    }
}
```

2. Update the code in the FLA file to set the text of the button to "Click me":

```
var myButton:RedButton = new RedButton("Click me");
myButton.x = 150;
myButton.y = 50;
addChild(myButton);
```

FIGURE 9.2 Sending a parameter to the class constructor

Now the button has a custom label as shown in **Figure 9.2**.

You can create new RedButton instances and easily give each one a unique label using the parameter you added to the constructor.

3. Add another instance and pass in the value "Or me" as the label:

```
var myButton:RedButton = new RedButton("Click me);

myButton.x = 150;

myButton.y = 50;

addChild(myButton);

var myOtherButton:RedButton = new RedButton("Or me");

myOtherButton.x = 150;

myOtherButton.y = 200;

addChild(myOtherButton);
```

CUSTOMIZING MULTIPLE PROPERTIES

With only two instances of the button, there is still a lot of code in the FLA. It would be nice if in addition to passing the custom label, you could pass the x and y coordinates to the function to have it position the button at a specific location. And you can.

To accept multiple values, you need to define them all and separate them with commas. You then need to apply those values that are passed into the to the x and y properties of the class instance. Notice in the code in the following step 1 you are accessing x and y directly. Remember, you are able to do this because your context or scope *is* the object, not the main timeline.

1. Update as the RedButton class with the following highlighted code:

```
package  {
    import flash.display.MovieClip;
    public class RedButton extends MovieClip {
        public function RedButton(newLabel:String,
        →  newX:Number, newY:Number) {
            trace("An instance of the RedButton class has been
            →  created.");
            labelText.text = newLabel;
            x = newX;
            y = newY;
        }
    }
}
```

Now when you create the instance of the variable, you can define the properties of all three.

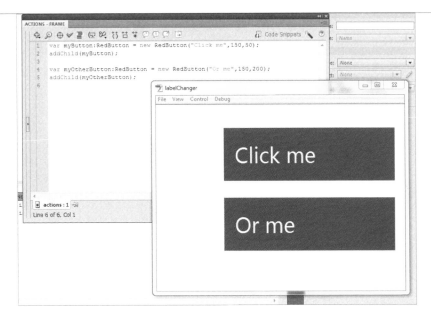

FIGURE 9.3 Sending different parameters to the unique constructor

2. Update the code in the timeline of the FLA to condense the code you had before with the following:

```
var myButton:RedButton = new RedButton("Click me",150,50);
addChild(myButton);
var myOtherButton:RedButton = new RedButton("Or me",150,200);
addChild(myOtherButton);
```

3. Run the project. You'll get something similar to **Figure 9.3**. As you can see, each instance has captured the three parameters of the constructor, and the class has repositioned each instance based on their unique values.

MAKING CONSTRUCTOR PARAMETERS OPTIONAL

Every time you create an instance you need to pass in these three values. If you provide only the custom button label text you would get an error.

1. Remove the x and y property variable values from the code on the timeline to read like this:

```
var myButton:RedButton = new RedButton("Click me");
addChild(myButton);
var myOtherButton:RedButton = new RedButton("Or me",150,200);
addChild(myOtherButton);
```

The first instance is created with only the label name, the other parameters aren't defined.

2. Run the project. You'll get the following error:

```
1136: Incorrect number of arguments.  Expected 3.
```

To prevent this, you can add default values to the parameter values that can give your classes greater flexibility. To do this, add an assignment operator to the constructor parameter definitions.

Parameter defaults are assignments you put in the constructor parameter definitions. If a value is not provided, the assignment operator takes over and assigns the parameter with the default value. If a value is passed in, the assignment is ignored, and the passed in value is used.

3. Update the RedButton class with the following highlighted parameter definitions:

```
package  {
    import flash.display.MovieClip;
    public class RedButton extends MovieClip {
        public function RedButton(newLabel:String,
            newX:Number=0, newY:Number=0) {
            trace("An instance of the RedButton class has been
                created.");
```

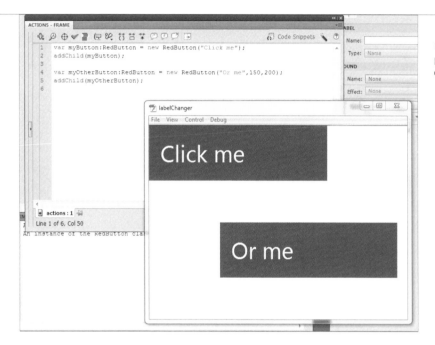

FIGURE 9.4 Using default parameters in class constructors

```
labelText.text = newLabel;
            x = newX;
            y = newY;
        }
    }
}
```

Now, if you fail to pass in the newX and newY parameters, they will get the value 0 automatically, and you'll not get an error when you run the project.

4. Run the project. The project runs without any errors, as shown in **Figure 9.4**.

It is important to note that if you don't pass anything inside the constructor you'll still get an error. This is because you have not provided a default value for the first parameter, so it is still required whenever you run the constructor.

CREATING METHODS

A method is a function that is part of class. In fact, there really is nothing different between a normal function and a method of a class. It is just that a method is exclusively part of a class.

To create a method, you define a function. Let's create a function that will handle changing the button label text. Edit your RedButton class with the following highlighted code:

```
package  {

    import flash.display.MovieClip;

    public class RedButton extends MovieClip {

        public function RedButton(newLabel:String, newX:Number=0,
            newY:Number=0) {

            trace("An instance of the RedButton class has been
                created.");

            x = newX;

            y = newY;

            changeLabel(newLabel);

        }

        public function changeLabel(newLabel:String):void

        {

            labelText.text = newLabel;

        }

    }

}
```

Notice that the public keyword appears again. For now, just make sure that it is listed before your function. You'll learn what it means in detail soon, I promise.

This function is accepting a parameter and is returning nothing. Notice that the constructor takes advantage of the new method that you created.

You can create as many methods as you want in your class. In future chapters, your methods will drive all the functionality in your projects.

ACCESSING METHODS FROM
OUTSIDE THE CLASS

FIGURE 9.5 Code completion assistance in the Actions panel

The example method you created here is being accessed from inside the class. You can access methods from outside the class as well.

Let's update the frame script with the following highlighted code to have it access the changeLabel method.

```
var myButton:RedButton = new RedButton("Click me");
addChild(myButton);
var myOtherButton:RedButton = new RedButton("Or me",150,200);
addChild(myOtherButton);
myOtherButton.changeLabel("New label!");
```

Notice that now you are accessing the method, or function, as part of myOtherButton instance. To access the method, you need to signify which instance you want to use first, insert a dot, list the method name, and then pass in any values that may be part of the method.

One of the best parts of working with classes is that the script editor has a lot more functionality. When you started typing ".changeLabel" after pressing the period, you may have noticed that a drop-down appeared with information about the class (**Figure 9.5**).

In the next section, you'll learn how to restrict methods from external access; that is what the private keyword is for that you have been using in your class definition.

WRAPPING **UP**

In this chapter, you learned how to take the stub code that Flash Professional creates for a new class and add behavior to it that is shared across all instances of the class. Here are some tips to help you get started working with classes:

- Classes start with the package `statement`, which is a group that holds the class and all the things that go with it.

- To use methods or classes that are outside the class, you need to use the `import` statement to make them accessible.

- A class needs to start with the `class` statement and be preceded by the `public` keyword.

- Every class has a constructor that has a name that matches the class name.

- When you save your class, it must have the same file name and spelling as the name of the class, have a .as file extension, and for now, be saved at the same location as your FLA.

- Just like with functions, you can pass in parameters to a constructor to help configure the instance as it is created.

- You can create methods, or functions, within the class using the function statement, prefixed by the `public` statement.

- Using the assignment operator, you can optionally add default values to function parameters if the data passed into the constructor or function call is missing.

- You can access classes outside the class through the instance name.

10

DOING MORE WITH **CLASSES**

When you program in ActionScript using classes, you are using a coding process known as Object-Oriented Programming (OOP). One of the tenets of OOP is that all your objects have an interface, or a way that you can access their actions, data, and procedures. This interface is defined through public and private controls on your attributes or methods.

There are techniques in ActionScript to restrict that interface, limiting access to properties or methods of a class to prevent errors or restrict the functionality of the project. In this chapter, you'll learn some of these techniques and learn how to create a streamlined interface for your application.

WHAT IS THE public KEYWORD FOR?

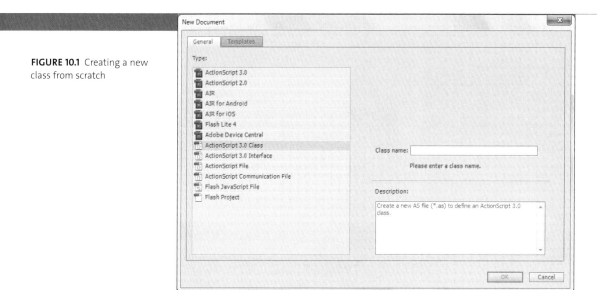

FIGURE 10.1 Creating a new class from scratch

In all the examples you have worked with so far, you have used the public statement. The public statement defines that the code that follows it is publicly accessible from outside the class. Let's start with a new class example and walk through it to see how the public statement works.

You will create a new ActionScript class from scratch; you aren't going to create it from an object in the Library.

1. Open Flash Professional CS5.5.

2. From the menu select File > New.

3. In the New Document dialog box, select ActionScript 3.0 class (**Figure 10.1**).

4. In the Class name field, enter **Cat** as the name of the class.

5. Click OK.

6. In the code editor, replace the stub code with the following code:

```
package {
    public class Cat {
        public var catName:String;
```

```
        public function Cat(newName:String):void {
            catName=newName;
        }
        public function getName():String {
            return catName;
        }
    }
}
```

7. Save the file as Cat.as in a new folder on your system. The Cat class is a basic class and doesn't extend any other classes, like MovieClip. To be honest though, it is extending the most basic class in ActionScript, the Object class. You could add extends Object to the class definition if you wanted to be verbose. When you create a generic class with no extensions of another class, you are creating what is called a *generic object*. Objects contain data and can calculate math and other basic functions. They can't be displayed on the Stage, and they don't have extensive events that can be listened for.

In the Cat class, you created a variable named catName. Notice you haven't assigned a value to it yet because you want to give it a value when you create an instance of it with the constructor. You can create variables without values in this way. This is called *defining* a variable, but not assigning it a value. This example is defining a variable called catName that will eventually hold a String.

You then create a constructor that accepts a newName parameter that you then give to the catName variable inside the function. Next, you have a method named getName that returns the value of the catName to whatever calls it. In this case, it is being called by the constructor.

You need to create a new project in which to use the class.

8. Create a new Flash Professional CS5.5 project.

9. Enter the following as a frame script:

```
import Cat;
var firstCat:Cat = new Cat("Hoover");
trace(firstCat.getName()); // Displays "Hoover"
```

10. Save this project in the same location as Cat.as.

11. Run the project. The Cat class and everything it can do will be imported into the project for you to access.

A new instance of the Cat class will be created called firstCat. You then pass a parameter to the constructor, which inside the class assigns to the catName property. Back in the FLA file, you display the name of the instance using the getName method of the firstCat instance.

In this example, everything is public. This includes the variable catName, the method getName, and the constructor. This could lead to problems. For instance, what if you changed the code to do this:

```
import Cat;
var firstCat:Cat = new Cat("Hoover");
trace(firstCat.getName()); // Displays "Hoover"
firstCat.catName = "BB";
trace(firstCat.catName); // Displays "BB"
```

Although at first glance, you might not find anything wrong with this code, but consider the reality of what you are doing: When you get a new pet cat, you give her a name just once; you don't rename her every now and then.

Unfortunately there is nothing in the Cat class that prevents this from happening. That is when you introduce the private statement.

RESTRICTING ACCESS
WITH private

In this example, the variable catName is publicly accessible. You want to restrict that and allow users the ability to access the catName variable only through the getName method.

If you make one simple change, you can get the desired effect.

1. Modify the Cat class with the highlighted code:

```
package {
    public class Cat {
        private var catName:String;
        public function Cat(newName:String):void {
            catName=newName;
        }
        public function getName():String {
            return catName;
        }
    }
}
```

2. In the frame script, comment out the second two lines:

```
var firstCat:Cat = new Cat("Hoover");
trace(firstCat.getName()); // Displays "Hoover"
/*
firstCat.catName = "BB";
trace(firstCat.catName);
*/
```

3. Run the project. Everything works as it did before.

4. Uncomment the last two lines. You'll get the following errors:

    ```
    1178: Attempted access of inaccessible property catName
    through a reference with static type Cat.
    ```

    ```
    1178: Attempted access of inaccessible property catName
    through a reference with static type Cat.
    ```

The errors occur because you are trying to access the catName variable to give it a new name, "BB," and you are trying to directly access the variable to get its value. However, you have defined the variable as private; you don't have the ability to directly access its value.

In the class, you are able to access the value, because a private variable is private internally to the class itself. Anywhere in the class you can access private variables and methods. To make methods private and exclusively accessible internally to the class, define them as private with the private statement instead of using the public statement.

USING **BEST PRACTICES** FOR **NAMING** PRIVATE MEMBERS

It is generally a best practice to prefix private variables and methods with an underscore to make it clear when you write your code that items are public or private.

You can update the code with this best practice by adding the underscores:

```
package {
    public class Cat {
        private var _catName:String;
        public function Cat(newName:String):void {
            _catName=newName;
        }
        public function getName():String {
            return _catName;
        }
    }
}
```

GETTERS AND SETTERS: KEEPING THINGS POLITE

Getting and setting are two basic principles for accessing values of properties in ActionScript. Let's expand the Cat class a bit with another variable:

```
package {
    public class Cat {
        private var _catName:String;
        private var _favoriteFood:String;
        public function Cat(newName:String):void {
            _catName=newName;
        }
        public function getName():String {
            return _catName;
        }
    }
}
```

You just added a new private variable named _favoriteFood. Unlike a name, a cat's favorite food might change as she gets older, so you need to make this property accessible outside the class for each unique instance.

Although you could make this a public variable, there is a good reason not to. Generally, granting public access to variables that are in a class is not a best practice. There can be variables that have certain restrictions in their value; for instance, a number variable representing someone's test score can only be between 0 and 100. If you had this as a public variable, you could assign anything to it that matches the variable type. You could also get whatever the value is, regardless of whether this is how you want the class to present the data.

Keeping variables private and having specific ways of setting values and getting values is called *keeping classes polite*. You give each class a specific interface that other classes and ActionScript can use to get meaningful values and set values that are error-free.

CREATING GETTER AND SETTER METHODS

To give external access to the _favoriteFood variable, you need to create two methods in the Cat class. The first will allow code external to the class to define the value of the variable, called a setter. The second, called a getter method, retrieves the value of the attribute and returns it to the caller.

1. Update the class to add these two methods for the new private _favoriteFood property you just added:

```
package {
    public class Cat {
        private var _catName:String;
        private var _favoriteFood:String;
        public function Cat(newName:String):void {
            _catName=newName;
        }
        public function getName():String {
            return _catName;
        }
        public function setFavoriteFood(newFood:String):void {
            _favoriteFood = newFood;
        }
        public function getFavoriteFood():String {
            return _favoriteFood;
        }
    }
}
```

Notice that you have two functions. The first one, setFavoriteFood, accepts a parameter that is then assigned to the private _favoriteFood variable inside the class. The second method, getFavoriteFood, gets the value of the private _favoriteFood variable and sends it outside the class through the return statement.

As you could probably surmise, the getName function is a getter, but unlike the food example, you don't have a setter function for the cat's name. Not all attributes need to have a matching getter/setter pair. Determining if you have one, the other, or both is based on the intention of the attribute or property.

2. Update the frame script to use the new functions:

```
import Cat;
var firstCat:Cat = new Cat("Hoover");
trace(firstCat.getName()); // Displays "Hoover"
firstCat.setFavoriteFood("tuna");
trace( firstCat.getName() + " loves " +
    firstCat.getFavoriteFood());
```

3. Run the project. The new getter and setter methods display "Hoover loves tuna" in the Output panel.

USING THE get AND set STATEMENTS

Although you have made the class *polite* using best practice getter and setter methods, you can't deny that visually, it is a lot easier to use the dot notation and access the variables themselves. Calling a specific method function to get a single value returned can seem a little clumsy. Luckily, ActionScript can make this easier using the get and set statements.

The get and set statements allow you to build an interface to the class that pretends you are accessing the variables directly, when in fact, you are routing the access to the values through getter and setter methods. To use these special statements, you need to adjust the getter and setter methods:

1. Update the Cat class with the following highlighted code:

```
package {
    public class Cat {
        private var _catName:String;
        private var _favoriteFood:String;
        public function Cat(newName:String):void {
            _catName=newName;
        }
        public function get catName():String {
            return _catName;
        }
        public function set favoriteFood(newFood:String):
            void {
            _favoriteFood = newFood;
        }
        public function get favoriteFood():String {
            return _favoriteFood;
        }
    }
}
```

You have changed the name of the getter and setter methods to be a specific name. The getter method is named catName. The favorite food getter and setter methods is named favoriteFood. In each of these methods, you need to define if the method is used to get or set the attributes you are building into the interface. In this case, you use get for the name method, and get and set to differentiate between the two methods for the food based on what you are doing. The set method is assigning a value to the attribute; the get method is returning a value to the caller.

Since you are using the get and set keywords, you can access the method names as if they were variables, and not need to use the function notion that you had previously.

2. Update the frame script as follows:

```
import Cat;
var firstCat:Cat = new Cat("Hoover");
trace(firstCat.catName);
firstCat.favoriteFood = "tuna";
trace(firstCat.catName + " loves " + firstCat.favoriteFood);
```

Now, instead of using function names, you can use simpler property notation while behind-the-scenes, you are still able to restrict access to the internally private variables.

If you tried to set the value of catName, which only has a getter method, you would get this error:

```
1059: Property is read-only.
```

That is because you have only defined a getter method, and not a setter.

GOING FRAME-SCRIPT-FREE: CREATING A DOCUMENT CLASS

So far, everything you have been doing in the FLA file is based on the frame script. Well, those days are now over. There is a special type of class you can use to move all the scripts you placed on frame 1 into a class. It is called the Document class. The Document class is the class that defines the entire FLA file, and contains methods and attributes that are part of the FLA file.

The easiest way to create your Document class is to do it after you created your FLA file.

FIGURE 10.2 The Properties panel for the document

1. Create a new Flash Professional CS5.5 ActionScript 3.0 project.

2. Name the file **MyPets.fla** and save it to the same location as the Cat class from before.

3. Without anything selected on the Stage, open the Properties panel (**Figure 10.2**).

4. In the Class field, enter **MyPets** as the class name, which is the exact spelling as the project file name but without the .fla file extension.

5. Click the Pencil icon to edit the class definition.

6. A new, empty class will be created for the Document class.

7. Save the file as **MyPets.as** in the same location as your FLA file, with the same name as the class name and FLA file name.

   Notice that the stub code that is created for the MyPets class already knows that this class will extend the MovieClip class. With the class name identified as part of the document properties, you have now created your first Document class.

   Test this to make sure that the Document class is working.

FIGURE 10.3 Setting the compile target from the document class

8. Update the ActionScript that is created automatically to output a confirmation message using the trace statement:

```
package  {
    import flash.display.MovieClip;
    public class MyPets extends MovieClip {
        public function MyPets() {
            // constructor code
            trace("MyPets constructed");
        }
    }
}
```

9. Now return to the FLA file and run the project. You should see the "MyPets constructed" message in the Output panel.

   Something helpful to know is that you can run the project from the Document class as well. At the top of the Document class window, you'll see a "target" drop down. This indicates which FLA project you want to run if you attempt to run the project from this file (**Figure 10.3**).

10. Create a new ActionScript file, name it **MyPets.as**, and include the following ActionScript:

```
package {
    public class MyPets extends MovieClip {
        public function MyPets():void {
        }
    }
}
```

CREATING AN INITIALIZATION METHOD

It is also a best practice to keep the code you are running out of the constructor and place it within a function named init (some people use others like main or initialize). You can execute the code from the constructor as a method.

Consider though that you don't want the init function publicly accessible. You want it to be available only inside the class. Just like with the properties of the classes, you can use the private statement to make entire methods accessible only within the class.

Working with the code you had before, create an init private method, and continue to build out the Document class.

1. Create an additional import statement to include the Cat class you created earlier.

2. Inside the constructor, insert a new method call for init().

3. Create a new private method after the constructor named init that will contain the startup code for the project.

4. Create some instances of the Cat class.

When you are finished, your Document class should look similar to the following code and your FLA file should not have any code on frame 1:

```
package {
    import flash.display.MovieClip;
    import Cat;
    public class MyPets extends MovieClip {
        public function MyPets():void {
            _init();
        }
        private function _init():void {
            var firstCat:Cat = new Cat("Hoover");
            firstCat.favoriteFood = "tuna"
            trace(firstCat.catName + " loves " +
                firstCat.favoriteFood);
            var secondCat:Cat = new Cat("BB");
            secondCat.favoriteFood = "chicken"
            trace(secondCat.catName + " loves " +
                secondCat.favoriteFood);
            var thirdCat:Cat = new Cat("Rocket");
            thirdCat.favoriteFood = "shoelaces"
            trace(thirdCat.catName + " loves " +
                thirdCat.favoriteFood);
        }
    }
}
```

5. Make sure now that the first frame in the FLA file contains no code.

6. Run your project. You'll find that everything runs just like it did before, but now you are fully using class-based coding. Congratulations!

WRAPPING **UP**

In this chapter, you expanded your basic knowledge of classes. Using the private statement, you can now create private methods and properties that are exclusively available inside the class. You learned how you can build an interface to the private properties inside the class using the get and set statements.

Finally, you learned how to create a Document class, which is the key for working almost exclusively in Flash Professional with ActionScript classes.

Here are some helpful tips to remember as you continue working with classes:

- Use the `private` statement to mark methods and properties as being inaccessible from outside a class.

- Create getter and setter methods to get and set your private attributes.

- Use the get and set statements to make it easier to work with class instance properties, but still protect their direct access using getter and setter methods.

- Name your private methods and properties with an underscore prefix to make distinguishing private and public members easier.

- Create a Document class to go with your FLA project to move all your non-frame-based ActionScript into a class.

- Use an initialization method to run startup code for your project in a private method.

11

ORGANIZING
YOUR CLASSES

So far, all the classes that you have used have been in the same location as the Flash Professional FLA project. This organization might work for simple projects, but as your projects become more complex, it can start to get confusing when you have potentially dozens of classes in the same place with no way to organize them. In this chapter, you'll learn how to organize your classes into folders called *packages* and learn how to include entire packages in your project.

YOUR PACKAGE HAS
BEEN DELIVERED

FIGURE 11.1 File structure with no packages...yet

When you create a Flash Professional FLA project and create a Document class that sits alongside it, you are working with the default package. The package represents the location relative to the project where the Flash Professional compiler can locate the class it needs. All the classes you have created so far are in this default package location.

You should use folders to organize your classes into logical groups.

CREATING A PACKAGE FOLDER

Packages are nothing more than folders on your computer. In fact, that is exactly how you create a package:

1. Create a new folder on your desktop named **Example Project**.

2. Create a new Flash Professional CS5.5 project.

3. Save the project with the name **MyProject.fla** in the Example Project folder on the desktop.

4. Create a Document class for the project named **MyProject.as** and save it in the same location as the FLA file (**Figure 11.1**).

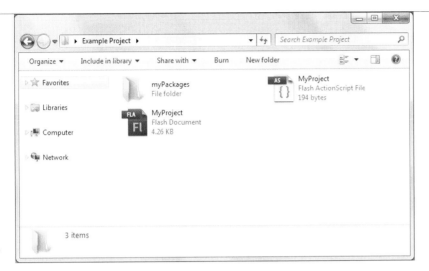

FIGURE 11.2 A shiny new package, ready to hold your classes!

5. Update the code in the Document class as follows:

```
package  {
    import flash.display.MovieClip;
    public class MyProject extends MovieClip {
        public function MyProject() {
            trace("My project is created!");
        }
    }
}
```

6. Save and run the project. You'll get the trace statement contents displayed in the Output panel.

   Pretty standard stuff; however, now you are going to create a new class and place it in a package.

7. In the folder where your FLA and Document class exist, create a new folder named **myPackages** (**Figure 11.2**).

8. In Flash Professional, select New from the File menu and create a new ActionScript 3.0 class.

When naming your class, you need to think of what is referred to as the *fully qualified package name*, meaning that you will refer to the class using its package structure.

Referring to package folder names is similar to referring to objects on the Stage; You use dot notation to represent children. Also, package folders must follow ActionScript naming rules, meaning there are no spaces or punctuation marks.

To name your new class correctly, you need to use the fully qualified package name.

9. Give the package the name **myPackages.CustomClass**.

10. Click OK.

Flash will know that you want to create the new class in the myPackages folder and will configure the starter code accordingly:

```
package myPackages {

    public class CustomClass {

        public function CustomClass() {

            // constructor code

        }

    }

}
```

As you can see, the package statement at the top now displays the name of the package that the class is within.

11. Add a trace statement to the class:

```
package myPackages {
    public class CustomClass {
        public function CustomClass() {
            trace("CustomClass created!");
        }
    }
}
```

12. Save the class.

Make sure you remember to save it in the myPackages folder, since that is how you defined the package statement in the class. If you put it in the wrong folder, it won't work!

Now you need to create an instance of this new class to see if it works.

13. Return to the MyProject Document class.

14. Update the code as highlighted:

```
package  {
    import flash.display.MovieClip;
    import myPackages.CustomClass;
    public class MyProject extends MovieClip {
        var myClass:CustomClass;
        public function MyProject() {
            trace("My project is created!");
            myClass = new CustomClass();
        }
    }
}
```

Since the class is not in the default package, you need to use the `import` state-ment to explicitly provide access to the class definition. As you can see, the `import` statement refers to the package name, followed by the class name. For the remain-ing code, you can refer to the class just by the name, and when you run the project, both `trace` statements will work, displaying the following in the Output panel:

```
My project is created!
CustomClass created!
```

REFERRING TO ALL CLASSES IN A PACKAGE

If you have more than one class in a package, it can become cumbersome to import each one individually. Let's update the project to illustrate.

1. Create a new class in the myPackages package named **AnotherCustomClass** using the same process used for the `CustomClass`.

2. Update the code as follows:

```
package myPackages {
    public class AnotherCustomClass {
        public function AnotherCustomClass() {
            trace("AnotherCustomClass created!");
        }
    }
}
```

3. Save the class in the myPackages folder.

4. Return to the MyProject Document class.

5. Update the code as shown:

```
package  {
    import flash.display.MovieClip;
    import myPackages.CustomClass;
    import myPackages.AnotherCustomClass;
    public class MyProject extends MovieClip {
        var myClass:CustomClass;
        var myOtherClass:AnotherCustomClass;
        public function MyProject() {
            trace("My project is created!");
            myClass = new CustomClass();
            myOtherClass = new AnotherCustomClass();
        }
    }
}
```

6. Run the project; you'll get output from the Document class and both custom classes you created:

```
My project is created!
CustomClass created!
AnotherCustomClass created!
```

As you can see, to import each class, you need to define these uniquely with two import statements. They can be merged together using the wildcard symbol, *.

7. Update the import statements, as highlighted below:

```
import flash.display.MovieClip;
import myPackages.*;
```

8. Run the project again.

The project will run the same as it did before. The wildcard is importing all of the classes within the selected package. Although this isn't a big time-saver when you have only two classes, it can be a huge savings if you have dozens or more that you need to import. You will see this used often with built-in classes to bring in all the flash.display package classes, or others.

CREATING NESTED PACKAGES

Just like with folders, you can create nested packages within other packages. To do this, you need to refer to the entire package chain, starting with the outer package and defining its nested children.

To show how this works, you'll update the previous example and move a class to a nested folder, update its definition, and then confirm that it still works.

1. Open the myPackages folder in Windows Explorer or the Finder.

2. Create a new folder named **more**.

3. Move the AnotherCustomClass class to the more folder.

4. Open AnotherCustomClass in Flash Professional CS5.5.

Since you moved the location of the class, you need to update the package reference in the class definition.

5. Update the code with the following highlighted code:

```
package myPackages.more {
    public class AnotherCustomClass {
        public function AnotherCustomClass() {
            trace("AnotherCustomClass created!");
        }
    }
}
```

6. Return to the MyProject Document class and add a new import statement to capture the new nested package:

```
package {
    import flash.display.MovieClip;
    import myPackages.*;
    import myPackages.more.*;
    public class MyProject extends MovieClip {
        var myClass:CustomClass;
        var myOtherClass:AnotherCustomClass;
        public function MyProject() {
            trace("My project is created!");
            myClass = new CustomClass();
            myOtherClass = new AnotherCustomClass();
        }
    }
}
```

7. Run the project.

You will find that the project works just as it did before, but now with a nested package structure. Plus, you learned how to refactor or change your project to keep it humming along. Good job!

CHANGING THE SOURCE PATH

Often, you'll want to keep a collection of classes that you use frequently across projects to which you can refer without needing to move them to your project folder. Using Flash Professional, you can do that by updating the source path.

If you keep your favorite classes in another folder or another hard drive, you can add that custom location to the source path, and it will be picked up by the compiler.

Let's update the previous example to see how this works.

1. Create a new folder on your Desktop named **Special**.

2. In Flash Professional, create a new ActionScript 3.0 class named **SpecialClass**.

3. Update the class code as shown:

```
package  {
    public class SpecialClass {
        public function SpecialClass() {
            trace("The amazing super special class!");
        }
    }
}
```

4. Save the class in the Special folder that you created on the Desktop.

5. Return to the MyProject Document class and update it as shown:

```
package  {
    import flash.display.MovieClip;
    import myPackages.*;
    import myPackages.more.*;
    public class MyProject extends MovieClip {
        var myClass:CustomClass;
        var myOtherClass:AnotherCustomClass;
        var mySpecialClass:SpecialClass;
        public function MyProject() {
            trace("My project is created!");
            myClass = new CustomClass();
            myOtherClass = new AnotherCustomClass();
            mySpecialClass = new SpecialClass();
        }
    }
}
```

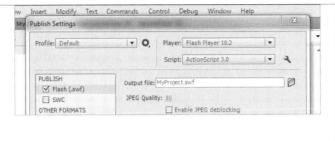

6. Run the project.

   You'll find that you can't run the project; it can't find the `SpecialClass` definition. As you can imagine, you are in a bit of a jam here, because the location of `SpecialClass` is completely outside the project folder, with no way to import it using traditional package definitions.

   This is when the source path configuration comes into play. With the FLA project open, you can adjust the ActionScript 3.0 compiler settings to include folders that are in different locations on your system.

7. Open the `MyProject.fla` file in Flash Professional CS5.5.

8. Select Publish Settings from the File menu.

9. In the Publish Settings window, click the wrench icon to the right of the Script drop-down (**Figure 11.3**).

10. In the Advanced ActionScript 3.0 settings window, click the folder icon within the Source Path tab area.

11. Browse and select the Special folder that you created on the Desktop (**Figure 11.4**).

FIGURE 11.3 Publish Settings window

FIGURE 11.4 Browsing for a folder to add to the source path

FIGURE 11.5 Setting the source
path for all projects

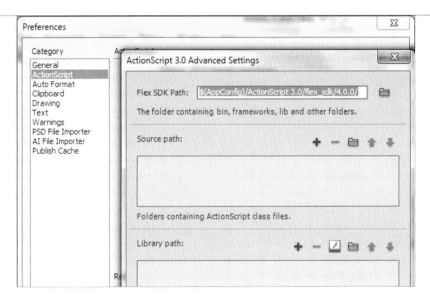

12. Click OK to select the folder.

13. Click OK to close the Advanced ActionScript 3.0 settings window.

14. Click OK again to close the Publish Settings window.

15. Run the project again.

The project works now, because you have told the compiler to specifically look for classes in a location that is outside your project folder. This setting is for the current project; you need to repeat this for other FLA files that might be working with the same external folder. If you want to make this an application-wide setting, you can do that from the Application Preferences window and define the source path location there. This setting will then be used for all projects in Flash Professional CS5.5 (**Figure 11.5**).

WRAPPING **UP**

In this chapter, you learned how to organize your classes into folders called packages. Packages are powerful ways to organize and manage your classes, which you can then easily access using package notation. In addition, configuring the source path for your project will give you the ability to include classes and packages that are located outside your project.

Here are some tips to help you work with packages:

- Packages and folders are synonymous. To create a package, simply create a folder for it within your project directory.

- Package folder names must be legal ActionScript names.

- When you define your class that is in the package, remember to refer to the package location in the package statement.

- To include classes that are in a package using the `import` statement, remember to provide the package name using dot notation.

- To include all the classes within a package, use the * wildcard symbol.

- For classes or packages that exist outside your project folder, update the source path option in the Advanced ActionScript 3.0 window to include these in your project.

PART 3

RESPONDING TO CONDITIONS AND WORKING WITH LOGIC

12

CONDITIONALS

Until now, all the examples you have been working with run in a straight line. You aren't changing courses during the execution of the code based on varying conditions. Often, you will want to do specific actions if certain conditions are met, and if they aren't met, you want to do other actions instead. This type of action is called Boolean logic.

In this chapter, you'll learn more about the Boolean variable type and see how you can use it to determine if certain conditions are true or false based on equality operators. You can then apply these operators to blocks of code that will execute differently based on the results of these evaluations.

BOOLEAN VARIABLES AND EQUALITY

Boolean variables can contain only two values: true or false. They can't contain numbers, strings, or other objects; just true or false.

To create a Boolean value, you define it as a Boolean variable type. Let's do that now in a new project:

1. Create a new project in Flash Professional CS5.5.

2. Create a new Document class called Booleans that extends the MovieClip class.

3. Update the Booleans class to contain the following code:

```
package {
    import flash.display.MovieClip;
    public class Booleans extends MovieClip {
        public function Booleans():void {
            _init();
        }
        private function _init():void {
            trace("Booleans Class Created");
        }
    }
}
```

To create a Boolean variable, you need to create a private variable named _isCorrect. A lot of Boolean variables begin with the word "is" because it helps form a question: "Is this correct?" To which there can be two responses, yes or no (true and false).

4. Add a private variable for the Boolean as highlighted in the code before:

```
package {
    import flash.display.MovieClip;
    public class Booleans extends MovieClip {
        private var _isCorrect:Boolean
        public function Booleans():void {
```

```
            _init();
        }
        private function _init():void {
            trace("Booleans Class Created");
        }
    }
}
```

Now you can assign a value to this variable using the keywords true or false.

5. Set the variable so the initial value is false as highlighted in the following code:

```
package {
    import flash.display.MovieClip;
    public class Booleans extends MovieClip {
        private var _isCorrect:Boolean
        public function Booleans():void {
            _init();
        }
        private function _init():void {
            trace("Booleans Class Created");
            _isCorrect = false;
        }
    }
}
```

Notice that when the value is set, you don't use quotation marks because this isn't a string, but a special value that is unique to the Boolean variable type.

You can use either true or false as the value for the Boolean variable type. Later in the chapter, you'll learn ways to generate these Boolean values.

From here on out, all the code you will be using is located within the init method of the class and the entire contents of the class won't be displayed unless there are updates outside the init method.

TESTING FOR EQUALITY

In ActionScript, you can test if two items are equal to each other using equality statements. These equality statements can come in several forms.

The first is the equality statement, or ==, which tests if items are equal to each other. Using the previous example, look how the code within the _init method is updated:

```
private function _init():void {
    _isCorrect = (5 == 5);
    trace(_isCorrect);
}
```

When this code runs, the Output panel displays true. You are testing whether the number 5 is equal to the number 5, which is true. The true value is generated by the equality statement == and is then assigned to the _isCorrect Boolean variable.

You can adjust this slightly to test for the equality of a variable's value. Update the code as highlighted below:

```
private function _init():void {
    var myValue:Number = 5;
    isCorrect = (myValue == 5);
    trace(_isCorrect);
}
```

Now you are testing to see if the value of the Number myValue is equal to 5. In this case it is, so you get the result true.

If the myValue changes, you get something different:

```
private function _init():void {
    var myValue:Number = 4;
    isCorrect = (myValue == 5);
    trace(_isCorrect);
}
```

Now you get the value of false, because myValue equals 4, which is not equal to 5. Since the equality test fails, it generates the value of false.

TESTING FOR INEQUALITY

Several operator statements can test varying conditions of inequality. Using these different operators you can test if two values are not equal, if one is greater than the other, if one is less than the other, or a combination of these:

```
private function __init():void {
    var myValue:Number = 4;
    trace ( myValue != 4 ); // false
    trace ( myValue < 5 );  // true
    trace ( myValue > 4 );  // false
    trace ( myValue <= 4 ); // true
    trace ( myValue >= 4 ); // true
}
```

Each of these statements tests for varying levels of inequality. Just like the equality statement, ==, these will result in either a true or a false.

Line 3 contains the inequality statement, !=.

```
    trace ( myValue != 4 ); // false
```

This asks a simple question, is this value not equal to the other? If they are not equal, then the statement evaluates as true; it is true that they are not equal. If they are equal, as they are in this example, the value violates the test and the result is false.

Lines 4 and 5 are testing if one value is greater or less than the other:

```
    trace ( myValue < 5 );  // true
    trace ( myValue > 4 );  // false
```

Line 4 is asking if the value 5 is greater than the variable myValue. Since myValue equals 4, the number 5 is indeed greater than myValue, so the result is true. Line 5 does the opposite, testing for if the value 4 is less than myValue. As you can see, it returns a value of false. That is because it technically isn't less than myValue, it is equal, so the test fails and results in false.

```
    trace ( myValue <= 4 ); // true
    trace ( myValue >= 4 ); // true
```

That is why both evaluate as true because the value of 4 is equal to the value of myValue. You'll notice that the less than or greater than symbol preceeds the equals sign. This won't work if they are in the wrong order, so be sure to put the equals sign last.

DEMONSTRATING EQUALITY AND INEQUALITY

To show how equality works, you're going to create a demo that combines drag and drop of an object and tests if it is dropped at a certain location. You'll use this to show how equality works as well as how you can use conditional statements based on the results of the conditional tests.

You first need to create an object to drag around.

1. In the FLA file, create a simple circle, and create a new linked object in the Library called DragCircle.

2. Convert the new object to a symbol and ensure the registration point is at the center (**Figure 12.1**).

   You have created the object in the Library, but you'll be re-creating it using ActionScript in the class, so you don't need it on the Stage.

3. Delete the object on the stage.

4. Create the following code in the Document class Booleans

```
package {
    import flash.display.MovieClip;
    import DragCircle;
    public class Booleans extends MovieClip {
        private var _isCorrect:Boolean;
        private var _dragCircle:MovieClip;
        public function Booleans():void {
            _init();
        }
```

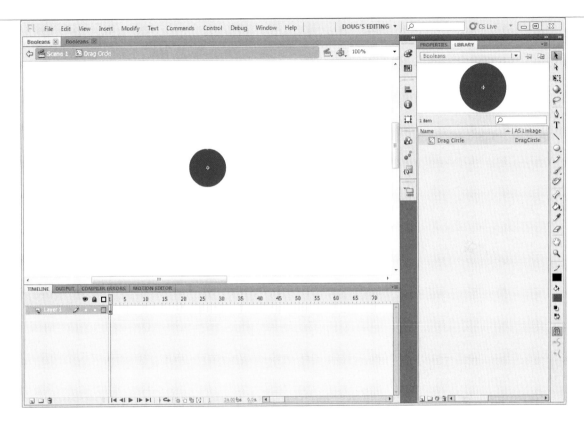

```
private function _init():void {
    _dragCircle = new DragCircle();
    _dragCircle.x = 100;
    _dragCircle.y = 100;
    addChild(_dragCircle);
    }
  }
}
```

FIGURE 12.1 Creating the DragCircle object

FIGURE 12.2 Running the project

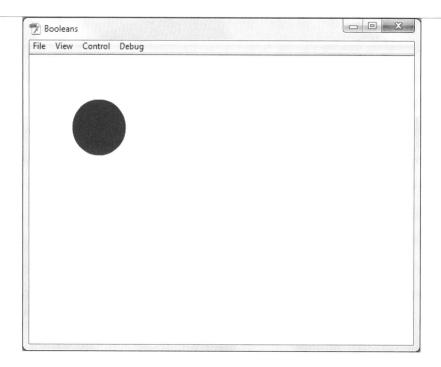

5. Run the project. You should see something similar to **Figure 12.2**.

Notice that you defined the instance of the circle in the class definition, and then created the instance with the new statement later on in the _init method. Also, for good measure, the DragCircle class was added at the top. This isn't required since the DragCircle is automatically created by Flash (since you haven't defined), but it makes the code clearer by including it here.

BUILDING DRAG AND DROP FOR THE MOUSE

You want to be able to drag and drop the object using the mouse. In ActionScript, every MovieClip has two methods that allow you to do exactly that: startDrag and stopDrag. You can use these methods in combination with the mouse events that you want to have trigger the beginning and ending of the drag action.

1. Add the code that will start the drag, as shown by the following highlighted code:

```
package {
    import flash.display.MovieClip;
    import DragCircle;
    import flash.events.MouseEvent;
    public class Booleans extends MovieClip {
        private var _isCorrect:Boolean;
        private var _dragCircle:MovieClip;
        public function Booleans():void {
            _init();
        }
        private function _init():void {
            _dragCircle = new DragCircle();
            _dragCircle.x = 100;
            _dragCircle.y = 100;
            addChild(_dragCircle);
            _dragCircle.addEventListener(MouseEvent.
                MOUSE_DOWN, drag);
            _dragCircle.addEventListener(MouseEvent.
                MOUSE_UP, drop);
        }
        private function drag(e:MouseEvent):void {
            e.target.startDrag();
        }
        private function drop(e:MouseEvent):void {
            e.target.stopDrag();
        }
    }
}
```

The new code adds two event listeners that are attached to the mouse down and mouse up events of the dragCircle instance. Each of these accesses the private methods named drag and drop. These methods accept a MouseEvent parameter that we call e. In the drag method, you access the target of the event (the _dragCircle instance) and use the startDrag method. This begins the drag action on the object. In the drop method, you discontinue the dragging of the object using the dropDrag method.

In order to prevent errors, you need to import the MouseEvent class at the top. They may have been added for you automatically as you typed your code.

2. Run the project. You can click and drag the circle around the screen. If you click and drag anywhere else, nothing will happen.

This is the basic code you'll build in the following examples.

ADDING FEEDBACK

Let's add a little feedback that reports the x and y coordinates of the object when you drop the circle.

1. Update the class code to send the x and y coordinate information to the Output panel:

```
package {
    import flash.display.MovieClip;
    import DragCircle;
    import flash.events.MouseEvent;
    public class Booleans extends MovieClip {
        private var _isCorrect:Boolean;
        private var _dragCircle:MovieClip;
        public function Booleans():void {
            _init();
        }
    }
```

```
            private function _init():void {
                _dragCircle = new DragCircle();
                _dragCircle.x = 100;
                _dragCircle.y = 100;
                addChild(_dragCircle);
                _dragCircle.addEventListener(MouseEvent.
                  ➝ MOUSE_DOWN, drag);
                _dragCircle.addEventListener(MouseEvent.
                  ➝ MOUSE_UP, drop);
            }
            private function drag(e:MouseEvent):void {
                e.target.startDrag();
            }
            private function drop(e:MouseEvent):void {
                e.target.stopDrag();
                trace("The circle is located at " + _dragCircle.x
                  ➝ + "," + _dragCircle.y);
            }
        }
    }
```

2. Run the project.

3. Drag the circle around the Stage and drop it. When you release the mouse, the Output panel will display the coordinates of the circle.

TESTING **CONDITIONS**

Now that you have the basics in place, let's add some condition testing and see how it works. Imagine you want to create a simple exercise that tests if the circle is dropped past 200 on the x axis. In other words, you want to test if the _dragCircle object's x coordinate is greater than 200.

1. Add a trace statement that will output the result of a simple conditional test based on the _dragCircle.x parameter:

```
package {
    import flash.display.MovieClip;
    import DragCircle;
    import flash.events.*;
    public class Booleans extends MovieClip {
        private var _isCorrect:Boolean;
        private var _dragCircle:MovieClip;
        public function Booleans():void {
            _init();
        }
        private function _init():void {
            _dragCircle = new DragCircle();
            _dragCircle.x = 100;
            _dragCircle.y = 100;
            addChild(_dragCircle);
            _dragCircle.addEventListener(MouseEvent.
              MOUSE_DOWN, drag);
            _dragCircle.addEventListener(MouseEvent.
              MOUSE_UP, drop);
        }
        private function drag(e:MouseEvent):void {
            _dragCircle.startDrag();
        }
```

```
private function drop(e:MouseEvent):void {
    _dragCircle.stopDrag();
    trace("The circle is located at " + _dragCircle.x
    →  + "," + _dragCircle.y);
    trace( _dragCircle.x > 200 );
}
    }
}
```

2. Drag the circle and drop it in various locations. You'll get the final location, but also a true or false indicating whether the x coordinate is greater than 200.

If you drag and drop the object at different locations, you'll get a variety of different responses:

```
The circle is located at 122,151
false
The circle is located at 365,107
true
The circle is located at 354,265
true
The circle is located at 279,176
true
The circle is located at 103,328
false
The circle is located at 65,72
false
```

Unfortunately, outputting true and false isn't very useful. You need to do some specific actions with the test result. This is where conditional statements come in, and the first one is called the if statement.

```
    (1)              (2)
if (_dragCircle.x > 200)
{
(3)     trace("The circle is past the 200 x coordinate.")
}                                    (4)
```

FIGURE 12.3 An example if
statement with callouts

THE **if** STATEMENT

The if statement does one thing. It asks a single question, and if the answer to
that question is true, it executes a branch of code. The code that tested for the
location of the circle worked, but it wasn't very useful. Using an if statement, you
can adjust the code so it can execute some specific code based on the results of the
conditional test. Refer to **Figure 12.3** as you step through the following anatomy
of an if statement.

You start an if statement with—you guessed it: if (callout 1). You then use
a set of parentheses around the conditional test you want to evaluate (callout 2).
You can evaluate only one condition at a time, so there can only be a single true or
false result in your condition. You then have a set of curly braces that denote the
code block that is placed after the if statement. If the condition is true, the code
inside the code block will run (callout 4). If it is false, it will ignore the code block
and keep running the program.

1. Insert the highlighted if statement in the example project:

```
package {
    import flash.display.MovieClip;
    import DragCircle;
    import flash.events.*;
    public class Booleans extends MovieClip {
        private var _isCorrect:Boolean;
        private var _dragCircle:MovieClip;
        public function Booleans():void {
```

```
        _ init();
    }
    private function _init():void {
        _dragCircle = new DragCircle();
        _dragCircle.x = 100;
        _dragCircle.y = 100;
        addChild(_dragCircle);
        _dragCircle.addEventListener(MouseEvent.
          MOUSE_DOWN, drag);
        _dragCircle.addEventListener(MouseEvent.
          MOUSE_UP, drop);
    }
    private function drag(e:MouseEvent):void {
        _dragCircle.startDrag();
    }
    private function drop(e:MouseEvent):void {
        _dragCircle.stopDrag();
        trace("The circle is located at " + _dragCircle.x
          + "," + _dragCircle.y);
        if ( _dragCircle.x > 200 ) {
            trace("The circle is placed after the
              200 x coordinate.");
        }
    }
}
}
```

2. Run the project. The Output panel will display something similar to the following:

```
The circle is located at 100,114
The circle is located at 209,134
The circle is placed after the 200 x coordinate.
The circle is located at 320,134
The circle is placed after the 200 x coordinate.
The circle is located at 68,200
```

This information is more useful than the previous true or false statements. Let's explore the if statement and learn how it works:

```
if ( _dragCircle.x > 200 ) {
    trace("The circle is placed after the 200 x coordinate.");
}
```

The if statement kicks off the question. Inside the parentheses, you create a single conditional statement that will evaluate as a single true or false. Then you start a new code block with curly braces and place the code that will run if the condition is true, followed by a closing curly brace.

This reads as: If dragCircle's x coordinate is greater than 200, then run this branch of code.

If your code block is only one line of code, you can omit the curly braces. You may encounter this in more complex code:

```
if ( _dragCircle.x > 200 ) trace("The circle is placed after the
→  200 x coordinate.");
```

Generally, programmers use the code blocks with the indented code, making the code easier to read.

THE if...else STATEMENT

So this code sample gives us feedback only if the coordinate is greater than 200. As you can see, when it isn't, it gives you nothing. What you want to do is have an alternative branch of code run if the condition is false. You can control this using the else statement.

1. Add the highlighted else statement in the following code:

```
package {
    import flash.display.MovieClip;
    import DragCircle;
    import flash.events.*;
    public class Booleans extends MovieClip {
        private var _isCorrect:Boolean;
        private var _dragCircle:MovieClip;
        public function Booleans():void {
            _init();
        }
        private function _init():void {
            _dragCircle = new DragCircle();
            _dragCircle.x = 100;
            _dragCircle.y = 100;
            addChild(_dragCircle);
            _dragCircle.addEventListener(MouseEvent.
                MOUSE_DOWN, drag);
            _dragCircle.addEventListener(MouseEvent.
                MOUSE_UP, drop);
        }
        private function drag(e:MouseEvent):void {
            _dragCircle.startDrag();
        }
        private function drop(e:MouseEvent):void {
            _dragCircle.stopDrag();
            trace("The circle is located at " + _dragCircle.x
                + "," + _dragCircle.y);
            if ( _dragCircle.x > 200 ) {
```

```
                    trace("The circle is placed after the
                    ⇢ 200 x coordinate.");
                } else {
                    trace("The circle is placed before or on the
                    ⇢ 200 x coordinate.");
                }
            }
        }
    }
```

The else statement is added after the end of the closing block of the if statement. If the condition that is tested at the start of the if statement is false, the first code block is ignored, and instead, the code block after the else statement runs.

Here is another way to look at it:

```
if (condition test)
{
    // Run this code if the condition test is true
} else {
    // Run this code if the condition test is false
}
```

As you can see from the code, either the first or the second code block is displayed:

```
The circle is located at 90,161
The circle is placed before or on the 200 x coordinate.
The circle is located at 283,174
The circle is placed after the 200 x coordinate.
The circle is located at 410,277
The circle is placed after the 200 x coordinate.
The circle is located at 39,317
The circle is placed before or on the 200 x coordinate.
```

THE if...else if STATEMENT

There is one final statement that you can use to evaluate code based on testing conditions, and that is the else if statement. The purpose of the else if statement is to continually test values until no more values work, and then end with an optional else statement.

For example, if you wanted to update the example to test if the dropped circle is past multiple specific points, you can adapt the code to continue evaluating conditions.

1. Update the code with the following highlighted code:

```
package {
    import flash.display.MovieClip;
    import DragCircle;
    import flash.events.*;
    public class Booleans extends MovieClip {
        private var _isCorrect:Boolean;
        private var _dragCircle:MovieClip;
        public function Booleans():void {
            _init();
        }
        private function _init():void {
            _dragCircle = new DragCircle();
            _dragCircle.x = 100;
            _dragCircle.y = 100;
            addChild(_dragCircle);
            _dragCircle.addEventListener(MouseEvent.
                MOUSE_DOWN, drag);
            _dragCircle.addEventListener(MouseEvent.
                MOUSE_UP, drop);
        }
```

```
private function drag(e:MouseEvent):void {
    _dragCircle.startDrag();
}
private function drop(e:MouseEvent):void {
    _dragCircle.stopDrag();
    trace("The circle is located at " + _dragCircle.x
    → + "," + _dragCircle.y);
    if ( _dragCircle.x > 400 ) {
        trace("The circle is placed after the
        → 400 x coordinate.");
    } else if ( _dragCircle.x > 200 ) {
        trace("The circle is placed after the
        → 200 x coordinate.");
    } else {
        trace("The circle is placed before or on the
        → 200 x coordinate.");
    }
}
```

2. Run the project. You'll get an Output similar to the following:

```
The circle is located at 142,111
The circle is placed before or on the 200 x coordinate.
The circle is located at 225,149
The circle is placed after the 200 x coordinate.
The circle is located at 495,185
The circle is placed after the 400 x coordinate.
The circle is located at 80,215
The circle is placed before or on the 200 x coordinate.
```

The application is testing multiple conditions in succession. First it is testing if the x coordinate is greater than 400. If it is, it runs the first code block; if it isn't, it tests another condition: is the x coordinate greater than 200? If it is, it runs the second code block; if it isn't, it runs the final code block after the else statement. The final else statement is optional and can be omitted if you don't want to have a catchall code block in your else if conditional test.

Again, to help illustrate this, here's an annotated version:

```
if (condition test 1)
{
    // Run this code if test 1 is true, then end
} else if (condition test 2) {
    // Run this code if test 1 is false, and test 2 is true, then end
} else {
    // Run this code if condition test 1 and 2 are false
}
```

Something you need to be careful of is that as soon as a condition is met, it ends the entire sequence. Take this for example:

```
if ( _dragCircle.x > 200 ) {
    trace("The circle is placed after the 200 x coordinate.");
} else if ( _dragCircle.x > 400 ) {
    trace("The circle is placed after the 400 x coordinate.");
} else {
    trace("The circle is placed before or on the 200 x coordinate.");
}
```

If the x coordinate is 500, the first condition tests true, but the second condition isn't tested at all, which is not what you wanted. To prevent this, you need to make sure that the conditions test in an order that makes sense, or if you are unsure, create multiple testing conditions with multiple if statements:

```
if ( _dragCircle.x > 200 ) {
    trace("The circle is placed after the 200 x coordinate.");
}
if ( _dragCircle.x > 400 ) {
    trace("The circle is placed after the 400 x coordinate.");
}
if ( _dragCircle.x <= 200 ){
    trace("The circle is placed before or on the 200 x coordinate.");
}
```

Now with these multiple testing conditions, all of them will be tested, regardless of whether any one of them are true or false. Generally, the elegance of the else statement will let you test if something is true and do something, or false and do something else; however there are times that you will want to create multiple if statement conditions as well.

WRAPPING **UP**

In this chapter you learned about working with Boolean values and using them to test for conditions using equality and inequality operators. Finally, you were able to use these new operators to build constructs in your code that let you execute different blocks of code based on the results of the conditional tests. As a bonus, you also learned how to use drag and drop behaviors with MovieClips. This was a lot for a single chapter, good job!

The following rules will help you work with Boolean variables and conditionals.

- Remember that Boolean values `true` and `false` do not use quotation marks.

- Use equality and inequality operators to test conditions between various values.

- Use the `startDrag` and `stopDrag` methods on MovieClip instances to create drag and drop examples.

- To execute specific code if a condition is true, use the `if` statement.

- To execute specific code if a condition is true, and another set if the condition is false, use the `if` statement in combination with the `else` statement.

- To test multiple conditions in a sequence, use the `if` and `else if` statements in a testing sequence.

- Plan your testing sequences, especially in more complex situations to ensure that the flow of the test will catch all the testing options. Map them out on paper before starting to write code.

13

ADVANCED **BOOLEAN LOGIC** AND **RANDOM** **NUMBERS**

Conditions give your applications the ability to change behaviors based on different circumstances. When working with more complex logic patterns, you need to use special operators. In this chapter, you'll review these operators and use them in conditional tests.

One of the most common ways to work with advanced logic is when you build random chance into your programs. This is customary for games and other interactive content. In this chapter, you'll learn how to generate random numbers and how to use them in your projects.

USING **LOGIC OPERATORS**

When you are testing conditions, you are limited to testing a pair of values. Oftentimes you want to test a combination of conditions in a single statement.

In the drag and drop example from Chapter 12, you were testing where an object was dropped based on the x axis. If you wanted to capture if the object was dropped within a specific region, you would have some pretty complex code:

```
package {
    import flash.display.MovieClip;
    import flash.events.MouseEvent;
    public class Booleans extends MovieClip {
        var circle:DragCircle;
        public function Booleans():void {
            _init();
        }
        private function _ init():void {
            circle = new DragCircle();
            circle.x = 50;
            circle.x = 50;
            addChild(circle);
            circle.addEventListener(MouseEvent.MOUSE_DOWN, drag);
            circle.addEventListener(MouseEvent.MOUSE_UP, drop);
        }
        private function drag(e:MouseEvent):void {
            circle.startDrag();
        }
        private function drop(e:MouseEvent):void {
            circle.stopDrag();
            if (circle.x > 100) {
                if (circle.y > 100) {
                    if (circle.x < 450) {
```

```
if (circle.y < 300) {
    trace("The circle is within the
    → rectangle!");
}
            }
        }
    }
}
```

Managing all of those nested condition statements to test the circle's location can get tricky, and you could easily have a situation where you test them in a different order and therefore exit the sequence prematurely.

To make this code easier to understand and more concise, you can use logical operators that can combine multiple testing pairs to create more complex tests.

THE AND OPERATOR

Probably the most common operator is the AND, which is represented by a pair of ampersands, &&. You can use these ampersands to link multiple conditional tests together. This operator requests that the conditions on either side must both be true for the entire test to be true.

Let's look at a section of code that highlights the AND operator:

```
trace ( 2 == 2 && 3 == 3 );
trace ( 2 == 3 && 3 == 3 );
```

These lines evaluate as the following in the Output panel:

```
true
```

```
false
```

This code evaluates each condition test, and when both are finished, it compares the results and asks if the one on the left AND the one on the right are both true. If they are, then the entire test is true. If they aren't, then the entire test is false.

In this case, 2 is equal to 2, and 3 is equal to 3, so you have two trues, which means that the whole test is true. In the second example, 2 is not equal to 3, so that is false, and the second test is true because 3 is equal to 3. Although the second test is true, the first is false, so when you use && the entire condition evaluates as false.

THE **OR** OPERATOR

In addition to AND, there is also the OR operator, which is represented by two vertical lines (also known as pipes), ||. In the following section of code, the test will pass if any of the individual tests are true:

```
trace ( 2 == 2 || 3 == 3 );
trace ( 2 == 3 || 3 == 3 );
```

These two lines evaluate to the following in the Output panel:

```
true
true
```

At least one of the tests on the left or right are true, so both tests pass.

THE **NOT** OPERATOR

The NOT operator is a little different from its siblings. It takes the current Boolean value of an object and reverses it. To use this, you take the variable that contains the Boolean value and you add an exclamation point, !, as a prefix to the variable name:

```
var myTest = 2 == 2 || 3 == 3;
trace ( !myTest );
```

This code produces the opposite of the test result:

```
false
```

The NOT operator is very helpful at creating toggle switches. MoveClips have several properties that have true or false values (visible is one example). Using the NOT operator, you can toggle between these values:

```
myMovie.visible = !myMovie.visible;
```

This code takes the current value, reverses it, and assigns it back to itself.

Now that you understand the AND and OR operators, you can adjust the drag and drop example to test if objects are dropped within a specific range of x and y coordinates:

```
package {
    import flash.display.MovieClip;
    import DragCircle;
    import flash.events.MouseEvent;
public class Booleans extends MovieClip {
        private var _isCorrect:Boolean;
        private var _dragCircle:MovieClip;
        public function Booleans():void {
            _init();
        }
        private function _init():void {
            _dragCircle = new DragCircle();
            _dragCircle.x = 100;
            _dragCircle.y = 100;
            addChild(_dragCircle);
            _dragCircle.addEventListener(MouseEvent.MOUSE_DOWN, drag);
            _dragCircle.addEventListener(MouseEvent.MOUSE_UP, drop);
        }
        private function drag(e:MouseEvent):void {
            e.target.startDrag();
        }
        private function drop(e:MouseEvent):void {
            e.target.stopDrag();
            if (_dragCircle.x > 100 && _dragCircle.x <
            ⇒ 450 && _dragCircle.y > 100 && _dragCircle.y < 300) {
                trace("The circle is within the rectangle!");
```

```
                    }
                }
            }
        }
```

Notice that you can string the && operators to create more complex examples. In this example, all four of the tests need to pass for the entire condition to pass. This format is much more concise and easier to understand than a set of nested if statements.

GENERATING RANDOM NUMBERS

As mentioned earlier, the principle of games is the element of random chance. To add that aspect to your project you need to work with random numbers. The Math class has a specific method that is critical for anyone adding random elements into a game or other application.

A random number generator creates numbers at random that add the element of chance to applications. The random number generator is accessed through the random method of the Math class.

1. Create a new project in Flash Professional CS5.5.

2. Create a Document class for the project (this example is named RandomNumber) and enter in the following ActionScript code:

```
package {
    import flash.display.MovieClip;
    public class RandomNumber extends MovieClip {
        public function RandomNumber():void {
            init();
        }
        private function init():void {
            trace ( Math.random() );
        }
    }
}
```

3. Run the project.

4. In the Output panel you will get a random decimal number that will resemble the following:

`0.5108420490287244`

The random method generates a decimal number between 0 and 1. You can use this number to create random numbers of different ranges. You can modify this to generate a number from 1 to 6, like a die.

5. Update the code, as follows:

```
package {
    import flash.display.MovieClip;
    public class RandomNumber extends MovieClip {
        public function RandomNumber():void {
            init();
        }
        private function init():void {
            trace ( Math.random() * 6 );
        }
    }
}
```

In this code, you are taking a randomly generated number and multiplying it by a factor of 6 to proportionally extend its range from 0 to 6.

6. Run the program several times, and you'll get a series of random numbers that resemble the following:

```
2.5428863195702434
4.439002267085016
2.601632511243224
1.4373473664745688
0.963768957182765
3.0498380083590746
1.1904680645093322
1.5892081037163734
```

Unfortunately, this isn't exactly what you want. A die doesn't have decimal values, so you need some way to drop the decimals. Luckily the Math class has a method that can help: the floor method.

7. Add the `floor` method to the previous code, as highlighted below:

```
package {
    import flash.display.MovieClip;
    public class RandomNumber extends MovieClip {
        public function RandomNumber():void {
            init();
        }
        private function init():void {
            trace ( Math.floor(Math.random() * 6) );
        }
    }
}
```

8. Run the project again a few times. You get something similar to the following:

3

2

5

0

1

4

You're close, but not quite there yet. Why? Because a die doesn't have the number 0, and if you run this over and over again, you'll notice that you'll never get the number 6. That is because you are stripping the decimal from the number. The random range is between 0 and 1. When you multiply this by 6, you will never get the number 6. You might get 5.9999, but when you use `floor`, you strip off the .9999 and get 5. You get a zero, because you could get a number like 0.9999, but that will become 0 when using the `floor` method. To correct this, simply add 1 and shift the range up by one digit.

9. Adjust the random number generator, as highlighted below:

```
package {
    import flash.display.MovieClip;
    public class RandomNumber extends MovieClip {
        public function RandomNumber():void {
            init();
        }
        private function init():void {
            trace ( Math.floor(Math.random() * 6) + 1 );
        }
    }
}
```

10. Run the project several times, and you will now get numbers that are like the numbers on a die:

4

6

6

3

5

1

That is more like it! You're ready for Vegas!

In addition to the floor method, the Math class contains two other ways to drop decimals: the ceil and round methods. The ceil method stands for ceiling, which bumps the value of the number to the next whole number if there is any decimal at all. So a number like 5.00001 would become 6 if you used the ceil method. The random method follows traditional rounding rules. If the number has a decimal of .5 or above, it is rounded up. If it is below .5, it is rounded down.

WRAPPING **UP**

In this chapter, you learned how to make complex logical evaluations using the AND and OR logical operators. In addition, you learned how to reverse Boolean values with the NOT operator. You learned how to generate random numbers using the `Math.random` method to build random chance in your programs.

Here are some tips to help you with the topics from this chapter:

- Use the AND and OR operators to combine conditional statements together to form a single true or false response.

- Use the AND operator, &&, if you want to ensure that all the conditions you are testing evaluate as true.

- Use the OR operator, | |, if you want to ensure that at least one of the conditions you are testing evaluates as true.

- Use the NOT operator, !, as a prefix on a variable name to reverse its Boolean value.

- Use the `Math.random` method to create a random decimal number from 0 to 1.

- Multiply and add values to your random number to adjust the range of your random number generator.

- Use the `Math.floor`, `Math.ceil`, or `Math.random` methods to drop decimals from your numbers.

14

WORKING WITH **TEXT** AND THE **KEYBOARD**

Working with text and working with the keyboard are skills that all Flash programmers need in their virtual tool belts. In this chapter, you'll learn how to use ActionScript to work with text fields, format them, and then respond to events from the keyboard. Working with text and the keyboard requires a high level of precision and accuracy. To help decipher all of this, you will use an interactive quiz to display ActionScript-based text and control the selection of answers through the keyboard.

WORKING WITH TEXT FIELDS

Before you learn how to work with keyboard events, let's cover the basics of working with text fields with ActionScript. The example for using the keyboard will be with a simple quiz where you'll ask a question and the user must press the button on the keyboard that corresponds to the answer. The text that displays in the quiz will be created entirely with ActionScript, without placing any text fields visually on the Stage in Flash Professional CS5.5.

WHAT ABOUT TLF? (TEXT LAYOUT FRAMEWORK)

This chapter is going to cover how to work with the basic text fields that are part of the Flash runtime. There is a new, more advanced text engine in Flash called the Text Layout Framework, or TLF. TLF is beyond the scope of this book; however, you can find more information about TLF on the Adobe website at: www.adobe.com/go/tlf.

As more projects are targeted for mobile devices, performance is a consideration as well. Currently, TLF does not perform well for mobile devices, because it was optimized for a laptop computer. Based on this, it is a good practice to work with the built-in text engine for now.

You could create dynamic text fields in the FLA file, but let's cover how to create these in ActionScript. Text fields are just like other objects in Flash—you create them using the var and new statements. In this example, there is an FLA file that uses a Document class called TextFields.

1. Create a Flash Professional project and a matching Document class named **TextFields**. Update the code in the class using the following code:

```
package {
    import flash.display.MovieClip;
    public class TextFields extends MovieClip {
        public function TextFields():void {
        }
    }
}
```

Now you want to create a text field that will contain the question you are going to ask the user in the quiz. You need to define the variable at the top that will contain the text field, and then add in the code to create the text field and update the text attribute.

2. Add the following highlighted code:

```
package {
    import flash.display.MovieClip;
    import flash.text.TextField;
    public class TextFields extends MovieClip {
        public var question:TextField;
        public function TextFields():void {
            _init();
        }
        private function _init():void {
            question = new TextField();
            question.x = 50;
            question.y = 50;
            question.width = 450;
            question.height = 100;
            question.text = "Which of these is the equality
            ⟶ statement?";
            addChild(question);
        }
    }
}
```

Let's review the code to see how it works.

First, you include the TextField class that is part of the flash.text package by inserting the import statement at the top of the class definition.

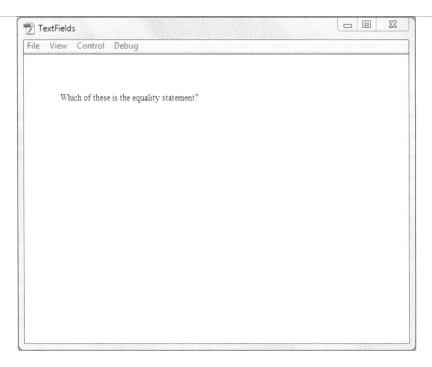

FIGURE 14.1 Creating your first text field using ActionScript

Next, you create an instance of the TextField class called question using the var statement. Notice that you are not creating an instance of it here, you do that later on in the init method.

In the _init method, a new TextField class instance is created, and some of the TextField instance properties are then modified. You set its location, its width and height, and then set the text contents with the text attribute.

Finally, you add the question TextField instance to the display stack.

3. Run the project. You'll get a line of text that contains the quiz question (**Figure 14.1**).

Unfortunately, the default text style isn't very interesting. In the next section, you'll learn how to create a text style and apply it to the text field.

CUSTOMIZING THE TEXT STYLE

The Flash Player built-in default font is similar to the Times New Roman. Unfortunately, it isn't very appealing. To make this project more interesting, you should give the quiz question a unique font, color, and size. You can do that using the TextFormat class.

The TextFormat class contains several properties that allow you to define the format of text. You can then apply that formatting to a text field, and all the text that appears from that point will use the format.

1. Update the package code with the following highlighted code:

```
package {
    import flash.display.MovieClip;
    import flash.text.TextField;
    import flash.text.TextFormat;
    public class TextFields extends MovieClip {
        public var question:TextField;
        public var format:TextFormat;
        public function TextFields():void {
            _init();
        }
        private function _init():void {
            question = new TextField();
            question.x = 50;
            question.y = 50;
            question.width = 450;
            question.height = 100;
            format = new TextFormat();
            format.font = "Verdana";
            format.color = 0xFF0000;
            format.size = 14;
            question.defaultTextFormat = format;
            question.text = "Which of these is the equality
                statement?";
```

FIGURE 14.2 Displaying the new font style

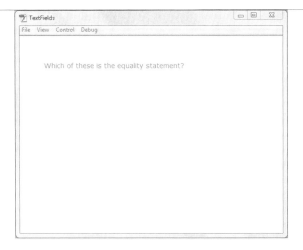

```
                    addChild(question);
                }
            }
        }
```

2. Run the project. You'll have the new font style applied (**Figure 14.2**).

The TextFormat class needs to be included in the opening import statements in the class definition and the variable needs to be defined as well.

When you create the instance of the TextFormat class, you can access the properties. In this example, you are accessing the font, color, and size properties of the format instance of the TextFormat class.

Then you add the format to the defaultTextFormat property of the question instance of the TextField class. When you add the text to it and then add the text field to the display stack, you see that the text is now using the Verdana font, that it is red, and that it is larger than before.

Notice that colors are defined using hexadecimal numbers. In ActionScript, you begin a hexadecimal number with the characters 0x, followed by the six-character value of the color. These are the same hexadecimal values used in HTML and CSS. So for a CSS formatted color of #00FF00, you would use 0x00FF00.

If you applied the text format after you added the text, the format won't look different. That is because you need to apply the format before you add the text to the field, otherwise you'll use the original format.

MAKING CHANGES TO STYLE LATER ON

In the last example, you set the default text format with the `defaultTextFormat` property and then added the string to the `text` property. Often there are situations when you need to adjust the style of the text field after it has been created.

You can't just change the text format property settings; you need to create a new text format, or update the old one, and reapply it to the text field. To reapply the format, use the `setTextFormat` method that is part of the `TextField` class. The `setTextFormat` method applies the format to the entire field, or you can add two optional parameters that define the start and end character that should have the format. So if you want to apply the text to only the second word of your string, you can count the number of characters and set the first and last character as the range that will accept the text format. Remember that the first character is 0, not 1, just like the elements of an array.

The following code is a example snippet that uses the `setTextFormat` method to update an existing text field with an alternative text format. Note the highlighted lines of code that changes the text using the different format:

```
myTextField = new TextField();

...

myTextFormat = new TextFormat();
myTextFormat.font = "Verdana";
myTextFormat.color = 0xFF0000;
myTextFormat.size = 24;
myTextField.defaultTextFormat = myTextFormat;
myTextField.text = "Text in Flash is pretty cool.";
myAlternateFormat = new TextFormat();
myAlternateFormat.font = "Times New Roman";
myAlternateFormat.color = 0x0000FF;
myAlternateFormat.bold = true;
myTextField.setTextFormat(myAlternateFormat,-1,13);
```

FIGURE 14.3 Using the setTextFormat method to update text format on an existing text field

FIGURE 14.4 The Font Embedding dialog box in Flash Professional CS5.5

This code produces the output shown in **Figure 14.3**.

CREATING YOUR OWN ACTIONSCRIPT FONTS

You'll find that if you attempt to run the previous examples on a computer that doesn't have the Verdana font, the program won't work correctly. This is because the font is not embedded in the application. To remedy this situation, you need to embed the font in the SWF so it is available to use on any system that renders it, regardless of whether it has the font.

There are a few extra steps required to embed a font, and they start with going back to the FLA file. Back in the FLA file, you need to create a new Font object in the Library, using a dialog box like the one shown in **Figure 14.4**.

Here is the step by step on how to embed a single font:

1. Right-click in the Library panel and select New Font.

2. Give your font a name in the Name field.

3. Select a font family.

4. Select a font style (each embedded font can be of a specific family *and* style).

5. Select the character range you want to embed.

   The character range is a good place to provide some more explanation. When you embed the font, you are taking the characters, or glyphs, of the font and embedding them in the SWF for use later on. Fonts can contain hundreds

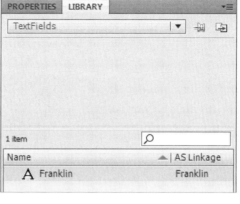

FIGURE 14.5 The ActionScript tab in the Font Embedding dialog box

FIGURE 14.6 An embedded font displayed in the Library panel

or even thousands of glyphs, so if you know that you won't need some, it is best to limit the range of glyphs you are embedding to keep your file size small. Typically, for English or Roman-based language projects, selecting the Basic Latin character range is sufficient. If you are working in other languages (for instance, Russian) you may need to embed additional characters.

6. Open the ActionScript tab (**Figure 14.5**).

7. Select Classic as the outline format.

8. Select the Export for ActionScript check box (the Class field should fill automatically).

9. Click OK.

If you look at the Library panel, you'll now see a new item for the embedded font (**Figure 14.6**).

With the font embedded in the project, you can use it in ActionScript. You first need to import the flash.text.Font class to use this new Library object. For good measure, you should import the Franklin class you created in the font embedding process shown in Figure 14.5 and 14.6. Next, you need to create an instance of the embedded font in your ActionScript. Finally, you replace the fontName property with the new custom Franklin font that was created earlier.

10. Update the project with the following highlighted code. Here is what the project should look like when you use the embedded font:

```
package {
    import flash.display.MovieClip;
    import flash.text.TextField;
    import flash.text.TextFormat;
    import Franklin;
    import flash.text.Font;
    public class TextFields extends MovieClip {
        public var question:TextField;
        public var format:TextFormat;
        public var questionFont:Font;
        public function TextFields():void {
            _init();
        }
        private function _init():void {
            question = new TextField();
            question.x = 50;
            question.y = 50;
            question.width = 450;
            question.height = 100;
            questionFont = new Franklin();
            format = new TextFormat();
            format.font = questionFont.fontName;
            format.color = 0xFF0000;
            format.size = 20;
```

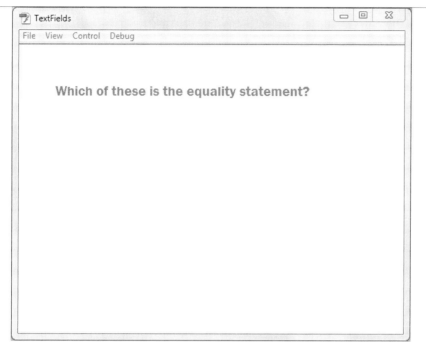

FIGURE 14.7 Displaying the embedded font

```
            question.defaultTextFormat = format;

            question.text = "Which of these is the equality
        ⇒ statement?";

            addChild(question);
        }
    }
}
```

11. Run the project. You'll see that the font changed to reflect the new embedded Franklin font (**Figure 14.7**).

CREATING THE QUIZ LAYOUT

Now that you know the basics of creating text fields, you can start creating the layout of the quiz example. The quiz is going to have three major text areas: the question, the responses, and the response that will display information to prompt the user to answer the question and report back whether the answer was correct.

Let's do this one stage at a time. You already created the question part as you were learning about text fields. You'll add the responses next. For simplicity, you'll use the same font as the question field, but adjust the color. You'll also clean up some variable names to avoid confusion.

1. Update the package code with the following highlighted text:

```
package {
    import flash.display.MovieClip;
    import flash.text.TextField;
    import flash.text.TextFormat;
    import Franklin;
    import flash.text.Font;
    public class TextFields extends MovieClip {
        public var question:TextField;
        public var responses:TextField;
        public var questionFormat:TextFormat;
        public var responsesFormat:TextFormat;
        public var quizFont:Font;
        public function TextFields():void {
            _init();
        }
        private function _init():void {
            // Format and display the quiz question
            question = new TextField();
            question.x = 50;
            question.y = 50;
```

```
question.width = 450;
question.height = 100;
quizFont = new Franklin();
questionFormat = new TextFormat();
questionFormat.font = quizFont.fontName;
questionFormat.color = 0xFF0000;
questionFormat.size = 20;
question.defaultTextFormat = questionFormat;
question.text = "Which of these is the equality
    statement?";
// Format and display the responses to the
    question
responses = new TextField();
responses.x = 50;
responses.y = 150;
responses.width = 450;
responses.height = 150;
responsesFormat = new TextFormat();
responsesFormat.font = quizFont.fontName;
responsesFormat.color = 0x000000;
responsesFormat.size = 14;
responses.defaultTextFormat = responsesFormat;
responses.text = "Question responses go here";
// Add text fields to the display stack
addChild(question);
addChild(responses);
            }
        }
    }
```

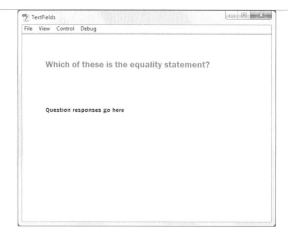

FIGURE 14.8 Updated quiz output with the responses added

> **TextFields**
> File   View   Control   Debug
>
> **Which of these is the equality statement?**
>
> **Question responses go here**

2. Run the project. You'll see the response text field displayed below the question text and in a different size and color (**Figure 14.8**).

HOW DO YOU PLAN LAYOUT IN CODE?

In this example, you were doing all the layout in code. You might wonder, and rightfully so, how on earth do I know where things need to go? Well, the answer is that I did some planning ahead of time. In fact, I do a lot of my layout on paper before I jump into code. I find that it makes the process much smoother.

I have a grid-ruled notebook that I use to sketch out the layouts of the projects I am working on. **Figure 14.9** shows the sketch I have for this chapter's example.

As you can see, I have each of the text fields laid out, showing their location and then their width and height. In this case, the journal grid lines represent 25 pixels. If I have a larger project, I'll adjust the scale accordingly.

A little planning ahead will pay dividends when you start coding. It is a practice I recommend you add to your workflow as soon as possible!

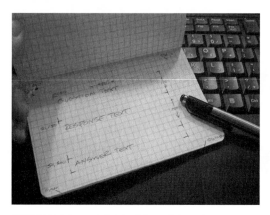

FIGURE 14.9 Journal sketch of the quiz layout

WORKING WITH ESCAPE SEQUENCES

Right now, the quiz example has only one line of text for responses. You are going to want four lines, each showing a possible answer to the multiple choice question. The problem is, how do you show multiple lines of text in a string sequence?

The answer is with escape sequences. *Escape sequences* are special two to four character combinations that are interpreted by ActionScript as directives on how to render the entire string. The most common is the new line character, or \n.

Here are the responses for the question and how you want to show them:

A) <=

B) ==

C) !=

D) >=

The new line character is placed where you want to show a line return. It is placed inside your string, and ActionScript will use it to show the line return, but not display the sequence as characters in your string.

Here are the responses with the new line escape sequence:

A) <=\n

B) ==\n

C) !=\n

D) >=

Now that the escape codes in the right places the line returns are not necessary. Here is what the string should look like:

A) <=\nB) ==\nC) !=\nD) >=

Looks like gibberish, doesn't it? That is why it is best to lay it out the way you want it first and then make the adjustments you need. Let's return to the project and make some adjustments.

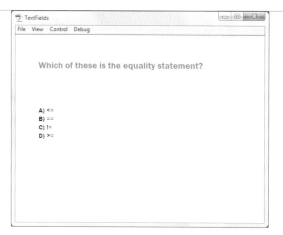

FIGURE 14.10 Displaying text using escape sequences

1. Update the response placeholder with the following highlighted code:

```
responses.text = "A) <=\nB) ==\nC) !=\nD) >=";
```

2. Run the project. You'll see that the escape sequences are replaced with new line returns (**Figure 14.10**).

There is one final step: Create the text field for the answer. This text field will give the user instructions on what to do when the question first displays, then indicate if the user was right or wrong.

You need to create a new text field and display the text, all things you have done before.

3. Update the package with the following highlighted code:

```
package {
    import flash.display.MovieClip;
    import flash.text.TextField;
    import flash.text.TextFormat;
    import Franklin;
    import flash.text.Font;
    public class TextFields extends MovieClip {
        public var question:TextField;
```

```
public var responses:TextField;
public var answer:TextField;
public var questionFormat:TextFormat;
public var responsesFormat:TextFormat;
public var answerFormat:TextFormat;
public var quizFont:Font;
public function TextFields():void {
    _init();
}
private function _init():void {
    // Format and display the quiz question
    question = new TextField();
    question.x = 50;
    question.y = 50;
    question.width = 450;
    question.height = 100;
    quizFont = new Franklin();
    questionFormat = new TextFormat();
    questionFormat.font = quizFont.fontName;
    questionFormat.color = 0xFF0000;
    questionFormat.size = 20;
    question.defaultTextFormat = questionFormat;
    question.text = "Which of these is the equality
    →  statement?";
    // Format and display the responses to the
    →  question
    responses = new TextField();
    responses.x = 50;
    responses.y = 150;
```

```
                responses.width = 450;
                responses.height = 150;
                responsesFormat = new TextFormat();
                responsesFormat.font = quizFont.fontName;
                responsesFormat.color = 0x000000;
                responsesFormat.size = 14;
                responses.defaultTextFormat = responsesFormat;
                responses.text = "A) <=\nB) ==\nC) !=\nD) >=";
                // Format and display the instructions/answer
                ⇒ response
                answer = new TextField();
                answer.x = 50;
                answer.y = 300;
                answer.width = 450;
                answer.height = 150;
                answerFormat = new TextFormat();
                answerFormat.font = quizFont.fontName;
                answerFormat.color = 0x0000FF;
                answerFormat.size = 14;
                answer.defaultTextFormat = answerFormat;
                answer.text = "Press the letter next to the
                ⇒ correct answer.";
                // Add text fields to the display stack
                addChild(question);
                addChild(responses);
                addChild(answer);
            }
        }
    }
```

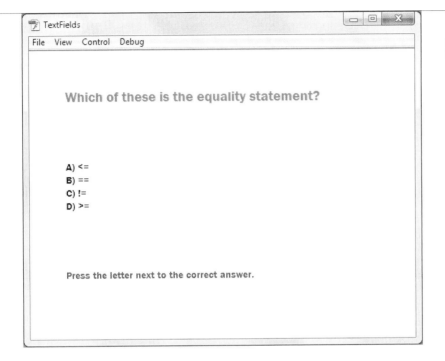

FIGURE 14.11 The final quiz layout

TextFields

File   View   Control   Debug

Which of these is the equality statement?

A) <=
B) ==
C) !=
D) >=

Press the letter next to the correct answer.

4. Run the project. You'll see the final layout (**Figure 14.11**).

You are all finished with the layout! In the next section you'll learn how to connect this to the keyboard so the user can answer the question and receive a response.

CREATING THE
KeyboardEvent HANDLER

The KeyboardEvent handler is like any other event—you need to create a listener and then a callback function that is triggered when the listener hears a specific type of event. To allow the user to use the keyboard to answer the quiz question, you need to use the KeyboardEvent to capture when the user presses a key on the keyboard.

To work with the keyboard event, you need to import the KeyboardEvent class, which is part of the flash.events package. Next, you need to add an event listener for the event. Since you don't have any objects that are necessarily linked to the event, you can attach the event listener to the Stage itself using the keyword stage. In the event listener, you want to listen for the event type. The KeyboardEvent class has a number of events. The two that are most common are KEY_DOWN and KEY_UP. The first, KEY_DOWN, is fired when the key is pressed down. The second, KEY_UP, is fired with the key is pressed and released. This example will use the KEY_DOWN event, since it is typically the behavior that you find in most programs. Finally, as with all other events, you need a callback function to run when the event occurs.

Update the code, as highlighted below, adding the KeyboardEvent event listener:

```
package {
    import flash.display.MovieClip;
    import flash.text.TextField;
    import flash.text.TextFormat;
    import Franklin;
    import flash.text.Font;
    import flash.events.KeyboardEvent;
    public class TextFields extends MovieClip {
        public var question:TextField;
        public var responses:TextField;
        public var answer:TextField;
        public var questionFormat:TextFormat;
        public var responsesFormat:TextFormat;
        public var answerFormat:TextFormat;
        public var quizFont:Font;
        public function TextFields():void {
```

```
        _init();
    }
    private function _init():void {
        // Format and display the quiz question
        question = new TextField();
        question.x = 50;
        question.y = 50;
        question.width = 450;
        question.height = 100;
        quizFont = new Franklin();
        questionFormat = new TextFormat();
        questionFormat.font = quizFont.fontName;
        questionFormat.color = 0xFF0000;
        questionFormat.size = 20;
        question.defaultTextFormat = questionFormat;
        question.text = "Which of these is the equality
         statement?";
        // Format and display the responses to the question
        responses = new TextField();
        responses.x = 50;
        responses.y = 150;
        responses.width = 450;
        responses.height = 150;
        responsesFormat = new TextFormat();
        responsesFormat.font = quizFont.fontName;
        responsesFormat.color = 0x000000;
        responsesFormat.size = 14;
        responses.defaultTextFormat = responsesFormat;
```

```
                    responses.text = "A) <=\nB) ==\nC) !=\nD) >=";
                    // Format and display the instructions/answer response
                    answer = new TextField();
                    answer.x = 50;
                    answer.y = 300;
                    answer.width = 450;
                    answer.height = 150;
                    answerFormat = new TextFormat();
                    answerFormat.font = quizFont.fontName;
                    answerFormat.color = 0x0000FF;
                    answerFormat.size = 14;
                    answer.defaultTextFormat = answerFormat;
                    answer.text = "Press the letter next to the correct
                      answer.";
                    // Add text fields to the display stack
                    addChild(question);
                    addChild(responses);
                    addChild(answer);
                    // Add keyboard event listener
                    stage.addEventListener
                      (KeyboardEvent.KEY_DOWN,_checkAnswer);
                }
            private function _checkAnswer(e:KeyboardEvent):void {
                if (e.keyCode == 65) {
                    answer.text = "You're wrong! Try again...";
                } else if (e.keyCode == 66) {
                    answer.text = "You're right! Congratulations";
                } else if (e.keyCode == 67) {
                    answer.text = "You're wrong! Try again...";
```

```
        } else if (e.keyCode == 68) {
            answer.text = "You're wrong! Try again...";
        }
    }
}
}
```

As mentioned earlier, you are attaching the listener to the Stage object. You need to attach to the Stage to give focus to the event listener from the beginning. If you don't, the listener won't work until you click once within the movie.

In the event listener, you are listening for the KEY_DOWN event. You want to trigger the callback function when the key has been pressed down. Again, when you typically use a keyboard, the key press is recognized when you press it down, not when you release it.

In the callback function, you have a series of if and else if statements that are testing a KeyboardEvent property that is passed into the function from the event listener.

In this example, you are using the event object, e, and you'll need to access it to determine which key was pressed as part of the event. In a simple keyboard event, only one key is pressed, so the event object has a property called keyCode that is a series of numbers that map to the keys on the keyboard.

For the quiz, you are concerned about the A, B, C, and D keys, since they are matching the responses for the quiz. These are mapped to the key codes 65, 66, 67, and 68 respectively.

> **NOTE:** Every key on a keyboard has a special number associated with it in ActionScript. These are called *key codes*. You can find the numeric code for each key in the ActionScript 3.0 reference guide on Adobe's website:
>
> ```
> http://help.adobe.com/en_US/AS3LCR/Flash_10.0/?flash/ui/
> Keyboard.html
> ```

When you have a key that matches, you send a congratulations response. If it doesn't match, you tell the user to try again.

DIFFERENCES BETWEEN CODE TYPES:
KEY CODES VERSUS CHARACTER CODES

There are two types of codes that are part of the KeyboardEvent object. The first is called the key code, which represents the specific key pressed by the user. The other is the character code, which is linked to the character created by the user with the keyboard.

You might wonder what the difference is. Let's look at an example to demonstrate this. This is the Document class for a new FLA file:

```
package {
    import flash.display.MovieClip;
    import flash.events.KeyboardEvent;
    public class KeyAndCharCodes extends MovieClip {
        public function KeyAndCharCodes():void {
            _init();
        }
        private function _init():void {
            stage.addEventListener
                (KeyboardEvent.KEY_DOWN,_getCodes);
        }
        private function _getCodes(e:KeyboardEvent):void {
            trace ("The key code is " + e.keyCode + " and the
                character code is " + e.charCode + " for the
                character " + String.fromCharCode(e.charCode));
        }
    }
}
```

The _getCodes method displays a line to the Output panel with the KeyboardEvent key code and character code, and shows how you can convert a character code to the actual letter it represents using the fromCharCode method of the String class.

When you run this, you can get something similar to the following:

```
The key code is 65 and the character code is 97 for the character a
The key code is 16 and the character code is 0 for the character
The key code is 65 and the character code is 65 for the character A
```

When the A button is pressed, it is represented by the key code 65 as the physical button. The character code, however, is linked to the generated character. In this case it is the lowercase a, which has a character code of 97.

The second line is when the Shift key is pressed, which has a key code of 16 but a character code of 0, because it doesn't create a character. When the A button is pressed with the Shift key, you get another key code of 65, but now, you are creating a capital A, which has a character code of 65.

When you build keyboard interfaces, you need to map to the key code since the character code can vary. If you build the quiz using the character code it wouldn't work if the user had caps lock on. Unless you specifically need to capture unique characters (like punctuation, for example) stick with key codes in your keyboard events.

RECOGNIZING SPECIAL KEYS

There are some special keys that you can access through shortcuts with the KeyboardEvent and Keyboard classes for buttons. The most common examples are the keyboard arrow keys. Using the Keyboard class, you can access these shortcuts using the keywords RIGHT, LEFT, UP, or DOWN as properties of the Keyboard class.

The following example is a project that contains a library object exported as a class called BlueSquare. The following defines the Document class for the project:

```
package {
    import flash.display.MovieClip;
    import flash.events.KeyboardEvent;
    import flash.ui.Keyboard;
    public class ArrowKeys extends MovieClip {
        var mySquare:BlueSquare;
        public function ArrowKeys():void {
```

```
        _init();
    }
    private function _init():void {
        mySquare = new BlueSquare();
        mySquare.x = 250;
        mySquare.y = 200;
        addChild(mySquare);
        stage.addEventListener
        ⤸ (KeyboardEvent.KEY_DOWN, _moveCircle);
    }
    private function _moveCircle(e:KeyboardEvent):void {
        if (e.keyCode == Keyboard.LEFT) {
            mySquare.x = mySquare.x - 5;
            trace("LEFT key pressed");
        } else if (e.keyCode == Keyboard.RIGHT) {
            mySquare.x = mySquare.x + 5;
            trace("RIGHT key pressed");
        } else if (e.keyCode == Keyboard.UP) {
            mySquare.y = mySquare.y - 5;
            trace("UP key pressed");
        } else if (e.keyCode == Keyboard.DOWN) {
            mySquare.y = mySquare.y + 5;
            trace("DOWN key pressed");
        }
    }
}
}
}
```

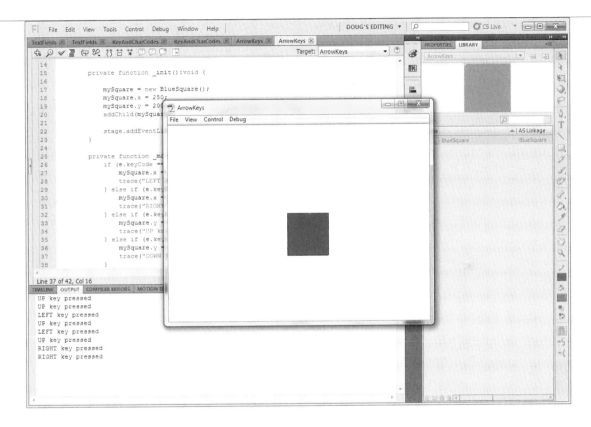

When this project runs, you'll get something similar to **Figure 14.12**.

Using the Keyboard class, you can access the keys for the arrow keys with the phrases LEFT, RIGHT, UP, and DOWN without needing to remember the key codes. These phrases are called constants and in fact contain the key code values, so when you test conditions, it is testing the KeyboardEvent key code against the stored key code in the constant.

FIGURE 14.12 Using keyboard arrow keys in your project

WRAPPING **UP**

In this chapter, you learned a lot about working with text, text formatting, and embedded fonts, and then learned how to work with the keyboard to create interactivity using keyboard keys.

Working with text in ActionScript gives you a lot of control over exactly how you want text to look and appear, but it can add complexity to working with the layout. It is important to consider your layout ahead of time, and sketching out a wireframe is a great way to plan ahead before you code.

Keyboard controls create an additional layer of interactive capabilities to your application, including controls for keyboard arrow keys.

Here are some tips to help you work with text and the keyboard in your project:

- Include the `flash.text.TextField` and `flash.text.TextFormat` classes using the `import` statement when working with text.

- Text fields have two parts: the text field itself and the text format. Define both and set the `defaultTextFormat` property before adding text to the text field.

- To make changes to text format and style after the text field is created, use the `setTextFormat` method of the `TextField` class.

- To embed fonts, add fonts to the Library and export for ActionScript. Create a new instance of the font in your ActionScript and use the `fontName` property to use the embedded font in your text format.

- Remember to include only the glyphs or characters you need when embedding fonts to keep your file size low.

- Sketch your layout on paper before creating code to save time refactoring later on.

- Use escape sequences like \n to create new line returns in text strings.

- When listening for keyboard events, determine if you want to use `KEY_DOWN` or `KEY_UP` as the event type.

- Remember the difference between key codes and character codes. Key codes are for the physical key, character codes are for the glyphs that are shown on the screen as the result of pressing a key (or combination of keys).

- Use shortcuts with the `Keyboard` class for special keys like the keyboard arrow keys.

15

CREATING GROUPS OF **OBJECTS** AND **REPEATING ACTIONS** USING **LOOPS**

In all the examples so far, you have been working with individual instances of objects. As you work with more complex projects that have multiple instances of objects, it can quickly become unworkable without some way to access properties or values with each instance in a logical group. For example, if you have a project with a couple instances of a Library object, it is pretty manageable. But what about when you have a dozen? A hundred? Or even a thousand? There needs to be some way to organize these into groups to make it easier for you as a coder to work with them.

In this chapter, you'll get an introduction to grouping objects into named sets called arrays. In addition, you'll look at how to use loops to execute blocks of code a repeated number of times based on a conditional test using the for loop.

WHAT ARE LOOPS?

FIGURE 15.1 A simple for loop

① ② ③ ④

```
for (var i:uint = 0; i < 10; i++)
    {
⑤       trace(i);
    }
```

A loop is a method in ActionScript to mark a block of code that will repeat a number of times based on a condition. The premise is that the loop of code will repeat continuously as long as the condition of the loop, defined by a Boolean conditional test, remains true.

Loops are used for a wide variety of functions. There are situations where you want to repeat the same action more than once, potentially thousands of times, and loops provide a concise and adjustable way to repeat code.

You can also use loops to go through groups or sets of objects called arrays. You'll learn about arrays in more detail in the second half of the chapter.

The most common loop you will encounter will ask for the test of a condition, and if that condition is true, run the block of code in the body of the loop, and then retest the condition, resulting in a cycle. If the condition proves to be false at some point, the loop stops executing. This is the basic premise of the for loop.

USING THE for LOOP

The for loop is the most basic of the loop types, and undoubtedly will be the one you will work with the most. As mentioned earlier, the basic architecture of a for loop starts with a Boolean conditional test. If the test is true, the loop executes. When the code of the loop is finished, it then retests the condition. If the condition is still true, the loop runs again. If the condition is false, the loop stops and continues to run the rest of the code.

Let's take a look at an example of a for loop and break down the parts using the callouts in **Figure 15.1**.

When you create a for loop, you start with the for statemen ❶. After the opening statement, you create a pair of parentheses that contain three sections, each separated by a semicolon.

The first statement ❷ defines a special variable used in a loop called an *iterator*. An iterator is a variable inside of a loop that defines how many times the loop will run. Typically, the iterator has the name of i, but you can use whatever variable name you want. You need to define the iterator to have a value to test against within the loop. Using the var statement, this loop creates the variable i, and sets it to a new object type, the uint type. This is a variation of the Number type. uint stands for unsigned integer, which states that the value will not contain decimals (also called an integer), and will only be positive (meaning that it can't have a negative or positive "sign" thus "unsigned").

The next section ❸ contains the conditional test itself. This is just like the conditional tests you have looked at before. In this case, you are asking to test if the variable i is less than the number 10.

For the conditional to test different situations, you need to change the iterator variable in some way. The final section ❹ is the step of the loop. The step defines how you modify the iterator at the end of a loop execution, but before the condition is retested and the loop runs again. If you didn't change the iterator in some way, you could potentially have a condition called an infinite loop that will run forever, because the testing condition will never become false. Infinite loops slow down your system, and eventually you'll be asked to kill or close your application.

Finally, you'll create a code block using braces that encapsulate the lines of code that will run with each iteration of the loop ❺.

Let's use this example in a Document class and see exactly how it works. Here is the Document class for the loop:

```
package  {
    import flash.display.MovieClip;
    public class Loops extends MovieClip {
        public function Loops() {
            for (var i:uint = 0; i < 10; i++)
            {
                trace(i);
            }
        }
    }
}
```

FIGURE 15.2 Output panel
from the loop

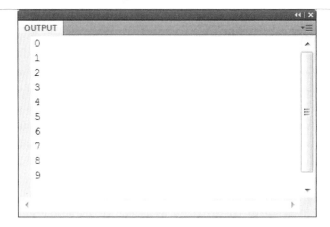

When this project runs, you'll get the messages displayed in **Figure 15.2**.

Let's step through this a few times and see exactly what takes place. First, you start the loop with the for statement and create an iterator variable that begins with the value 0. You test the condition: Is 0 less than 10? The answer is true, so you run the loop.

The loop code sends the current value of the iterator variable to the Output panel. The loop code is then finished.

The loop processes the step, which increments the iterator by 1, resulting in 1. The loop starts again, retesting the condition, running the code, and sending the value of the iterator to the Output panel.

The iterator eventually equals 9, displays in the Output panel, and then increments by 1, resulting in 10. You retest the condition: Is 10 less than 10? No, it isn't—it is equal, so the result is false. Since the conditional test failed, the loop ends, and the program finishes.

Using this basic model, you can create loops that will run a known number of times (as in the example), or test against a variable that could run a different number of times based on different conditions.

For example, if you wanted to have a specific action, like a calculation, change multiple times, you would use a loop to do this. Later in the chapter, you'll learn about arrays, which are groups of objects you can use to repeat the same action over each object in the group. For example, if you wanted to change the location of several MovieClips, you could put them in a group, and using the loop, move through all the objects within the group and run the same piece of code to change the location.

CONTROLLING THE FLOW OF LOOPS WITH **break** AND `continue`

You might have situations where you want to alter the flow of a loop. Using the break and continue statements, you can suspend execution of code in the loop body, or end the loop early.

The break statement exits out of the loop immediately, regardless of the result of your loop conditional test. Use this whenever you want to exit a loop. The continue statement suspends the execution of the loop code body, applies the step to the iterator, and restarts the loop again.

Here is an updated example that uses the break and continue statements in conjunction with a couple if statements:

```
package  {
    import flash.display.MovieClip;
    public class Loops extends MovieClip {
        public function Loops() {
            for (var i:uint = 0; i < 10; i++)
            {
                if (i == 5) continue;
                if (i == 7) break;
                trace(i);
            }
        }
    }
}
```

In this example, if the iterator is equal to 5, you are skipping the rest of the loop code using the continue statement. When the iterator equals 7, you will exit out of the loop entirely using break, even though the loop condition is still true.

Notice that you have the break and continue statements on the same line as the if statement. Because you are running only a single command for the conditional, you can omit the braces and put everything on the same line.

FIGURE 15.3 Using break and continue to alter the flow of a loop

```
OUTPUT
0
1
2
3
4
6
```

Figure 15.3 shows the result when you run this new code.

As you can see, the code never outputs the number 5, because you are skipping that part of the loop body using the continue statement. You also never get any numbers greater than 7 because you exit out of the loop using break.

NESTING LOOPS

It is possible to nest loops inside of each other. In nested loops, the inner loop runs a set number of times for each execution of the outer loop. Here is an example:

```
package  {
    import flash.display.MovieClip;
    public class NestedLoops extends MovieClip {
        public function NestedLoops() {
            _init();
        }
        private function _init():void
        {
            for (var i:uint = 0; i < 3; i++)
            {
                trace ("Outer loop #" + i);
```

```
        for (var ii:uint = 0; ii < 3; ii++)
        {
            trace ("Inner loop #" + ii);
        }
    }
  }
 }
}
```

This code creates the following in the Output panel:

```
Outer loop #0
Inner loop #0
Inner loop #1
Inner loop #2
Outer loop #1
Inner loop #0
Inner loop #1
Inner loop #2
Outer loop #2
Inner loop #0
Inner loop #1
Inner loop #2
```

The outer loop starts, with the iterator at 0, then runs the inner loop three times before it goes back and reruns the outer loop.

When you work with nested loops, make sure that you are working with the right iterator variables. As you can see in this example, unique iterator variable names are used for each nested loop. This is required, otherwise your inner loop, will change the iterator of the outer loop. Also, inner loops must be completely self-contained, meaning they are completely within the code block's curly brackets of the outer loop. If they aren't they won't work correctly.

ANOTHER STYLE OF LOOPS, THE **do** LOOP

When using the for loop, there is a chance that the code within the loop will never run. If the conditional results in false at the start of the first execution of the loop, the loop will be skipped entirely. If you have a loop that you want to run at least once, and then test the loop condition at the end, there is an option for you called the do loop, sometimes referred to as the do...while loop.

Another difference with the do loop is that it doesn't have an iterator variable defined inside the loop, so if you are running something based on an existing variable, the do loop might be the right fit.

Here is a simple example using a do loop:

```
package  {
    import flash.display.MovieClip;
    public class DoLoop extends MovieClip {
        public function DoLoop() {
            var myValue:uint = 0;
            do
            {
                trace(myValue);
            } while (myValue != 0)
        }
    }
}
```

In this example, you use the do statement to start the body of the loop, which sends a statement to the Output panel. At the end, you use the while statement to cue up the conditional test that you want to use to determine if the loop runs again. If the condition is true, the loop runs again, testing the condition again at the end.

In this case though, the condition test will be false, even after the first time you run the loop; however, unlike the for loop, the loop will run at least once, even though the test will be false in the end.

CREATING GROUPS OF ITEMS WITH ARRAYS

Often, you'll have multiple objects in your application that you need to work with. Having a few or even hundreds of objects can be difficult to manage. ActionScript can make managing multiple objects easier by grouping objects into named groups called arrays.

Arrays are collections of objects that have a specific order. You can refer to any object within the collection and even loop through the objects in the array. Arrays can contain strings, numbers, or even MovieClips, which makes it perfect to house groups of objects that you are showing on the Stage.

Let's start with a basic example using strings (the names of some of my current and past pets), and you can evolve it from there. This example is within a new Document class:

```
package {
    import flash.display.MovieClip;
    public class SimpleArray extends MovieClip {
        public var myArray:Array;
        public function SimpleArray() {
            myArray = ["Binky", "Hoover", "BB", "Rocket"];
            trace(myArray);
        // "Binky", "Hoover", "BB", "Rocket"
            trace(myArray[0]);        // "Binky"
            trace(myArray.length);    // 4
        }
    }
}
```

Just like with any object in ActionScript, you need to create a named variable to refer to it. In this case, you are using the name myArray and are typing it as an Array.

To create the initial set of array items, you assign to the array a set of objects encapsulated in square brackets and separated by commas.

```
myArray = new Array("Binky", "Hoover", "BB", "Rocket");
```

You can send the entire array to the `trace` statement, which lists the items that are inside it.

In this array, you have four specific strings inside the collection. You now need a way to access the objects within the array. Each item that is contained in array is assigned a number, which is called its *index*. The index number is automatically assigned when you create an array. The index numbers start with 0 and each item then counts up from there.

Knowing that, the string "Binky" is element 0 of the `myArray` object. "Hoover" is element 1, "BB" is element 2, and finally, "Rocket" is element 3.

You can access the elements of the array using the index number. When you attach the square brackets to the end of the name of the array and include the index number (or an evaluation that will result in a number), you are able to point to that specific item in the array and work with it.

Using the statement `myArray[0]`, you are able to access the 0 index, which is the string "Binky", and then send that to the `trace` statement.

The final `trace` statement is accessing a property of the array. The `length` property returns the total number of elements that are in the array collection, which in this case is 4.

MODIFYING AN ARRAY

After you create an array, you'll undoubtedly want to make changes to the contents at some point. If you use the assignment operator and use bracket notation, you'll overwrite the existing contents of the array.

So, to make changes to existing items you can use the index element selector and assign a new value to it. Here is an example:

```
package  {
    import flash.display.MovieClip;
    public class SimpleArray extends MovieClip {
        public var myArray:Array;
        public function SimpleArray() {
            myArray = ["Binky", "Hoover", "BB", "Rocket"];
```

```
            trace(myArray[2]);
            myArray[2] = "Tilly";
            trace(myArray[2]);
        }
    }
}
```

The result will output:

```
BB
Tilly
```

In this example, you are accessing index 2 of the array and are overwriting its value using the assignment operator.

Now, this is fine if you need to change values to existing array items, but if you want to add items to the collection and make the collection larger, this won't work. Luckily, there is a method of the Array class that you can use called push() that will add an item to the end of the array collection and give it a new index number.

Here is an example:

```
package  {
    import flash.display.MovieClip;
    public class SimpleArray extends MovieClip {
        public var myArray:Array;
        public function SimpleArray() {
            myArray = ["Binky", "Hoover", "BB", "Rocket"];
            trace(myArray);
            myArray.push("Tilly");
            trace(myArray);
        }
    }
}
```

When you run this example, you'll get the following in the Output panel:

```
Binky,Hoover,BB,Rocket
Binky,Hoover,BB,Rocket,Tilly
```

The push() method accepts new items and adds them to the end of the collection. You can add multiple items in a single statement. Just separate them using commas within the push() method call.

That covers how to add items, but what about removing them? Interesting thing about removing items—when you remove an item, you will need to shift the index numbers of all of the other items. And guess what? There's a method for that! The splice() method of the Array class allows you to select one or more items and remove them from the group. The array will then rearrange itself and renumber the remaining elements so there are no gaps in element IDs. The splice() method asks for the first element you want to remove, using the element's index number, and then the number of items that you want to remove.

Below is an example:

```
package  {
    import flash.display.MovieClip;
    public class SimpleArray extends MovieClip {
        public var myArray:Array;
        public function SimpleArray() {
            myArray = ["Binky", "Hoover", "BB", "Tilly", "Rocket"];
            trace(myArray);
            myArray.splice(3,1);
            trace(myArray);
        }
    }
}
```

When you run this example, you'll see the following in the Output panel:

```
Binky,Hoover,BB,Tilly,Rocket
Binky,Hoover,BB,Rocket
```

As you can see, you were able to remove Tilly from the group. (Poor Tilly!) You were able to do that using the `splice()` method and indicate you wanted to remove starting with the index 3 element, and you wanted to remove just one item. You could omit the second parameter if you wanted to remove everything after the indicated index.

USING LOOPS TO CREATE ARRAYS

Now that you know how to create groups or collections of items, let's look at a common case that you might come across. In this example, there is an object in the Library called BlueCircle that is exported for ActionScript. In order to work with these instances, they need to be positioned and then event listeners need to be added to each. The following code shows a way to do this without using loops:

```
package  {
    import flash.display.MovieClip;
    import flash.events.MouseEvent;
    public class ManyCircles extends MovieClip {
        public var circle1:BlueCircle;
        public var circle2:BlueCircle;
        public var circle3:BlueCircle;
        public var circle4:BlueCircle;
        public var circle5:BlueCircle;
        public function ManyCircles() {
            _init();
        }
        private function _init():void {
            circle1 = new BlueCircle();
```

```
                          circle1.x = 50;
                          circle1.y = 50;
                          circle1.addEventListener(MouseEvent.CLICK, _toggleVisible);
                          addChild(circle1);
                          circle2 = new BlueCircle();
                          circle2.x = 150;
                          circle2.y = 50;
                          circle2.addEventListener(MouseEvent.CLICK, _toggleVisible);
                          addChild(circle2);
                          circle3 = new BlueCircle();
                          circle3.x = 250;
                          circle3.y = 50;
                          circle3.addEventListener(MouseEvent.CLICK, _toggleVisible);
                          addChild(circle3);
                          circle4 = new BlueCircle();
                          circle4.x = 350;
                          circle4.y = 50;
                          circle4.addEventListener(MouseEvent.CLICK, _toggleVisible);
                          addChild(circle4);
                          circle5 = new BlueCircle();
                          circle5.x = 450;
                          circle5.y = 50;
                          circle5.addEventListener(MouseEvent.CLICK, _toggleVisible);
                          addChild(circle5);
                      }
                      private function _toggleVisible(e:MouseEvent):void
                      {
                          if (e.target.alpha == 1)
```

```
        {
            e.target.alpha = .25;
        } else {
            e.target.alpha = 1;
        }
    }
  }
}
```

Obviously, you are doing the same actions many times in this example, and if you wanted to change the number of circles, you'd quickly find that the code isn't very flexible. Using arrays, you can create collections that hold instances of objects for you to work with later. You also can use the array notation as a way to refer to the objects within them, without working with instance names, which gives us a lot more flexibility.

The following is the same application rewritten to take advantage of arrays:

```
package  {
    import flash.display.MovieClip;
    import flash.events.MouseEvent;
    public class ManyCirclesWithLoops extends MovieClip {
        public var circleCollection:Array;

        public function ManyCirclesWithLoops() {
            _init();
        }
        private function _init():void {
            circleCollection = new Array();
            for (var i:uint = 0; i < 5; i++)
            {
                trace("Adding circle #" + i);
```

```
                var tempCircle:BlueCircle = new BlueCircle();
                tempCircle.x = 50 + (100*i);
                tempCircle.y = 50;
                tempCircle.addEventListener(MouseEvent.CLICK,
                →  _toggleVisible);
                addChild(tempCircle);
                circleCollection.push(tempCircle);
            }
            trace(circleCollection);
        }
        private function _toggleVisible(e:MouseEvent):void
        {
            if (e.target.alpha == 1)
            {
                e.target.alpha = .25;
            } else {
                e.target.alpha = 1;
            }
            trace ("Click on " + e.target + e.target.name);
        }
    }
}
```

In this example, an array called circleCollection is created for the purpose of holding the new BlueCircle instances. In the initialization function, you have a loop that will run five times. Each time you run the loop, you create a new "fresh" instance of the BlueCircle class, temporarily called tempCircle. You define its parameters, including a dynamic calculation of the x property based on the iterator variable, and add an event listener to the object. You then add the object to the display stack. Before the loop ends, you pass the instance to the circleCollection array using the push() method. This adds the instance to the array and then ends the loop.

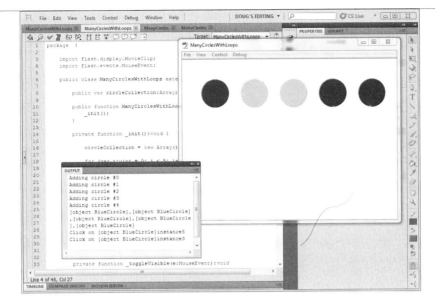

FIGURE 15.4 Output from array example

After the last execution of the loop finishes, you output the contents of the array.

In the event callback function, you use the event object to toggle the alpha level of the object broadcasting the event. You send a confirmation message to the Output panel as well.

When you run the project, you'll get something similar to what is shown in **Figure 15.4**.

You'll see that you add each instance of the object, starting with 0 and ending with 4, then you send the entire array to the Output panel, which shows it as a collection of BlueCircle objects.

When you click a circle, the event callback sends a message to the console. You'll see that you send the object itself first, sending [object BlueCircle]. Then you pass the e.target.name property. This is the instance name assigned to the item. As you know, all objects have an instance name—but in the course of the example, you never had a specific instance name defined. Fear not, an instance name was created automatically for the objects, which you can see is named instance5 and instance3 for the objects that were clicked in this example. Although instance names were created, because you are using the array, you can use the array bracket notation to point to specific objects, or again, to loop through all the objects that you have.

LOOPING THROUGH AN ARRAY

In the previous example, you used loops to build the array, but how do you use them to loop through objects that are already in an array? With the for loop, you can use the iterator and condition test to work with the array's length property to run for each object in the array. You then use the iterator to select an item from the array using the bracket notation.

Here is an updated example that adds a keyboard event listener to report the status of all the circles in the array:

```
package  {
    import flash.display.MovieClip;
    import flash.events.MouseEvent;
    import flash.events.KeyboardEvent;
    public class ManyCirclesWithLoops extends MovieClip {
        public var circleCollection:Array;
        public function ManyCirclesWithLoops() {
            _init();
        }
        private function _init():void {
            circleCollection = new Array();
            for (var i:uint = 0; i < 5; i++)
            {
                trace("Adding circle #" + i);
                var tempCircle:BlueCircle = new BlueCircle();
                tempCircle.x = 50 + (100*i);
                tempCircle.y = 50;
                tempCircle.addEventListener
                    (MouseEvent.CLICK, _toggleVisible);
                addChild(tempCircle);
                circleCollection.push(tempCircle);
            }
```

```
            trace(circleCollection);
            stage.addEventListener
            →  (KeyboardEvent.KEY_DOWN, _reportStatus);
        }
        private function _toggleVisible(e:MouseEvent):void
        {
            if (e.target.alpha == 1)
            {
                e.target.alpha = .25;
            } else {
                e.target.alpha = 1;
            }
            trace ("Click on " + e.target + e.target.name);
        }
        private function _reportStatus(e:KeyboardEvent):void
        {
            for (var i:uint = 0; i < circleCollection.length; i++)
            {
                if (circleCollection[i].alpha == 1)
                {
                    trace("Circle " + i + " is solid.");
                } else
                {
                    trace("Circle " + i + " is partially
                    →  transparent.");
                }
            }
        }
    }
}
```

When this code runs and you click on a few circles and then press a key on the keyboard, the Output panel will display something similar to the following:

```
Adding circle #0
Adding circle #1
Adding circle #2
Adding circle #3
Adding circle #4
[object BlueCircle],[object BlueCircle],[object BlueCircle],
  [object BlueCircle],[object BlueCircle]
Click on [object BlueCircle]instance3
Click on [object BlueCircle]instance5
Circle 0 is solid.
Circle 1 is partially transparent.
Circle 2 is partially transparent.
Circle 3 is solid.
Circle 4 is solid.
```

When you press a key on the keyboard, the callback function springs to life and loops through each object in the array, starting with element 0. Ultimately the loop ends when the iterator is equal to the length property of the array. Remember, this works because the first element is numbered 0, not 1.

WRAPPING **UP**

In this chapter, you learned how to repeat actions using loops. You covered two types of loops: the for loop where you define your iterator variable, condition test, and step for the loop; and the do loop that allows your loop to run at least once and then tests a condition at the end of the loop.

In addition to loops, you also covered how you can create arrays, or collections of objects, including objects that you display on the Stage. Using these arrays, you can then loop creation and manipulation actions across the items in the collection to make repetitive actions easier to manage.

Here are some tips to help make working with loops and arrays easier:

- To loop through a collection of ActionScript commands a specific number of times, use the for loop.

- The for loop requires three parameters: the iterator variable, the condition test, and the step. Each are separated by semicolons in the loop definition.

- For a loop that you want to run at least once, consider the do loop.

- A do loop tests the conditional at the end after the while statement.

- Remember to check your condition test to ensure that it will exit at some point; otherwise you have an infinite loop that will run forever.

- You can nest loops within each other; just make sure you manage your iterators and keep the loops entirely self-contained.

- Creating an array allows you to have a name for a collection of objects.

- Access objects within the array using bracket notation and identify an element index number.

- Use the push() method to add items to the array.

- Use the splice() method to remove one or more items from the array.

- Remember that the first item in an array has the element index number 0.

- The length property of an array returns the number of items in the array. Use this number to help loop through objects in an array using a for loop.

PROJECT 2

DICEOUT!

Over the last several chapters, you have learned the basics of working with classes and object-oriented programming with ActionScript. Now it is time to put your skills to the test with a little game called DiceOut.

What is different about this project, compared to the first, is that you'll have a design file to start from, which will introduce a common workflow for teams. Often a designer might create a non-interactive version of the project and pass it along to the interactive designer to add the logic and controls to make everything work.

Part of this project will use some elements of the clock that you created in Project 1. It will be helpful to familiarize yourself with the previous project, or if you skipped it, go back and complete it as part of building Project 2. Let's get started!

PROJECT SPECIFICATION:
DICEOUT

DiceOut is a game of chance based on rolling three six-sided dice. The game begins with a display of three dice. The user starts the game with a button on the screen.

After starting the game, the user then has 12 seconds, displayed on an analog clock, to get the highest roll possible for the game.

With each roll, the game scores the dice based on the following rules:

- 50 points for any doubles

- 100 points for triple *1s*

- 200 points for triple *2s*

- 300 points for triple *3s*

- 400 points for triple *4s*

- 500 points for triple *5s*

- 600 points for triple *6s*

- 0 points for other combinations

After the 12-second timer runs out, the game displays the final score and ends.

VISUAL DESIGN REVIEW:
DICEOUT

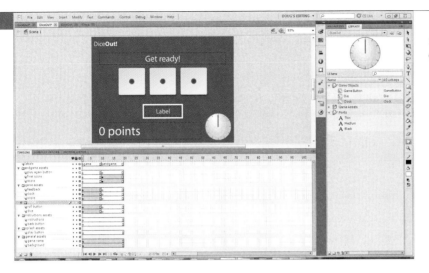

FIGURE P2.1 DiceOut overview—start of project

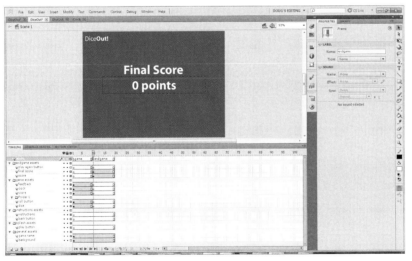

FIGURE P2.2 DiceOut overview—end of game

A Flash designer has already created the design of the project and has provided it to you at the following location: www.peachpit.com/actionscript3dd.com.

You ask the designer for a review of the project. He agrees to sit with you and provides an overview of the project (**Figure P2.1**).

The timeline (**Figure P2.2**) is organized into folders indicating the areas of the application. These folder are called endGame assets, game assets, instructions assets, splash assets, and general assets. The project has two main sections, labeled in a labels timeline row. The first is named "game."

- There is a text field at the top of the Stage called feedbackText used to display prompts to the user, and to show what type of roll they scored after rolling the dice.

- The three dice are named die1, die2, and die3; each is an instance of a MovieClip that contains six frames, each frame showing a unique face of the die.

- The button to start the game is named rollButton and is an instance of a generic Game Button Library object. Within this Game Button Library object is a text field called buttonLabel.

- The points are displayed in a text field called scoreText.

- The clock is a variation of the clock you created earlier for a previous client and is being reused here.

The second section of the project is labeled "endgame."

- In this section is some static text and a dynamic text field named finalScore to display the final score.

KICK-OFF **MEETING NOTES**:
DICEOUT

Before getting started, as part of the kick-off process a number of people from the team including designers, developers, and architects hold a quick meeting called the "kick off" to discuss the project, get ideas from each other on how to approach the design and development, and to answer any open questions that might not be addressed in the project specification. Below are the notes from this meeting.

To work efficiently with the dice, you should add them into an array so you can loop through them.

Testing for the face of the dice will require that you have a way to store the value of the roll somehow in each die, otherwise you won't have a way to know what the score is.

After talking with another developer, you learn a new way to work with events that might be helpful. Apparently, you can create your own custom events that you can broadcast from any MovieClip. To do this, you use the `dispatchEvent` method, and then create a new Event, adding a string that would be used to identify the event.

She gave me this code as an example:

```
dispatchEvent(new Event("endGame"));
```

This line of code is in the class that broadcasts the event. You need to create a listener attached to that object to capture the event like this:

```
clock.addEventListener("endGame", endGame);
```

Instead of working with a built-in event like `MouseEvent.CLICK`, you should enter the string that matches the string used to create the event. It might come in handy for the clock to tell the game when it runs out of time.

With the kick-off finished, it is time to get started. Try to create the project on your own, and when you are finished, read on and I'll explain how I created the project and why I chose the methods I did.

SOLUTION AND WALKTHROUGH: DICEOUT

Whew! Working with another person's project adds an interesting twist to everything, doesn't it?

In addition to using the skills you have learned so far, through working with others on the team you also learned some new things about ActionScript; specifically, how to create your own custom events that you can broadcast from a MovieClip.

With that, here is one way to solve this challenge. Because there are so many open-ended ways to approach this project, this is just an example—but it may introduce some solutions that you hadn't considered.

OVERVIEW OF THE DOCUMENT CLASS

In this finished example, the DiceOut Document class contains most of the game functionality. The work to manage the countdown timer, the rolling of each die, and the button labels changes were offloaded into custom classes for those objects.

Let's start with a review of how I created the Document class:

```
package
{
    import flash.display.MovieClip;
    import flash.events.MouseEvent;
    import flash.events.Event;
    public class DiceOut extends MovieClip
    {
        /*
        Objects on stage:
        - rollButton:GameButton;
        - die1:Die;
        - die2:Die;
        - die3:Die;
        - scoreText:TextField;
        - feedbackText:TextField;
        - clock:Clock;
```

```
*/
private var gameDice:Array;
private var score:uint = 0;
public function DiceOut()
{
    stop();
    setupDice();
    setupButtons();
    setupListeners();
}
private function setupDice():void
{
    gameDice = new Array(die1,die2,die3);
}
private function setupButtons():void
{
    rollButton.setLabel("Roll");
}
private function setupListeners():void
{
    rollButton.addEventListener(MouseEvent.CLICK, rollDice);
    clock.addEventListener("endGame", endGame);
}
public function rollDice(e:MouseEvent):void
{
    clock.startClock();
    var currentRoll:Array = [];
    for (var i:uint = 0; i < gameDice.length; i++)
```

```
        {
            currentRoll[i] = gameDice[i].rollDie();
        }
        scoreRoll(currentRoll);
    }
    public function scoreRoll(newRoll:Array):void
    {
        if (newRoll[0] == newRoll[1] && newRoll[1] ==
            newRoll[2])
        {
            if (newRoll[0] == 1)
            {
                score +=  100;
                scoreText.text = score + " points";
                feedbackText.text = "Triple 1";
            } else if (newRoll[0] == 2)
            {
                score +=  200;
                scoreText.text = score + " points";
                feedbackText.text = "Triple 2";
            } else if (newRoll[0] == 3)
            {
                score +=  300;
                scoreText.text = score + " points";
                feedbackText.text = "Triple 3";
            } else if (newRoll[0] == 4)
            {
                score +=  400;
```

```
                    scoreText.text = score + " points";
                    feedbackText.text = "Triple 4";
            } else if (newRoll[0] == 5)
            {
                score +=  500;
                scoreText.text = score + " points";
                feedbackText.text = "Triple 5";
            } else if (newRoll[0] == 6)
            {
                score +=  600;
                scoreText.text = score + " points";
                feedbackText.text = "Triple 6";
            }
        }
        else if (newRoll[0] == newRoll[1] ||
      →  newRoll[1] == newRoll[2] ||
      →  newRoll[0] == newRoll[2])
        {
            score +=  50;
            scoreText.text = score + " points";
            feedbackText.text = "Doubles!";
        }
        else
        {
            feedbackText.text = "";
        }
    }
    public function endGame(e:Event):void
```

```
        {
            gotoAndStop("endgame");
            finalScore.text = score + " points";
        }
    }
}
```

WALKTHROUGH OF THE DOCUMENT CLASS

Let's start with the contents before the constructor:

```
/*
Objects on stage:
- rollButton:GameButton;
- die1:Die;
- die2:Die;
- die3:Die;
- scoreText:TextField;
- feedbackText:TextField;
- clock:Clock;
*/
private var gameDice:Array;
private var score:uint = 0;
```

First, the class has an opening comment that lists the objects that are on the Stage. This is helpful when working with a visually laid out project and prevents the need to flip back and forth to find out the name of an object on the Stage.

Next are two private variables that are created; the first is an array to hold the dice, and the second to hold the player's score.

Let's jump to the constructor next:

```
public function DiceOut()
```

```
{
    stop();
    setupDice();
    setupButtons();
    setupListeners();
}
```

To prevent the project from playing the main timeline, I added a stop action when the object is constructed, then three helper functions to get everything up and running. The first is the setupDice method:

```
private function setupDice():void
{
    gameDice = new Array(die1,die2,die3);
}
```

This method uses the gameDice array and populates it with the MovieClips that are on the Stage. By having these in the array, I felt it would be easier to loop through them to roll each die and get its score.

You then configure the rollButton instance on the Stage:

```
private function setupButtons():void
{
    rollButton.setLabel("Roll");
}
```

This is running a public method that is part of a GameButton custom class you created and is shown below:

```
package {
    import flash.display.Sprite;
    public class GameButton extends Sprite {
        /*
        Objects on stage:
```

```
    - buttonLabel:MovieClip
    */
    public function GameButton() {
        // constructor code
    }
    public function setLabel(newLabel:String):void
    {
        buttonLabel.text = newLabel;
    }
  }
}
```

The method is accepting a label and is assigning it to the text property of the buttonLabel text field that is in the MovieClip.

Ok, back to the Document class, the next step is to set up the event listeners:

```
private function setupListeners():void
{
    rollButton.addEventListener(MouseEvent.CLICK, rollDice);
    clock.addEventListener("endGame", endGame);
}
```

Here, there is an event listener for when rollButton is clicked, which then executes a callback function called rollDice. An event listener is then added for a custom event broadcasted from the clock called endGame, which executes the endGame callback function.

Let's take a look at the Clock class that is linked to the countdown clock on the Stage:

```
package   {

    import flash.display.MovieClip;
    import flash.utils.Timer;
```

```
import flash.events.TimerEvent;
import flash.events.Event;
public class Clock extends MovieClip {
    /*
    Objects on stage:
    - second:MovieClip
    */
    private var clockTimer:Timer;
    public function Clock() {
        setupTimer();
    }
    private function setupTimer():void
    {
        clockTimer = new Timer(1000,12);
        clockTimer.addEventListener(
        →  TimerEvent.TIMER, tickClock);
        clockTimer.addEventListener(
        →  TimerEvent.TIMER_COMPLETE, endClock);
    }
    public function startClock():void
    {
        clockTimer.start();
    }
    public function tickClock(e:TimerEvent):void
    {
        second.rotation += 30;
    }

    public function endClock(e:TimerEvent):void
```

```
        {
            dispatchEvent(new Event("endGame"));
        }
    }
}
```

In this custom class, there is a single private variable, the timer itself, named clockTimer.

The constructor executes the setupTimer method, which configures the timer and adds the TimerEvent.TIMER and TimerEvent.TIMER_COMPELTE event listeners.

I created a public function called startClock to gets everything up and running. It starts the clock, which will then start broadcasting events.

The first event is the TimerEvent.TIMER, which has a callback function named tickClock. This changes the angle of the hand of the clock by adding 30 degrees.

The second event is the TimerEvent.TIMER_COMPELTE which has a corresponding callback function named endClock. To create a custom event from scratch, you need to use the dispatchEvent statement. Within this, create a new instance of the Event class, and provide it with a string that you want to use to identify the event. Remember, this string is what the event listener is going to "hear" when the custom event is dispatched. The endgame event is what the Document class is listening to.

Cool! Back to the Document class.

When the user clicks the rollButton object, the rollDice callback function begins:

```
public function rollDice(e:MouseEvent):void
{
    clock.startClock();
    var currentRoll:Array = [];
    for (var i:uint = 0; i < gameDice.length; i++)
    {
        currentRoll[i] = gameDice[i].rollDie();
    }

    scoreRoll(currentRoll);
}
```

Here, the clock is started and an array is created within the method that will hold the roll of the dice. There is a for loop that moves through all the items in the gameDice array and executes a rollDie method for each.

The rollDie method is a public method of the Die class that is attached to each instance of the dice on the Stage:

```
package  {
    import flash.display.MovieClip;
    public class Die extends MovieClip {
        /*
        Objects on stage:
        - none
        */
        public function Die() {
            stop();
        }
        public function rollDie():uint
        {
            var dieRoll:uint;
            dieRoll = Math.random()*6+1;
            this.gotoAndStop(dieRoll);
            return dieRoll;
        }
    }
}
```

To prevent the die from playing the main timeline a stop action is added to the Die class when it is created. In the public rollDie method, a variable is created to hold the die value. It receives a random number from 1 to 6, and the die then displays the matching die face corresponding to the random number.

The method then returns the value of the die back to the caller, which is back in the rollDie method in the Document class.

Back in the Document class, the returned value is added to the currentRoll array. When all three dice have been rolled, that currentRoll array is sent to the scoreRoll method to evaluate the results and award points to the player:

```
public function scoreRoll(newRoll:Array):void
{
    if (newRoll[0] == newRoll[1] && newRoll[1] == newRoll[2])
    {
        if (newRoll[0] == 1)
        {
            score +=  100;
            scoreText.text = score + " points";
            feedbackText.text = "Triple 1";
        } else if (newRoll[0] == 2)
        {
            score +=  200;
            scoreText.text = score + " points";
            feedbackText.text = "Triple 2";
        } else if (newRoll[0] == 3)
        {
            score +=  300;
            scoreText.text = score + " points";
            feedbackText.text = "Triple 3";
        } else if (newRoll[0] == 4)
        {
            score +=  400;
            scoreText.text = score + " points";
            feedbackText.text = "Triple 4";
        } else if (newRoll[0] == 5)
```

```
        {
            score +=  500;
            scoreText.text = score + " points";
            feedbackText.text = "Triple 5";
        } else if (newRoll[0] == 6)
        {
            score +=  600;
            scoreText.text = score + " points";
            feedbackText.text = "Triple 6";
        }
    }
    else if (newRoll[0] == newRoll[1] || newRoll[1] ==
    →  newRoll[2] || newRoll[0] == newRoll[2])
    {
        score +=  50;
        scoreText.text = score + " points";
        feedbackText.text = "Doubles!";
    }
    else
    {
        feedbackText.text = "";
    }
}
```

The newRoll array contains the values of the dice.

First, a test runs to determine if the three dice equal each other. Through the laws of association, if die1 equals die2, and die1 equals die3, then all three are the same. If that condition is true, then the value of die1 will determine what all three of the dice are, which can be either 1, 2, 3, 4, 5, or 6.

FIGURE P2.3 Displaying a winning score

FIGURE P2.4 The end of the game. Better luck next time!

Based on the value of that die, the score is increased, the score display is updated, and feedback text is shown to the user.

If the three don't equal each other, then the next step is to see if there are doubles. This is done by seeing if die1 equals die2, or if die2 equals die3, or if die1 equals die3. If any of these conditions are true, then the score is increased, the score display is updated and feedback text is shown to the user as shown in **Figure P2.3**.

If none of these scoring conditions is met, then the feedback text is cleared, since the player didn't have any winning combinations.

The final piece is to end the game. This happens when the clock broadcasts the custom endGame event, which the Document class is listening for. When it hears it, the Document class runs the endGame method:

```
public function endGame(e:Event):void
{
    gotoAndStop("endgame");
    finalScore.text = score + " points";
}
```

Here, the main timeline is moved to the "endgame" label, and the final score is displayed to the user (**Figure P2.4**).

With this project, there are several elements that were employed. The first was tying in the interaction of the user's mouse to trigger the rolling of the dice using event listeners. Then, through random number generation, the numbers were "rolled" and based on the conditional logic added, the roll was tested against the scoring rules and then assigned points based on certain combinations.

Through using a timer, the clock is able to time the user's play and end the game after a specific amount of time.

Good job! As you can see, even after learning just a small bit of ActionScript, you can create some pretty cool projects. In the next section of the book, you'll learn more and your next project will challenge you to make a mobile application using Flash Professional CS5.5, ActionScript, and Adobe AIR.

PART 4

GETTING **CREATIVE** WITH **ACTIONSCRIPT**

16

DRAWING WITH ACTIONSCRIPT

You might have thought that ActionScript didn't have a creative side—up until this chapter, that would seem true. But you can be just as creative with Action-Script as you can be with the Pen tool. In fact, a whole class of art that is generated by code is growing in popularity.

In this chapter, you'll start to crack open the creative part of coding and learn the basics for unleashing the graphics API of Action-Script to draw directly in your project—all with code.

DRAWING AND CODE

The Flash runtime includes an application programming interface, or API, that allows you to create generative artwork in projects. The statements and properties of the API are pretty expansive, and you might be surprised to learn that they have been part of every MovieClip that you have worked with in the past.

So far, you have been using the drawing tools in Flash Professional CS5.5 to create the artwork for your various MovieClips. In this chapter, you won't use the drawing tools at all—in fact, you will be using only Flash Professional to create your Document class to link to your FLA, and doing everything else in code.

SPRITES: MOVIECLIPS WITHOUT TIMELINES

When you create a MovieClip, it contains an internal timeline that you can animate using Flash Professional tools. These tools allow you to create tweens and add frame events, labels, and other information using the Timeline and Actions panels. When using code to animate your MovieClip, you won't be using the Timeline or Actions panels. Instead, you will be working with graphics that don't have timelines, and you will create interactions on them using event handlers like you have done before. These graphics without timelines are called *sprites*, and there is a unique class that you will use to create them.

Let's create a basic sprite and see how they are created.

1. Create a new project in Flash Professional CS5.5.

2. Create a new Document class (the one below is called FirstSprite).

3. Enter the following code in the Document class:

```
package {
    import flash.display.MovieClip;
    import flash.display.Sprite;
    public class FirstSprite extends MovieClip {
        public var myFirstSprite:Sprite;
        public function FirstSprite() {
            myFirstSprite = new Sprite();
            trace(myFirstSprite);
            // myFirstSprite.gotoAndStop(2);
```

```
            }
        }
    }
```

4. Run the project and look at the Output panel.

When you run this project, you'll see [object Sprite] in the Output panel. This is because you are now creating a Sprite object, not a MovieClip. This all is pretty elementary. You first need to import the flash.display.Sprite class at the top using the import statement and create the variable container for your Sprite object. Then create a new sprite and voilà, you have a new Sprite.

Remember, the Sprite doesn't have a timeline—to prove this, you can uncomment the gotoAndStop method call near the end of the code. If you do, you'll get an error when you attempt to run the project:

```
1061: Call to a possibly undefined method gotoAndStop through a
reference with static type flash.display:Sprite.
```

This is because there is no gotoAndStop method in the Sprite class. It doesn't need one because there isn't a timeline!

YOUR FIRST SHAPE

Remember when you learned your shapes as a baby? No, I don't either; however, we can relive all of that by learning how to create your first shape again—this time with ActionScript.

When you work with the graphics API in ActionScript, you will be using a special property called the graphics property. All MovieClips and sprites contain a graphics property and inside are a bunch of methods that you can use to build shapes and graphics.

Update the example from the previous section and create your first shape.

1. Change the code from the previous example with the following highlighted code:

```
package  {
    import flash.display.MovieClip;
    import flash.display.Sprite;
```

FIGURE 16.1 A simple shape

```
public class FirstSprite extends MovieClip {
    public var myFirstSprite:Sprite;
    public function FirstSprite() {
        myFirstSprite = new Sprite();
        myFirstSprite.graphics.lineStyle(1,0x000000);
        myFirstSprite.graphics.drawRect(10,10,50,100);
        addChild(myFirstSprite);
    }
}
```

2. Run the project. You'll see the rectangle as in **Figure 16.1**.

Congratulations! You have created your first shape!

As you can see, you are accessing the graphics property of the sprite that was created and are executing specific functions to create the graphics. First, you are defining the parameters of the stroke, creating a rectangle, and defining its location and size. You'll learn more about each of these steps in more depth later in the chapter.

EXTENDING THE **Sprite** CLASS

Drawing in ActionScript is pretty cool—but it can get cumbersome quickly if you don't plan ahead. As you know, you can create custom classes that extend built-in functionality. In fact, every time you create an object in the Library you are doing exactly that. You are extending the MovieClip class and are adding design information in your custom class definition.

Without the help of the Library panel, though, you will need to perform this extension yourself in code. To do so is pretty simple, and the previous example can be updated to use this custom class.

1. Select New from the File menu.

2. Select ActionScript 3.0 Class from the list in the dialog box.

3. On the right, enter **SimpleRectangle** as the Class name and click OK.

4. Save the file as **SimpleRectangle.as** in the same location as your FLA and Document class.

5. Enter the following code and save the class:

```
package  {
    import flash.display.Sprite;
    public class SimpleRectangle extends Sprite {
        public function SimpleRectangle() {
            graphics.lineStyle(1,0x000000);
            graphics.drawRect(10,10,50,100);
        }
    }
}
```

Notice that you are calling the graphics property directly because you are inside the graphic already.

6. Open the Document class again and update the code with the following highlighted code:

```
package  {
    import flash.display.MovieClip;
    import flash.display.Sprite;
    public class FirstSprite extends MovieClip {
        public var myFirstSprite:SimpleRectangle;
        public function FirstSprite() {
            myFirstSprite = new SimpleRectangle();
            addChild(myFirstSprite);
        }
    }
}
```

7. Run the project. You'll get the exact same output that you had before. This time, you have moved the code for drawing the graphics to a unique class, and as with any class, you can create multiple instances of it.

8. Edit the Document class again and update with the following highlighted code:

```
package  {
    import flash.display.MovieClip;
    import flash.display.Sprite;
    public class FirstSprite extends MovieClip {
        public var myFirstSprite:SimpleRectangle;
        public var mySecondSprite:SimpleRectangle;
        public function FirstSprite() {
            myFirstSprite = new SimpleRectangle();
            addChild(myFirstSprite);
            mySecondSprite = new SimpleRectangle();
            mySecondSprite.x = 50;
```

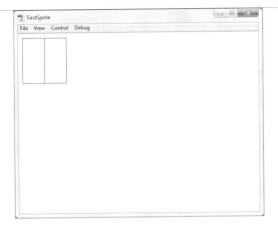

FIGURE 16.2 Creating another instance of SimpleRectangle

```
        addChild(mySecondSprite);
    }
  }
}
```

9. Run the project again. You'll see two rectangles display in your project (**Figure 16.2**).

This is because you have moved the code to draw the graphics into a reusable class that extends the Sprite class. This class can be used over and over again, and you only have to write the drawing code once.

DRAWING LINES AND WORKING WITH STROKES

The most basic object you can create with the drawing API is a simple line. To create a line, there are two things that you need to consider:

- What is the stroke of the line?

- Where does the line start and end?

Strokes are the basis of the color, style, and corner parameters of the line. Strokes are also the basis for the outlines of shapes that you will learn to create later in the chapter. To define the stroke of a line, you will need to use the lineStyle method of the graphics property.

The previous example used following line to define the rectangle's line style:

```
graphics.lineStyle(1,0x000000);
```

The first property, 1, defines the width of the stroke in pixels. The second property defines the color of the stroke. Color is defined using hexadecimal numbers. If you have worked with CSS and HTML before, you'll know that hexadecimal numbers are used to define color for various objects. The same exists with ActionScript. Unlike HTML, the # sign is replaced with 0x when writing color values in hexadecimal. If you need to find the hexadecimal value for a color, check out Adobe kuler at http://kuler.adobe.com. The kuler website displays color values in a number of formats, including hexadecimal, or hex. The Color panel in Flash also displays hexadecimal colors, but it is disabled when you are editing ActionScript classes.

You can add a third property to define the alpha, or transparency, of the stroke. Valid property values are decimals from 0 to 1, with 0 being fully transparent and 1 being fully opaque.

To draw a line with these strokes, you'll use a sequence of new commands to draw on the screen with a virtual pen. You'll need to create a new class that extends Sprite.

1. Create a new ActionScript 3.0 class from the File menu.

2. Call the class **SomeLines**.

3. Add the following code to the class, saving the file as **SomeLines.as** at the same location as the FLA and other class files:

```
package  {
    import flash.display.Sprite;
    public class SomeLines extends Sprite {
        public function SomeLines() {
            graphics.lineStyle(1,0xFF0000);
            graphics.moveTo(100,100);
            graphics.lineTo(200,200);
        }
    }
}
```

FIGURE 16.3 A single red line

4. Update the Document class to work with this new SomeLines class as highlighted below:

```
package  {
    import flash.display.MovieClip;
    import flash.display.Sprite;
    public class FirstSprite extends MovieClip {
        public var mySprite:SomeLines;
        public function FirstSprite() {
            mySprite = new SomeLines();
            addChild(mySprite);
        }
    }
}
```

5. Run the project. You'll get a single red line as shown in **Figure 16.3**.

The first line of the SomeLines function defines the width and color of the line's stroke. In the next two lines, you are working with a virtual pen that is in every Sprite and MovieClip. By default, the pen is located at the coordinate 0,0; so to draw with the pen, you need to move it to the location where you want to start drawing a line, put the pen down, and draw the line to another point:

```
graphics.moveTo(100,100);
graphics.lineTo(200,200);
```

The moveTo method moves the virtual pen to a new location without drawing on the Stage. The lineTo method tells the pen to draw from its existing location to a specific point, using the defined parameters in the lineStyle method.

You can string a number of lines together using additional moveTo methods.

6. Update this section of code as highlighted below:

```
package  {
    import flash.display.Sprite;
    public class SomeLines extends Sprite {
        public function SomeLines() {
            graphics.lineStyle(1,0xFF0000);
            graphics.moveTo(100,100);
            graphics.lineTo(200,200);
            graphics.lineTo(150,300);
            graphics.lineTo(400,50);
        }
    }
}
```

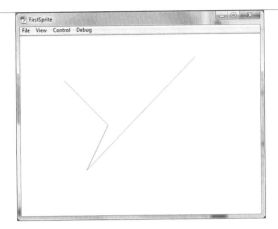

FIGURE 16.4 Stringing together multiple lineTo methods

7. Run the project. You'll notice that additional lines have been created that were strung together (**Figure 16.4**).

You can see how the virtual pen is working. With each lineTo method, you are telling the pen to draw to another location. If you wanted to stop drawing and move the pen to a different location, you would need to add in a moveTo method to temporarily stop the virtual pen from drawing.

SAVING CODING TIME WITH…WELL…with

As you can see when you work with the drawing API, you type the property name graphics a bunch of times. Luckily, ActionScript has a way to save you from typing it over and over again using the with statement.

The with statement captures an object, property, or class and puts it in front of the objects within a nested code block. Update the previous example using the with statement, as highlighted in the following code:

```
package  {
    import flash.display.Sprite;
    public class SomeLines extends Sprite {
        public function SomeLines() {
            with (graphics)
            {
```

```
                    lineStyle(1,0xFF0000);
                    moveTo(100,100);
                    lineTo(200,200);
                    lineTo(150,300);
                    lineTo(400,50);
                }
            }
        }
}
```

The with statement captures the reference you want to use throughout the code block inside the opening parenthesis, in this case the graphics property. It then automatically appends that to the beginning of the statements inside, eliminating the need to repeat it on each line. Using the with statement can be a big time saver!

DRAWING AHEAD OF THE CURVE

So far, everything you have drawn has been a straight line, but you can draw curves using the drawing API with the curveTo method. The curveTo method draws a curved line from the current location of the virtual pen to an anchor point, but the line is curved based on a control point that acts like a magnet for the line.

The curveTo method takes four parameters. The first two are the x and y coordinates of the control point—this is the invisible point that the line will use as a way to build the curve. The last two parameters are the x and y coordinates of the anchor point, which is where the line will end.

Let's see how the curveTo statement works.

1. Update the code from the previous section with the following highlighted code:

```
package {
    import flash.display.Sprite;
    public class SomeLines extends Sprite {
        public function SomeLines() {
            with (graphics)
```

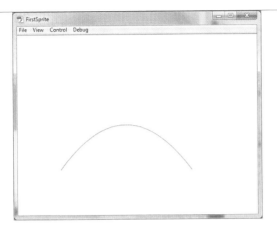

FIGURE 16.5 Drawing a curved line using ActionScript

```
        {
                lineStyle(1,0xFF0000);
                moveTo(100,300);
                curveTo(250,100,400,300);
        }
    }
  }
}
```

2. Run the project. You'll see what is in **Figure 16.5**.

   As you can see, the curve is drawn from left to right with an attraction in the middle to this invisible control point.

   Let's see how the control point affects the curve.

3. Modify the code to add in multiple curves with different control points, as in the following highlights:

```
package  {
    import flash.display.Sprite;
    public class SomeLines extends Sprite {
        public function SomeLines() {
```

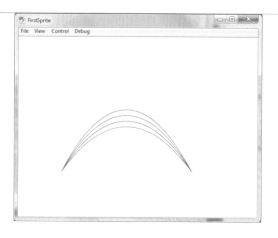

FIGURE 16.6 Showing the effect of the control point on curved lines

```
with (graphics)
{
    lineStyle(1,0xFF0000);
    moveTo(100,300);
    curveTo(250,100,400,300);
    moveTo(100,300);
    curveTo(250,75,400,300);
    moveTo(100,300);
    curveTo(250,50,400,300);
    moveTo(100,300);
    curveTo(250,25,400,300);
}
}
}
}
```

4. Run the project again. You'll see the output displayed in **Figure 16.6**.

As you move the control point up, the arc of the curve becomes more pronounced.

There are specific equations that are used to calculate exactly how this curve works, but I doubt you are in the mood for a trigonometry lesson, so I will spare you the details. Needless to say, with some practice, you'll be able to create some interesting effects with the curveTo method.

DRAWING SHAPES

While you can draw shapes using the lineTo and curveTo methods, the drawing API offers shortcuts for creating a lot of common objects. In this section you'll review four of the most common ones. Start by creating a new custom class extending the sprite and entering in some code.

1. Create a new ActionScript 3.0 class from the File menu.

2. Name the class **SomeShapes**.

3. Add the following code to the class, saving the file as **SomeShapes.as** in the same location as the FLA and other class files:

```
package  {
    import flash.display.Sprite;
    public class SomeShapes extends Sprite {
        public function SomeShapes() {
            with (graphics)
            {
                // Rectangle
                lineStyle(1,0xFF0000);
                drawRect(10,10,200,100)
                // Rounded Rectangle
                lineStyle(1,0x00FF00);
                drawRoundRect(10,200,100,100,20);
                // Rounded Rectangle with Pixel Hinting On
                lineStyle(1,0x000000,1,true);
                drawRoundRect(120,200,100,100,20);
```

```
                            // Circle
                            lineStyle(1,0x0000FF);
                            drawCircle(350,200,50);
                            // Ellipse
                            lineStyle(1,0x00FFFF);
                            drawEllipse(350,200,50,25);
                        }
                    }
                }
            }
```

4. Update the Document class to work with this new SomeLines class, as highlighted below:

```
package {
    import flash.display.MovieClip;
    import flash.display.Sprite;
    public class FirstSprite extends MovieClip {
        public var mySprite:SomeShapes;
        public function FirstSprite() {
            mySprite = new SomeShapes();
            addChild(mySprite);
        }
    }
}
```

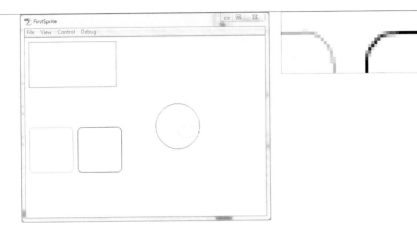

FIGURE 16.7 Some shapes created using shape drawing methods.

FIGURE 16.8 Closeup showing the differences in curve detail between rounded rectangles

5. Run the project. You'll get the results shown in **Figure 16.7**. In the next few sections, you'll cover how each of these works.

RECTANGLES

The first section of code marked with the //Rectangles comment uses the drawRect method. This works pretty simply. You define the coordinates of the upper-left corner of the rectangle, followed by the width and height of the rectangle. It adopts the stroke defined by the most recent lineStyle method.

Since the drawRect method always starts in the upper-left corner, you need to factor that in if you are trying to center an object around a specific point.

ROUNDED RECTANGLE

The drawRoundRect method is similar to the drawRect method, except it adds a corner radius parameter at the end. You can optionally add another corner property if you want the width and height to be different, but that is not required.

What you will find is that the green rounded rectangle has some odd pixel artifacts in the corners that don't appear in the black one (**Figure 16.8**).

This is caused by how Flash draws using defaults. To improve the drawing of these corners and other curves, you can update the format of the stroke using additional parameters in the lineStyle method. In the second example of the drawRoundRect method, you entered a couple other parameters in the lineStyle method. The first new parameter was the alpha of the stroke, this doesn't have any effect, but you must include it since the next parameter is what you want to change.

The last parameter is the pixel hinting toggle. I'll spare you the geeky details, but *pixel hinting* is a function of the Flash runtimes that "snaps" your lines and drawings to whole pixels, reducing blur and artifacts when working with curves and angles. By default, pixel hinting is off. When you turn that on by setting the parameter to true, you will see an improvement in the curve quality of a number of graphics that you draw with the API. This is why the curves in the second rectangle that is black look better than the one that is green.

CIRCLES AND ELLIPSES

The last two examples use the drawCircle and drawEllipse methods. The first is drawCircle. To use this method, you define the center point of the circle and then define the radius. The radius is the distance from the center of the circle to the edge. So if you want a 100-pixel wide circle (100 pixels in diameter), you want a 50-pixel parameter for the radius.

The final example uses drawEllipse which operates differently from drawCircle. The biggest difference is that you define the ellipse from the top-left "corner" of the circle, and then the width and height. To help understand, think of when you use the circle tool in Flash Professional or Illustrator. You click the mouse and start dragging to create the circle. The first two parameters define the coordinates of where you click the mouse, then the width and height define the size when you move the mouse from the starting point.

USING FILLS

Working with fills is similar to working with strokes. You need to define the fill before you draw a line or a shape. To create a fill, you will use the beginFill method. You can use the previous example's code to see how this works.

1. Update the code from the previous example with the highlighted changes:

```
package  {
    import flash.display.Sprite;
    public class SomeShapes extends Sprite {
        public function SomeShapes() {
```

```
with (graphics)
{
    // Rectangle
    lineStyle(1,0xFF0000);
    beginFill(0x00FF00)
    drawRect(10,10,200,100);
    endFill();
    // Rounded Rectangle with Pixel Hinting On
    lineStyle(1,0x000000,1,true);
    beginFill(0xFF0000,.5)
    drawRoundRect(120,200,100,100,20);
    endFill();
    // Multi-line shape
    lineStyle(1,0x0000FF);
    moveTo(350,200);
    beginFill(0x000000);
    lineTo(400,25);
    lineTo(450,300);
    lineTo(425,250);
    lineTo(350,200);
    endFill();
}
        }
    }
}
```

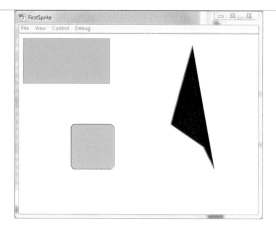

2. Run the project. You'll see that there are now three filled strokes (**Figure 16.9**).

Notice that the fill begins by executing the beginFill method before it draws a shape. Inside the first object, the rectangle, you defined the fill as green (or 0x00FF00 for those hexadecimal speakers out there). When the shape finishes drawing, you end the fill using the endFill method.

Using the endFill method after finishing the shape isn't always necessary. However, if you are doing a lot of ActionScript drawing, I highly recommend it. Otherwise you might wind up with some weird fill situations, especially if you are working with curves and lines.

The second example is the rounded rectangle. This time the beginFill method is accepting two properties. The first is the color, in this case red (or 0xFF0000). The second defines the alpha property of the fill, which is .5, making this 50% transparent/opaque.

The third and final example demonstrates how fills work with lines and strokes. If you define and start a fill before you start drawing a line, and the virtual pen returns to the starting point, the object will be filled in with the requested color and transparency. There are a bunch of rules that govern how fills work with mult-lined shapes, but the simplest case is when you create a multi-lined object; if you end the shape where you start it, and don't cross any paths, the entire shape will get a fill inside of it.

BUILDING GRADIENTS

While solid color fills can get you pretty far, they are lacking something—pizazz. Luckily, Flash offers a number of other options that you can use to spice up your shapes, including gradient fills that can be applied to achieve special effects.

Gradients are formed by three basic building blocks: stops, alphas, and colors. You define a gradient by defining the location of stops along a continuum. Then at each stop, you define color properties that will be meshed against all the other gradient stops in the sequence. A gradient can have a minimum of two stops and a maximum of fifteen.

Creating a gradient is a multi-step process, and you'll use the `beginGradientFill` method to bring it all together. To start, you'll update the fill of one of the earlier shapes with a simple two-stop gradient fill.

1. Update the code from the previous example as highlighted below:

```
package  {
    import flash.display.Sprite;
    import flash.display.GradientType;
    import flash.geom.Matrix;
    public class SomeShapes extends Sprite {
        public function SomeShapes() {
            var myMatrix = new Matrix();
            myMatrix.createGradientBox(200,100);
            with (graphics)
            {
                // Rectangle
                lineStyle(1,0xFF0000);
                beginGradientFill(GradientType.LINEAR,
                                  [0x00FF00,0x0000FF],
                                  [1,1],
```

```
                                    [0,255],
                                    myMatrix);
                    drawRect(10,10,200,100);
                    endFill();
                    // Rounded Rectangle with Pixel Hinting On
                    lineStyle(1,0x000000,1,true);
                    beginFill(0xFF0000,.5);
                    drawRoundRect(120,200,100,100,20);
                    endFill();
                    // Multi-line shape
                    lineStyle(1,0x0000FF);
                    moveTo(350,200);
                    beginFill(0x000000);
                    lineTo(400,25);
                    lineTo(450,300);
                    lineTo(425,250);
                    lineTo(350,200);
                    endFill();
                }
            }
        }
    }
```

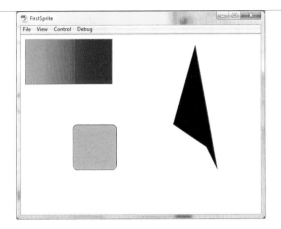

FIGURE 16.10 Creating a gradient using ActionScript

2. Run the project. You'll get what is shown in **Figure 16.10**.

    Ok, so this one is going to need some explaining—let's do it line by line. Skip the myMatrix variable for now; let's start the explanation of the fill with the beginGradientFill method:

    ```
    beginGradientFill(GradientType.LINEAR,[0x00FF00,0x0000FF],
        [1,1],[0,255], myMatrix);
    ```

    You first need to define what type of gradient you want to make. In this case, you are creating a LINEAR type gradient. Next, you want to define the two colors that will make up the gradient: green and blue. Notice that these are grouped in square brackets. Since there can be up to fifteen colors in a gradient, the method needs a flexible way to use multiple items as a single parameter. What object can have multiple items but still have a single name? You guessed it. An array.

    You need to use more arrays for the next two parameters for the same reason. The next parameter defines the alpha transparency at each of the stops, and then the third defines the location of the stops. The location of the stops are defined from a range of 0 to 255. So if you want one color to be all the way on one side, and the other all the way on the other, you'll use the array [0,255].

FIGURE 16.11 Effect of reducing the size of the gradient box

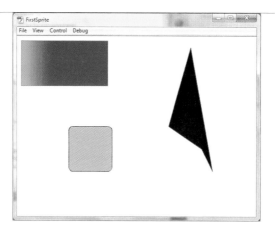

This final parameter is a bit of an odd one, it is called a *matrix*. Simply put, this parameter will determine the size of the gradient box. The gradient box is different than the fill. The gradient box can be smaller, larger, or the same size as the fill, but a gradient box can be used for multiple fills and it would look the same. The simplest properties for the gradient box are to keep it the exact same as the fill, which is what is in the example. To create the gradient box, an instance of the `Matrix` class needs to be created, and then you define the gradient box using the `createGradientBox` method, which asks for the width and height of the box. This is defined before the `with` statement, since you don't want to confuse it with the other items.

As a result, you get a basic two-stop gradient. Let's take a look at how the gradient box works.

3. Update the `createGradientBox` statement as follows:

```
myMatrix.createGradientBox(100,100);
```

The box is now half the width it was before.

4. Run the project again and notice the difference (**Figure 16.11**).

The gradient is now tighter, that is because the gradient box is now smaller than it was before. In fact, it now takes half as many pixels to get from green to blue than it did before. Why? Because the gradient box is half the width.

DEGREES

For those of you who skipped geometry and trigonometry in school, here's a quick lesson: A circle has 360 degrees. A degree is just a unit of measure, and a circle has 360 of them. A radian is another form of measurement of an angle, and a circle has 2π of them. Remember π, or pi? It is a special number used in circular geometry, it is approximately 3.14. Take a look at **Figure 16.12** and hear me out:

FIGURE 16.12 Angles of a circle using radians

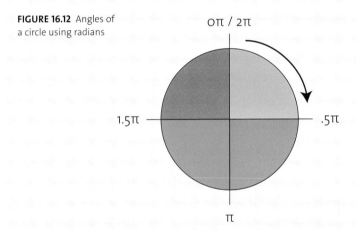

What most people would refer to as 90 degrees would be referred to as .5π radians. To rotate 180 degrees is π, 270 is 1.5π, and to go a complete 360 is 2π radians. In Flash, you can use the Math class to help work with π, using the expression Math.PI.

You can also modify the gradient box by rotating it. This will alter the flow of the gradient at an angle that you can then use for your fill. However, unlike the rotation property on a MovieClip or sprite, the gradient box defines rotation in radians not degrees.

You can apply angular measurements to the gradient box properties to rotate the gradient.

FIGURE 16.13 Rotating the gradient box

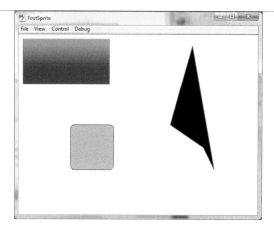

5. Update the createGradientBox method again as follows:

```
myMatrix.createGradientBox(100,100 ,.5*Math.PI);
```

6. Run the project. The gradient is now rotated (**Figure 16.13**).

CAN YOU CREATE RADIAL GRADIENTS?

The answer is yes, but the explanation on how they work can be pretty tricky. If you want to play with radial gradients, change the gradient type to GradientType.RADIAL and experiment with the various values.

LOOPING WITH THE DRAWING API

Now that you have learned the basics of drawing with the drawing API, you can use it to create some generative graphics in your projects. Remember that loops are used to repeat ActionScript actions numerous times. This can be ten times or ten thousand. You can use loops to create some interesting effects.

Let's get started and make some graphics. I encourage you to take this example and tweak it to experiment with the drawing API in ActionScript.

1. Create a new Flash Professional CS5.5 project and give it a Document class name. In this example, you'll call it **SoManyBoxes**.

FIGURE 16.14 Five simple random lines

2. Enter the following code as the Document class:

```
package  {
    import flash.display.MovieClip;
    public class SoManyBoxes extends MovieClip {
        public function SoManyBoxes() {
            for (var i:uint = 0; i < 5; i++)
            {
                with (graphics)
                {
                    lineStyle(1,Math.random()*0xFFFFFF,
                    ➝  Math.random());
moveTo(Math.random()*stage.stageWidth,
➝  Math.random()*stage.stageHeight);
lineTo(Math.random()*stage.stageWidth,
➝  Math.random()*stage.stageHeight);
                }
            }
        }
    }
}
```

3. Run the project. You'll see something similar to **Figure 16.14**.

Your project won't look the same, because this example uses random numbers to always create a different output each time.

If you look at the code, you'll see that the code is looping five times using the for loop. Inside the loop, the stroke is being defined using lineStyle. Within lineStyle, there are three parameters. The stroke will always be one pixel wide, defined by the first property. The second line of code within the with statement is to create a random color for the fill. By using the Math.random method, you can scale that up to the maximum color by using the 0xFFFFFF hexadecimal number as the multiplier. The last option defines the transparency, which already is in the same range as the Math.random method without modification.

Break the code that creates the line into two parts. First, you want to move the virtual pen, but not draw the line with the moveTo method. Inside here you are generating numbers for the x and y coordinate for the moveTo method. To make sure you get a number in range of the Stage, the code uses the stage object's stageWidth and stageHeight properties to get the right number. These two properties of the stage object will return the current dimensions of the project.

The next line of code draws the line, using the random color and transparency defined in the lineStyle statement to a random point calculated using the stage object's stageWidth and stageHight properties.

Pretty cool, right?

Well, since this is a loop, you can make this even cooler.

4. Change the for statement in the loop as follows:

```
for (var i:uint = 0; i < 1000; i++)
```

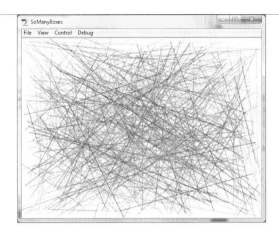

FIGURE 16.15 One thousand lines, one simple tweak

5. Run the program. You'll see something a little more interesting (**Figure 16.15**).

This is a basic example, but as you can see, you can create some cool effects with a little ActionScript and a lot of imagination.

WRAPPING **UP**

With just a little bit of ActionScript knowledge, you can start to crack the shell of Flash to reveal some creative coding pieces. With the basics learned here you are only bound by your creativity and imagination. Here are some tips to help you work with the graphics API of ActionScript 3.0:

- All graphics commands start with the graphics property, which is part of the MovieClip or Sprite classes.

- The Sprite class is identical to the MovieClip, but it doesn't contain a timeline or controls for a timeline.

- Colors in ActionScript are defined using hexadecimal numbers that are prefixed with 0x.

- To create your own reusable shapes and objects, extend the Sprite class in a custom class and place your graphics API code inside.

- When drawing shapes, remember the differences in where the shapes "start." Specifically, that the circle shape is drawn from the center, where other shapes draw from the upper-left corner down and to the right.

- Drawing lines means working with the virtual pen. To draw, use the lineTo method. To pick up and move without drawing, use moveTo.

- When working with gradients remember the differences between the gradient box and the area of the fill.

- To find out the Stage height and width, use the stage object's stageWidth and stageHeight properties.

- To repeat a number of lines with the same property or object, use the with statement.

17

ANIMATION USING ACTIONSCRIPT

Animation on the timeline is very powerful, and it has been the cornerstone of Flash Professional since it was first created. As scripting and coding have become more advanced, the need for dynamically created animations that are driven by data or random events has also evolved.

This chapter will introduce you to creating animations using ActionScript. As the saying goes, this is just the tip of the iceberg. There are countless implementations, evolutions, and mind-blowing examples of how you can extend the basics of code-based animation, including new 3D capabilities in the Flash runtimes. When you finish this chapter, you'll have a pretty cool ActionScript animation example—an animated starfield that looks like you are traveling at warp speed!

ACTIONSCRIPT **ANIMATION** = **LOCATION** + TIME

Animation is a basic concept, and there are a number of various forms. *Cell-based animation* is like a cartoon or film; you draw an object as if you took photos of its movements in rapid succession. *Tween-based animation* uses the computer to calculate the changes from a start point to an end point over a set amount of time and automatically fill in the gaps between. *Time-based animation* is what you'll cover in this chapter. It is the concept of taking an object and determining its location and other properties on the Stage at a given period of time.

Let's create a starting point for a warp speed starfield.

1. Create a new Flash Professional project called **Starfield**, give it a black background, and set the frame rate, or FPS, to **60**.

2. Create a Document class for the project.

3. Create a new custom class named Star that extends the Sprite class.

4. Enter the following as the code for the new Star class:

```
package  {
    import flash.display.Sprite;
    public class Star extends Sprite {
        public function Star() {
            // Create a basic star with (graphics)
            {
                lineStyle(0);
                beginFill(0xFFFFFF);
                drawCircle(0,0,3);
            }
        }
    }
}
```

This class will draw a three-pixel-wide white circle centered at the registration point of the sprite.

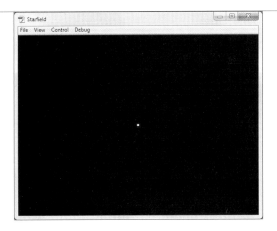

FIGURE 17.1 A single lonely star

5. Enter the following code for the Starfield Document class:

```
package  {
    import flash.display.MovieClip;
    public class Starfield extends MovieClip {
        private var _starCollection:Array;
        public function Starfield() {
            var newStar:Star = new Star();
            newStar.x = stage.stageWidth / 2;
            newStar.y = stage.stageHeight / 2;
            addChild(newStar);
            _starCollection = new Array();
            _starCollection.push(newStar);
        }
    }
}
```

This class will create an array to hold all the instances of the Star class (you will create more later in the project). It then creates a new instance of the Star class, centers it based on the Stage width and height, adds it to the display stack, and then pushes it to a newly created array.

6. Run the project. The results are shown in **Figure 17.1**.

MOVING AN OBJECT USING A TIMER

The basis of working with time-based animation is, you guessed it, time. In this project, you'll use ActionScript to move an object (star) around the screen, changing its location over time. You can use the `Timer` class and the `TimerEvent.TIMER` to create a callback function that will move the object slightly with each interval of the timer.

Since you are going to create more complex functionality, you should follow best practice and move some code outside of the constructor.

1. Update the code from the previous section with the following code:

```
package  {
    import flash.display.MovieClip;
    import flash.utils.Timer;
    import flash.events.TimerEvent;
    public class Starfield extends MovieClip {
        private var _starCollection:Array;
        private var _animateTimer:Timer;
        public function Starfield() {
            _createCollection();
            _configureTimer();
            _createStars();
            _startTimer();
        }
        private function _createCollection():void
        {
            _starCollection = new Array();
        }
        private function _configureTimer():void
        {
            _animateTimer = new Timer(100);
```

```
        _animateTimer.addEventListener
    →      (TimerEvent.TIMER, _animateStars);
    }

    private function _createStars():void
    {
        var newStar:Star = new Star();
        newStar.x = stage.stageWidth / 2;
        newStar.y = stage.stageHeight / 2;
        addChild(newStar);
        _starCollection.push(newStar);
    }
    private function _startTimer():void
    {
        _animateTimer.start();
    }
    //// Event Callbacks
    private function _animateStars(e:TimerEvent):void
    {
        _starCollection[0].x += 1;
    }
    }
}
```

Let's walk through this and discover exactly what is going on.

If you follow the flow of the constructor, you'll see that you first create the array collection object by assigning an empty array to it. Next, you config-ure the timer to an interval of 100 milliseconds. The timer will continue infinitely so an interval count is not required. The event listener is then created, accessing a callback function when the TimerEvent.TIMER event is broadcasted. The next section is the same as you had before, creating the star instance in a temporary variable and pushing it to the array as a new element. The timer is then started.

The callback event for the timer is where the animation happens. Every 100 milliseconds, this function will execute. Its function is to move the location of the stars in the array (for now there is only one) to give the appearance that they are moving. The equation that is used increases the x property of the selected array element by one.

2. Run the project. You'll find that the star slowly moves across the screen to the left.

   The callback function is determining the direction of the animation. You can modify that by changing the location properties.

3. Alter the _animateStars method as shown here:

```
private function _animateStars(e:TimerEvent):void
{
    _starCollection[0].x += 2;
    _starCollection[0].y += 1;
}
```

   This now affects both the x and y coordinates of the star.

4. Run the project again. You'll see the star slowly move down and to the right.

CREATING RANDOM ANIMATIONS

The animation so far is less than interesting, mostly because the star is moving in a constant direction at a constant speed. You can adjust and provide some interest by changing the slope of the animation.

The slope is a measurement of a line that determines changes along the x axis and y axis. You might remember it from geometry class as "rise over run." When creating time-based animation, the slope determines the direction and the speed of the animation.

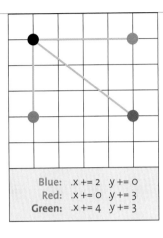 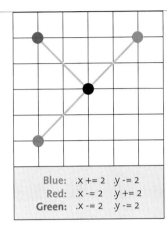

FIGURE 17.2 Various slope examples

Blue:	.x += 2	.y += 0
Red:	.x += 0	.y += 3
Green:	.x += 4	.y += 3

Blue:	.x += 2	.y -= 2
Red:	.x -= 2	.y += 2
Green:	.x -= 2	.y -= 2

Take a look at **Figure 17.2**.

Let's start with the graph on the left. In this example, the black dot represents the current location of the star on the screen. There are various changes you can make to the star that will move it on the screen. You can move it directly to the right by increasing x as shown with the blue dot. The dot can move directly down by increasing y as shown using the red dot. You could also move both x and y at the same time, causing a diagonal movement, as shown with the green dot.

The amount you change it will determine the speed at which the animation will take place. If you create a smaller number of x or y changes, the animation will run slower. The more you increase the amount of change to x and y, the faster the animation will run. Think about it: If you change the increase of x from 1 to 2, the speed at which the animation moves will double.

These examples are all using positive changes, and as a result, you can see that the movement is either to the right, down, or a combination of both. If you want to move the object in any direction, you will need to use a combination of positive and negative changes to x and y.

The graph on the right of Figure 17.2 shows how these other changes will work. If you want to move an object up and to the right, you increase x, but decrease y, as shown with the blue dot. The red dot is moving down and to the left, which is an increase in y, but a decrease in x. Finally, to move up and to the left, as shown with the green dot, you need to decrease x and y.

Whew! Enough of the geometry lesson for now. What you want to do is create an animation that will go in all directions, but what would make it better would be to make it random at the same time.

FIGURE 17.3 Modifying a
random number generator

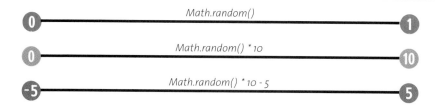

To introduce some randomness, you need to generate two random numbers for the star. The rate you want x to change, and the rate you want y to change. These will then be used to calculate the change you want for the star. Now the trick is to pick a range that is positive and negative, otherwise you'll only have animations that move right and down.

Figure 17.3 shows how you can take a starting random number range and get what you want.

First, you start with the base random number generator, which gives you a range of decimals from 0 to 1. You then scale that range to go up to 10 by multiplying it. You then shift the range so that the midpoint of the range is 5 by reducing it by half of the scale you expanded it by.

Now, you can get a random number in the range of -5 to 5. Since you need to store both numbers, you can use a nested array to hold the numbers. Why an array, you ask? It might seem like overkill, but it will make perfect sense later in the chapter.

1. Update the code from the previous example, as shown below:

```
package {
    import flash.display.MovieClip;
    import flash.utils.Timer;
    import flash.events.TimerEvent;
    public class Starfield extends MovieClip {
        private var _starCollection:Array;
        private var _rateCollection:Array;
        private var _animateTimer:Timer;
        public function Starfield() {
            _createCollection();
            _configureTimer();
```

```
    _createStars();
    _startTimer();
}
private function _createCollection():void
{
    _starCollection = new Array();
    _rateCollection = new Array();
}
private function _configureTimer():void
{
    _animateTimer = new Timer(100);
    _animateTimer.addEventListener
        (TimerEvent.TIMER, _animateStars);
}
private function _createStars():void
{
    var newStar:Star = new Star();
    newStar.x = stage.stageWidth / 2;
    newStar.y = stage.stageHeight / 2;
    addChild(newStar);
    _starCollection.push(newStar);
    var newXRate:Number = Math.random()*10-5;
    var newYRate:Number = Math.random()*10-5;
    var newRate:Array = [newXRate,newYRate];
    _rateCollection.push(newRate);
}
private function _startTimer():void
{
```

```
                    _animateTimer.start();
                }
                //// Event Callbacks
                private function _animateStars(e:TimerEvent):void
                {
                    _starCollection[0].x += _rateCollection[0][0];
                    _starCollection[0].y += _rateCollection[0][1];
                }
            }
        }
```

Let's walk through this to better understand. First, you are creating a new array to hold the rate changes (even though you have only one for now). When you create the star in the _createStars method, you also create a new rate for both x and y coordinates using the equation you created earlier. You then create a new temporary array to hold these and push that array inside as a new array element. As a result, you'll have an array, _rateCollection, whose first element contains an array of two elements, the first is the rate of change for x, the second is the change of y.

In the callback function, you apply these rate changes to the x and y location of the star. You access the nested arrays by stacking the element brackets against each other. In this case, accessing the first element's first element as the rate of change for x, and then the first element's second element as the rate of change for y.

Whew!

2. Run the project and see what happens.

3. Run the project again. You'll see that each time you run the project, the star will move in a random direction.

Now wouldn't it be cool if there were more stars? Why yes, I think it would.

ANIMATING MULTIPLE OBJECTS WITH LOOPS

Now you'll discover why the star and rates of change are stored in arrays. It is to allow you to easily add multiple instances of stars to the example without needing to refactor extensive amounts of code.

You already have the arrays to store the stars and the rates of change. All you need to do is add the loops, and it should all work. Let's find out.

1. Update the code, as highlighted, to add the loops you need—let's start with 10 stars:

```
package  {
    import flash.display.MovieClip;
    import flash.utils.Timer;
    import flash.events.TimerEvent;
    public class Starfield extends MovieClip {
        private var _starCollection:Array;
        private var _rateCollection:Array;
        private var _animateTimer:Timer;
        public function Starfield() {
            _createCollection();
            _configureTimer();
            _createStars();
            _startTimer();
        }
        private function _createCollection():void
        {
            _starCollection = new Array();
            _rateCollection = new Array();
        }
```

```
private function _configureTimer():void
{
    _animateTimer = new Timer(100);
    _animateTimer.addEventListener
        (TimerEvent.TIMER, _animateStars);
}
private function _createStars():void
{
    for (var i:uint = 0; i < 10; i++)
    {
        var newStar:Star = new Star();
        newStar.x = stage.stageWidth / 2;
        newStar.y = stage.stageHeight / 2;
        addChild(newStar);
        _starCollection.push(newStar);
        var newXRate:Number = Math.random()*10-5;
        var newYRate:Number = Math.random()*10-5;
        var newRate:Array = [newXRate,newYRate];
        _rateCollection.push(newRate);
    }
}
private function _startTimer():void
{
    _animateTimer.start();
}
//// Event Callbacks
```

FIGURE 17.4 Warp speed captain!

```
private function _animateStars(e:TimerEvent):void
{
    for (var i:uint = 0; i < 10; i++)
    {
        _starCollection[i].x += _rateCollection[i][0];
        _starCollection[i].y += _rateCollection[i][1];
    }
}
```

As you can see, you didn't need to change much.

2. Run the project. You'll see a bunch of stars start to animate (**Figure 17.4**).

Congrats! But you aren't finished—as you may have found out, when the stars move off the screen they disappear forever. So sad! How do you detect when the stars move off the Stage, place them back in the center, and create a new random rate of movement so you can keep moving forward at Warp 10?

The answer: Use a conditional to determine the location and see if it is within the range of the Stage. If it is, animate it as usual, if not, adjust it.

3. Update your code, as highlighted below:

```
package  {
    import flash.display.MovieClip;
    import flash.utils.Timer;
    import flash.events.TimerEvent;
    public class Starfield extends MovieClip {
        private var _starCollection:Array;
        private var _rateCollection:Array;
        private var _animateTimer:Timer;
        public function Starfield() {
            _createCollection();
            _configureTimer();
            _createStars();
            _startTimer();
        }
        private function _createCollection():void
        {
            _starCollection = new Array();
            _rateCollection = new Array();
        }
        private function _configureTimer():void
        {
            _animateTimer = new Timer(100);
            _animateTimer.addEventListener
                (TimerEvent.TIMER, _animateStars);
        }
        private function _createStars():void
        {
```

```actionscript
        for (var i:uint = 0; i < 10; i++)
        {
            var newStar:Star = new Star();
            newStar.x = stage.stageWidth / 2;
            newStar.y = stage.stageHeight / 2;
            addChild(newStar);
            _starCollection.push(newStar);
            var newXRate:Number = Math.random()*10-5;
            var newYRate:Number = Math.random()*10-5;
            var newRate:Array = [newXRate,newYRate];
            _rateCollection.push(newRate);
        }
    }
    private function _startTimer():void
    {
        _animateTimer.start();
    }
    //// Event Callbacks
    private function _animateStars(e:TimerEvent):void
    {
        for (var i:uint = 0; i < 10; i++)
        {
            with (_starCollection[i]) {
                if (x < 0 || x > stage.stageWidth ||
                    y < 0 || y > stage.stageHeight)
                {
                    x = stage.stageWidth / 2;
                    y = stage.stageHeight / 2;
```

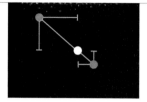

FIGURE 17.5 Calculating random position and rate of location change

```
        _rateCollection[i][0] =
            Math.random()*10-5;

        _rateCollection[i][1] =
            Math.random()*10-5;

    } else {

        _starCollection[i].x +=
            _rateCollection[i][0];

        _starCollection[i].y +=
            _rateCollection[i][1];

    }

  }

 }

 }

}
```

Well look at that, all that stuff you learned before is starting to come in handy, isn't it? With the use of an if statement, you are able to detect if the x coordinate is less than 0, greater than the Stage width, or if the y coordinate is less than 0, or greater than the Stage height. If it is, plop it back in the center and create a new rate of change for the star.

4. Run the project. You'll find that as soon as a star disappears from the window, it is back in the center and keeps moving.

FINE-TUNING ANIMATIONS

You have done a lot so far, and the fundamentals are all in place, but there are some adjustments you can make to really polish this example. The first thing you can do is adjust the starting location of the stars. They all appear in the center—the exact center of the screen. This isn't very realistic; in fact, it is downright odd. To fix this, you can create a random location on the screen and use this to evaluate the rate of change you want to use to move the star. Take a look at **Figure 17.5**.

In this illustration, the white dot represents the center of the Stage, otherwise known as the coordinate `stage.stageWidth/2, stage.stageHeight/2`. You can position an object anywhere in the Stage using the `stageWidth` and `stageHeight` methods with the random number generator. You now need to calculate the slope, or the difference of x and y from the center of the Stage to the random location. You can do that by taking the random x and y coordinate and subtracting the location of the center of the Stage. This is the slope of the position of the star relative to the center of the Stage. You can scale down this slope to calculate the rate of change for x and y.

1. Update the project with the code highlighted below:

```
package  {
    import flash.display.MovieClip;
    import flash.utils.Timer;
    import flash.events.TimerEvent;
    public class Starfield extends MovieClip {
        private var _starCollection:Array;
        private var _rateCollection:Array;
        private var _animateTimer:Timer;
        public function Starfield() {
            _createCollection();
            _configureTimer();
            _createStars();
            _startTimer();
        }
        private function _createCollection():void
        {
            _starCollection = new Array();
            _rateCollection = new Array();
        }
```

```actionscript
private function _configureTimer():void
{
    _animateTimer = new Timer(100);
    _animateTimer.addEventListener
        (TimerEvent.TIMER, _animateStars);
}
private function _createStars():void
{
    for (var i:uint = 0; i < 10; i++)
    {
        var newStar:Star = new Star();
        newStar.x = Math.random()*stage.stageWidth;
        newStar.y = Math.random()*stage.stageHeight;
        addChild(newStar);
        _starCollection.push(newStar);

        var newXRate:Number =
            (newStar.x - stage.stageWidth/2) * .1;
        var newYRate:Number =
            (newStar.y - stage.stageHeight/2) * .1;
        var newRate:Array = [newXRate,newYRate];
        _rateCollection.push(newRate);
    }
}
private function _startTimer():void
{
    _animateTimer.start();
}
//// Event Callbacks
```

```
private function _animateStars(e:TimerEvent):void
{
    for (var i:uint = 0; i < 10; i++)
    {
        with (_starCollection[i]) {
            if (x < 0 || x > stage.stageWidth ||
            →  y < 0 || y > stage.stageHeight)
            {
                x = Math.random()*stage.stageWidth;
                y = Math.random()*stage.stageHeight;
                _rateCollection[i][0] =
                →  (x - stage.stageWidth/2) * .1;
                _rateCollection[i][1] =
                →  (y - stage.stageHeight/2) * .1;
            } else {
                _starCollection[i].x +=
                →  _rateCollection[i][0];
                _starCollection[i].y +=
                →  _rateCollection[i][1];
            }
        }
    }
}
```

As you can see, there were only a couple modifications required.

2. Run the project. You'll see that the stars don't always fly out from the direct center of the stage, and the direction of movement follows the slope they were already on based on their random location.

But you aren't finished yet. There are a few more tweaks you can do. The next adjustment is to change the brightness, or alpha property, of the stars as they animate. Remember, you are flying through space, so they stars shouldn't be as bright when they first display, but get brighter as the viewer "moves" towards them.

You can create this effect by defining the initial alpha property at a low value, and adding another rate of change to the array. This time it will be a rate of change of alpha.

3. Update the project as highlighted below to add this new animation effect:

```
package  {
    import flash.display.MovieClip;
    import flash.utils.Timer;
    import flash.events.TimerEvent;
    public class Starfield extends MovieClip {
        private var _starCollection:Array;
        private var _rateCollection:Array;
        private var _animateTimer:Timer;
        public function Starfield() {
            _createCollection();
            _configureTimer();
            _createStars();
            _startTimer();
        }
        private function _createCollection():void
        {
            _starCollection = new Array();
            _rateCollection = new Array();
        }
        private function _configureTimer():void
```

```
{
    _animateTimer = new Timer(100);

    _animateTimer.addEventListener
    ⇒ (TimerEvent.TIMER, _animateStars);
}
private function _createStars():void
{
    for (var i:uint = 0; i < 10; i++)
    {
        var newStar:Star = new Star();
        newStar.x = Math.random()*stage.stageWidth;
        newStar.y = Math.random()*stage.stageHeight;
        newStar.alpha = 0;
        addChild(newStar);
        _starCollection.push(newStar);
        var newXRate:Number =
        ⇒ (newStar.x - stage.stageWidth/2) * .1;
        var newYRate:Number =
        ⇒ (newStar.y - stage.stageHeight/2) * .1;
        var newARate:Number = Math.random() * .1;
        var newRate:Array =
        ⇒ [newXRate,newYRate, newARate];
        _rateCollection.push(newRate);
    }
}
private function _startTimer():void
{
    _animateTimer.start();
}
//// Event Callbacks
```

```actionscript
private function _animateStars(e:TimerEvent):void
{
    for (var i:uint = 0; i < 10; i++)
    {
        with (_starCollection[i]) {
            if (x < 0 || x > stage.stageWidth ||
                y < 0 || y > stage.stageHeight)
            {
                x = Math.random()*stage.stageWidth;
                y = Math.random()*stage.stageHeight;
                alpha = 0;
                _rateCollection[i][0] =
                    (x - stage.stageWidth/2) * .1;
                _rateCollection[i][1] =
                    (y - stage.stageHeight/2) * .1;
                _rateCollection[i][2] =
                    Math.random() * .1;
            } else {
                _starCollection[i].x +=
                    _rateCollection[i][0];
                _starCollection[i].y +=
                    _rateCollection[i][1];
                _starCollection[i].alpha +=
                    _rateCollection[i][2]
            }
        }
    }
}
```

4. Run the project again. Now the stars will fade in as they get "closer" to you.

   You can probably guess what I'm going to say next, and your right—"But wait! There's more!" As you play the animation, you'll notice it needs to be a little less choppy. If you remember, the interval that the objects move at is determined by the timer interval. You can adjust this to make a more fluid animation.

5. Adjust the timer interval in the following line of code:

   ```
   _animateTimer = new Timer(10);
   ```

6. Run the project again.

   Woah! What is this? Warp 20?! It is clear that the animation is running too quickly—but it is flowing much better that it was before. You can adjust the speed by adjusting the rate of the movement of the stars with each interval. This was calculated as a proportion of the slope based on the original random location of the star against the center of the Stage. Since the interval is now a tenth of what it used to be (10 milliseconds instead of 100), to achieve the same effect you had before you need to reduce the rate of change by a tenth as well.

7. Adjust the code, as shown below, to apply the fix:

   ```
   package  {
       import flash.display.MovieClip;
       import flash.utils.Timer;
       import flash.events.TimerEvent;
       public class Starfield extends MovieClip {
           private var _starCollection:Array;
           private var _rateCollection:Array;
           private var _animateTimer:Timer;
           public function Starfield() {
               _createCollection();
               _configureTimer();
   ```

```actionscript
        _createStars();
        _startTimer();
    }
    private function _createCollection():void
    {
        _starCollection = new Array();
        _rateCollection = new Array();
    }
    private function _configureTimer():void
    {
        _animateTimer = new Timer(10);
        _animateTimer.addEventListener
            (TimerEvent.TIMER, _animateStars);
    }
    private function _createStars():void
    {
        for (var i:uint = 0; i < 10; i++)
        {
            var newStar:Star = new Star();
            newStar.x = Math.random()*stage.stageWidth;
            newStar.y = Math.random()*stage.stageHeight;
            newStar.alpha = 0;
            addChild(newStar);
            _starCollection.push(newStar);
            var newXRate:Number =
                (newStar.x - stage.stageWidth/2) * .01;
            var newYRate:Number =
                (newStar.y - stage.stageHeight/2) * .01;
            var newARate:Number = Math.random() * .01;
```

```
            var newRate:Array =
              [newXRate,newYRate, newARate];
            _rateCollection.push(newRate);
        }
    }
    private function _startTimer():void
    {
        _animateTimer.start();
    }
    //// Event Callbacks
    private function _animateStars(e:TimerEvent):void
    {
        for (var i:uint = 0; i < 10; i++)
        {
            with (_starCollection[i]) {
                if (x < 0 || x > stage.stageWidth ||
                   y < 0 || y > stage.stageHeight)
                {
                    x = Math.random()*stage.stageWidth;
                    y = Math.random()*stage.stageHeight;
                    alpha = 0;
                    _rateCollection[i][0] =
                       (x - stage.stageWidth/2) * .01;
                    _rateCollection[i][1] =
                       (y - stage.stageHeight/2) * .01;
                    _rateCollection[i][2] =
                       Math.random() * .01;
                } else {
                    _starCollection[i].x +=
                       rateCollection[i][0];
```

```
                                        _starCollection[i].y +=
                                     →   rateCollection[i][1];

                                        _starCollection[i].alpha +=
                                     →   rateCollection[i][2]

                                }

                          }

                    }

              }

        }
```

8. Run the project again. You'll see that the rate of the animation is back to what it was before, but now it is much smoother than it originally was.

Ok, one more change—this one is simple. You need more stars. Update the following line so you can have a (partial) universe of stars:

```
package  {
    import flash.display.MovieClip;
    import flash.utils.Timer;
    import flash.events.TimerEvent;
    public class Starfield extends MovieClip {
        private var _starCollection:Array;
        private var _rateCollection:Array;
        private var _animateTimer:Timer;
        public function Starfield() {
            _createCollection();
            _configureTimer();
            _createStars();
            _startTimer();
        }
```

```
private function _createCollection():void
{
    _starCollection = new Array();
    _rateCollection = new Array();
}
private function _configureTimer():void
{
    _animateTimer = new Timer(10);
    _animateTimer.addEventListener
        (TimerEvent.TIMER, _animateStars);
}
private function _createStars():void
{
    for (var i:uint = 0; i < 500; i++)
    {
        var newStar:Star = new Star();
        newStar.x = Math.random()*stage.stageWidth;
        newStar.y = Math.random()*stage.stageHeight;
        newStar.alpha = 0;
        addChild(newStar);
        _starCollection.push(newStar);
        var newXRate:Number =
            (newStar.x - stage.stageWidth/2) * .01;
        var newYRate:Number =
            (newStar.y - stage.stageHeight/2) * .01;
        var newARate:Number = Math.random() * .01;
        var newRate:Array =
            [newXRate,newYRate, newARate];
        _rateCollection.push(newRate);
```

```
        }
}
private function _startTimer():void
{
    _animateTimer.start();
}
//// Event Callbacks
private function _animateStars(e:TimerEvent):void
{
    for (var i:uint = 0; i < 500; i++)
    {
        with (_starCollection[i]) {
            if (x < 0 || x > stage.stageWidth ||
                y < 0 || y > stage.stageHeight)
            {
                x = Math.random()*stage.stageWidth;
                y = Math.random()*stage.stageHeight;
                alpha = 0;
                _rateCollection[i][0] =
                    (x - stage.stageWidth/2) * .01;
                _rateCollection[i][1] =
                    (y - stage.stageHeight/2) * .01;
                _rateCollection[i][2] =
                    Math.random() * .01;
            } else {
                _starCollection[i].x +=
                    _rateCollection[i][0];
                _starCollection[i].y +=
                _rateCollection[i][1];
```

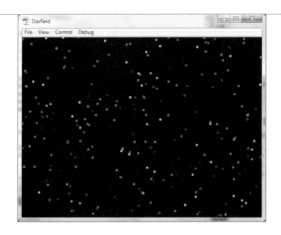

FIGURE 17.6 Traveling the galaxy, courtesy of ActionScript

```
                        _starCollection[i].alpha +=
                            _rateCollection[i][2]
                    }
                }
            }
        }
    }
}
```

9. Run the project again, and sit back, you are well on your way to Alpha Centauri.

Oh, OK, one more change—you are such a good student, you can do one more little tweak. Remember when I said that you would want to adjust the alpha because the star was farther away? Well, that would adjust the size too, wouldn't it? You can adjust that with an easy tweak.

10. Update the code as follows:

```
package  {
    import flash.display.MovieClip;
    import flash.utils.Timer;
    import flash.events.TimerEvent;
    public class Starfield extends MovieClip {
```

```
private var _starCollection:Array;
private var _rateCollection:Array;
private var _animateTimer:Timer;
public function Starfield() {
    _createCollection();
    _configureTimer();
    _createStars();
    _startTimer();
}
private function _createCollection():void
{
    _starCollection = new Array();
    _rateCollection = new Array();
}
private function _configureTimer():void
{
    _animateTimer = new Timer(10);
    _animateTimer.addEventListener
        (TimerEvent.TIMER, _animateStars);
}
private function _createStars():void
{
    for (var i:uint = 0; i < 500; i++)
    {
        var newStar:Star = new Star();
        newStar.x = Math.random()*stage.stageWidth;
        newStar.y = Math.random()*stage.stageHeight;
        newStar.alpha = 0;
```

```
            newStar.scaleX = newStar.scaleY = 0;

            addChild(newStar);

            _starCollection.push(newStar);

            var newXRate:Number =
            ⇢  (newStar.x - stage.stageWidth/2) * .01;

            var newYRate:Number =
            ⇢  (newStar.y - stage.stageHeight/2) * .01;

            var newARate:Number = Math.random() * .01;

            var newRate:Array =
            ⇢  [newXRate,newYRate, newARate];

            _rateCollection.push(newRate);

        }

    }


    private function _startTimer():void

    {

        _animateTimer.start();

    }

    //// Event Callbacks

    private function _animateStars(e:TimerEvent):void

    {

        for (var i:uint = 0; i < 500; i++)

        {

            with (_starCollection[i]) {

                if (x < 0 || x > stage.stageWidth ||
                ⇢  y < 0 || y > stage.stageHeight)

                {

                    x = Math.random()*stage.stageWidth;

                    y = Math.random()*stage.stageHeight;
```

```
                                alpha = 0;
                                scaleX = scaleY = 0;
                                _rateCollection[i][0] =
                                   (x - stage.stageWidth/2) * .01;

                                _rateCollection[i][1] =
                                   (y - stage.stageHeight/2) * .01;

                                _rateCollection[i][2] =
                                   Math.random() * .01;

                           } else {
                                _starCollection[i].x +=
                                   _rateCollection[i][0];

                                _starCollection[i].y +=
                                   _rateCollection[i][1];

                                _starCollection[i].alpha +=
                                   _rateCollection[i][2];

                                if (_starCollection[i].alpha > 1)
                                   _starCollection[i].alpha = 1;

                                _starCollection[i].scaleX =
                                   _starCollection[i].alpha;

                                _starCollection[i].scaleY =
                                   _starCollection[i].alpha;

                           }
                       }
                   }
               }
           }
       }
```

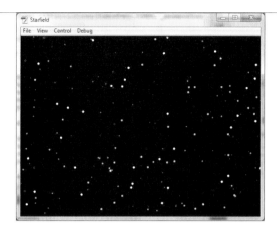

FIGURE 17.7 Engage!

Now the star's size is determined using scaleX and scaleY, which will adjust the size relative to its natural dimensions. Notice that you added an `if` statement near the end. This is because the `alpha` property is constantly going up, in fact, it is going above 1. While the `alpha` property can deal with this since it treats any value over 1 as 1, scaleX and scaleY are a different story. They will accept values over 1 and scale them above their natural dimensions.

Another trick that is used is assigning a value to multiple values in a single line:

```
scaleX = scaleY = 0;
```

This is the same as writing it out on two lines:

```
scaleX = 0;
scaleY = 0;
```

Another quick shortcut that you can use—free of charge!

Ok—enough—I hear you loud and clear.

11. Run the Project.

The result of all your hard work is a cool animated warp speed starfield effect (**Figure 17.7**). Congratulations.

WRAPPING **UP**

In this chapter, you learned some of the basics of creating time-based animation using ActionScript. Using a few simple concepts, you can create some interesting animated effects.

Here are some helpful tips to help you work with time-based animation using ActionScript:

- Time-based animation has a basic principle: Change the location of an object based on a rate of location change over a series of timer intervals.

- To define the speed of the animation requires two factors. The first is the rate of movement change (sometimes called slope) and the second is the frequency of intervals that apply that rate of change.

- The slope of an object is based on the change in x and the change in y.

- The rate of change when moving in all directions away from a center point will require positive or negative changes to x and y.

- When animating a series of objects, use arrays and loops to repeat animations actions and keep your code easier to scale and change.

- Experiment! Animation is about creativity—play with different effects, properties, timings, and objects. Happy mistakes are fun to discover!

18

WORKING WITH EXTERNAL **MEDIA**

Flash is one of the most expressive ways to create interactive content and media across multiple devices. ActionScript is a core part of connecting with media, and gives designers and developers the ability to work with images, audio, and video to make any experience more immersive and compelling.

In this chapter, you'll learn how to load images, audio, and video and control their display and playback in your applications.

USING **IMAGES**

When working with images, you have two options: You can import them into your Library and place instances of them on the Stage, or you can load them dynamically using ActionScript. Both options have advantages and disadvantages.

When importing images into the Library, you make the process of visually laying out your project much easier; but keeping your project small for fast loading on a web browser can be complex. For mobile or desktop applications images are typically embedded into the application, so this isn't as much of a concern, but it can affect startup time of a project published on the web. Another limitation is that the images are static, and you still need to work with ActionScript to change them.

Loading images with ActionScript keeps your images separate from the rest of the project, making it easier to change images outside of Flash if you need to make updates or other changes. It also ensures that your published project is smaller since the images aren't embedded with the SWF. The disadvantage of using ActionScript is that layout needs to be handled with code. It varies between people, but there is often a personal preference to have graphics visually laid out in Flash Professional, or have it handed through ActionScript. There is no right or wrong way, just find the balance that is right for you and your project.

In the next few sections, you'll learn how to load images and media assets into a project using ActionScript. You'll learn to work with images and other SWF files.

You can load images from an external location. The most common are graphics files, including JPEG, GIF, and PNG files. You can load PNGs with transparency without any problems. You can also load another SWF file and it will be treated like any other graphic file.

A special class called the `ProLoader` class manages the loading and unloading of images and SWFs. You'll use the `ProLoader` class in the following example.

1. Create a new Flash Professional project named `FirstProLoader` and a matching Document class.

2. Add the following code to your Document class:

```
package  {
    import flash.display.MovieClip;
    import fl.display.ProLoader;
    import flash.net.URLRequest;
    public class FirstProLoader extends MovieClip {
```

```
private var _imageLoader:ProLoader;
public function FirstProLoader() {
    _loadImage();
}
private function _loadImage():void
{
    // Create a variable to store the URL of the file
    →  to load
    var imageURL:URLRequest = new URLRequest("http://
    →  www.helpexamples.com/flash/images/image1.jpg");
    // Create the ProLoader
    _imageLoader = new ProLoader();
    // Position the ProLoader on the stage
    _imageLoader.x = 10;
    _imageLoader.y = 10;
    // Load the file at the URL stored
    _imageLoader.load(imageURL);
    // Add the loader to the display stack
    addChild(_imageLoader);
    }
  }
}
```

Let's step through this code and look at what is going on. The _loadImage method is where all the action happens, so you'll focus there.

First, you need a variable that will store the URL of the file that you'll load. In this case, it is a JPEG file that is being loaded. ActionScript has a specific class that is used to hold URLs, called the URLRequest class.

FIGURE 18.1 Loading an image using the ProLoader class

The ProLoader is constructed and then positioned on the Stage. The ProLoader is like any other display object so you can manipulate its appearance on the Stage (**Figure 18.1**) like any other image, Sprite, or MovieClip.

The load method loads the file at the URL location. Finally the ProLoader is added to the display stack.

3. Run the project. You'll see an image of a flower appear in the project, this is the image at the location of the URL that is part of the URLRequest.

See? Not that hard when you understand all the parts. The ProLoader class is new to Flash Professional CS5.5, and is pretty easy and flexible to use.

You'll undoubtedly want to include audio with your projects at some time. Action-Script offers an easy way to play sound files including MP3 files as a response to user events in your projects.

In this section, you are going to start a new project and create a simple play button that will start the playback of the audio file.

1. Create a new Flash Professional project called **PlayAudio** and create a matching Document class.

2. Add the following code to your Document class:

```
package  {
    import flash.display.MovieClip;
    import flash.display.Sprite;
    import flash.events.MouseEvent;
    public class PlayAudio extends MovieClip {
        var playAudioButton:Sprite;
        public function PlayAudio() {
            playAudioButton = new Sprite();
            playAudioButton.graphics.beginFill(0xFF0000);
            playAudioButton.graphics.drawRect(0,0,50,50);
            playAudioButton.graphics.endFill();
            addChild(playAudioButton);
            playAudioButton.x = playAudioButton.y = 20;
            playAudioButton.addEventListener
                (MouseEvent.CLICK, controlSound);
        }
        public function controlSound(e:MouseEvent):void
        {
        }
    }
}
```

You created a sprite called playAudioButton, drew the button using the drawing API, and then added an event listener for the MouseEvent.CLICK event type.

The process of working with audio is very similar to working with images, with two exceptions. First, you will be working with the Sound class, not the ProLoader class. Like the ProLoader, you need to define the URL of where the audio file is located with an instance of the URLRequest class. Also, you have to explicitly tell the sound to play; it won't start automatically when you load it.

3. Update the Document class, as highlighted below:

```
package   {
    import flash.display.MovieClip;
    import flash.display.Sprite;
    import flash.events.MouseEvent;
    import flash.media.Sound;
    import flash.net.URLRequest;
    public class PlayAudio extends MovieClip {
        var playAudioButton:Sprite;
        var soundURL:URLRequest;
        var mySound:Sound;
        public function PlayAudio() {
                playAudioButton = new Sprite();
playAudioButton.graphics.beginFill(0xFF0000);
playAudioButton.graphics.drawRect(0,0,50,50);
                playAudioButton.graphics.endFill();
                addChild(playAudioButton);
                playAudioButton.x = playAudioButton.y = 20;
                soundURL = new URLRequest("http://www.
                 ⇨ helpexamples.com/flash/sound/song3.mp3");
                mySound = new Sound(soundURL);
```

```
playAudioButton.addEventListener
   (MouseEvent.CLICK, controlSound);

   }
   public function controlSound(e:MouseEvent):void

   {

       mySound.play();

   }

}

}
```

4. Run the project. When you click the button, you'll hear a groovy little tune play on your speakers.

FIGURE 18.2 The Flash Professional Components panel

There are a few ways you can work with video on the web including progressive, streaming, or embedded. In addition there are a number of controllers you can use to play back video. The flexibility for what and how to play video is one reason why Flash is such a successful way to deliver video on the web.

This section will cover how to work with the FLVPlayback component that is part of Flash Professional CS5.5. The FLVPlayback component is an object that you can include on the Stage or in the Library, populate with a video source, and use the built-in player controls to control the video experience in your project. In addition, you can create your own playback controls using some easy-to-use methods that are part of the FLVPlayback component

You need to add the FLVPlayback component to your project:

1. Create a new Flash Professional CS5.5 project.

2. Open the Components panel from the Window menu (**Figure 18.2**).

3. Drag the FLVPlayback 2.5 component to the Library.

   With the component added to your project, you can configure it to play back video using ActionScript.

   The FLVPlayback component has an extensive API to allow you to control how you want to play and display video. Let's start with pointing the component to a video file on the web.

4. Create a Document class for your project.

5. Update the Document class with the following highlighted code:

```
package  {
    import flash.display.MovieClip;
    import fl.video.FLVPlayback;
    public class PlayFLV extends MovieClip {
        var myVideo:FLVPlayback;
        public function PlayFLV() {
            _setupVideo();
        }
        private function _setupVideo():void
        {
            myVideo = new FLVPlayback();
            myVideo.x = myVideo.y = 10;
            addChild(myVideo);
            myVideo.source = "http://www.helpexamples.com/
            → flash/video/water.flv";
        }
    }
}
```

FIGURE 18.3 Video playing in the project using the FLVPlayback component

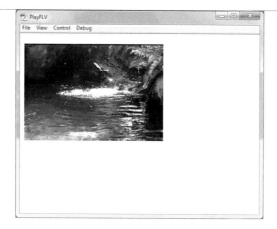

6. Run the project. You'll see a serene video play in the corner of your project (**Figure 18.3**).

Let's step through the code to discover how it works.

First, you need to create an instance of the FLVPlayback component that is in the Library. It is linked to the FLVPlayback class that is located in the fl.video class package, imported at the top of the class definition.

Next, you need to position and add the component to the display stack like any other visual object.

At that point, you provide the URL for the video file that will play. The file in this example is an FLV video that is on a web server. You can work with any of the files that are supported by the FLVPlayback component including FLV, F4V, or H.264 encoded video files. You set this location using the source property.

ALTERING THE PLAYBACK
OF VIDEO

When using the FLVPlayback component, you have an API available to control the video. To get started, we need to create a button you can use for the project.

1. Create a new custom class called VideoButton and save it at the same location as your FLA.

2. Update the code in VideoButton as follows:

```
package  {
    import flash.display.Sprite;
    import flash.text.TextField;
    import flash.text.TextFormat;
    public class VideoButton extends Sprite {
        var buttonLabel:TextField;
        var buttonFormat:TextFormat;
        public function VideoButton(newLabel:String) {
                graphics.beginFill(0xCCCCCC);
                graphics.drawRect(0,0,100,20);
                graphics.endFill();
                buttonLabel = new TextField();
                buttonLabel.width = 100;
                buttonLabel.height = 20;
                buttonLabel.selectable = false;
                addChild(buttonLabel);
                buttonFormat = new TextFormat();
                buttonFormat.font = "Verdana";
                buttonLabel.defaultTextFormat = buttonFormat;
                setLabel(newLabel);
        }
        public function setLabel(newLabel:String)
        {
```

```
                    buttonLabel.text = newLabel;
                }
            }
        }
```

You are drawing a background of the button using the drawing API. Then, you are creating a text field, formatting it, populating it from a string passed into the class constructor and assigned using the helper function setLabel.

You now need to update the Document class to use this new shiny button, and then control the playback of the video. Since the video immediately plays when you load it, you need to stop it immediately after you load it.

3. Alter the Document class as follows:

```
package {
    import flash.display.MovieClip;
    import fl.video.FLVPlayback;
    import flash.events.MouseEvent;
    public class PlayFLV extends MovieClip {
        var myVideo:FLVPlayback;
        var playButton:VideoButton;
        public function PlayFLV() {
            _setupVideo();
        }
        private function _setupVideo():void
        {
            myVideo = new FLVPlayback();
            myVideo.autoPlay = false;
            myVideo.x = myVideo.y = 10;
            addChild(myVideo);
            myVideo.source = "http://www.helpexamples.com/
                flash/video/water.flv";
```

```
            playButton = new VideoButton("Play");

            playButton.x = 400;

            playButton.y = 50;

            addChild(playButton);

            playButton.addEventListener
            → (MouseEvent.CLICK, playVideo);

        }

        public function playVideo(e:MouseEvent):void

        {

            myVideo.play();

        }

    }

}
```

Here, you created a new instance of the VideoButton that you created in step 2, and positioned it on the screen, providing it with the label "Play." After defining the video source, you immediately stopped the playback with the stop method of the FLVPlayback class.

To play the video when the button is clicked, you added an event listener listening for the MouseEvent.CLICK event type. The callback method for the event, playVideo, then executes the play method of the FLVPlayback class.

FIGURE 18.4 Starting a video using the FLVPlayback API

4. Run the project. You'll be able to play the video using the new play button you created (**Figure 18.4**).

PAUSING VIDEO

To add pause functionality to the video, you need to consider if you want the pause to be a toggle button. Typically, while a video is playing, if the user clicks pause, the video stops; if the user clicks pause again, the video continues.

You can do this by creating a conditional that will test if the movie is paused or not using the paused property. In addition, it is helpful to give the user feedback on what the button will do, so using the VideoButton class, you can use the setLabel method to change the button label accordingly.

1. Update the Document class with the following highlighted code:

```
package {
    import flash.display.MovieClip;
    import fl.video.FLVPlayback;
    import flash.events.MouseEvent;
    public class PlayFLV extends MovieClip {
        var myVideo:FLVPlayback;
        var playButton:VideoButton;
        var pauseButton:VideoButton;
```

```
public function PlayFLV() {
    _setupVideo();
}
private function _setupVideo():void
{
    myVideo = new FLVPlayback();
    myVideo.autoPlay = false;
    myVideo.x = myVideo.y = 10;
    addChild(myVideo);
    myVideo.source = "http://www.helpexamples.com/
    ➡ flash/video/water.flv";
    playButton = new VideoButton("Play");
    playButton.x = 400;
    playButton.y = 50;
    addChild(playButton);
    pauseButton = new VideoButton("Pause");
    pauseButton.x = 400;
    pauseButton.y = 100;
    addChild(pauseButton);
    playButton.addEventListener
    ➡ (MouseEvent.CLICK, playVideo);
    pauseButton.addEventListener
    ➡ (MouseEvent.CLICK, pauseVideo);
}
public function playVideo(e:MouseEvent):void
{
    myVideo.play();
}
public function pauseVideo(e:MouseEvent):void
{
```

```
            if (!myVideo.paused)
            {
                myVideo.pause();
                pauseButton.setLabel("Resume");
            } else {
                myVideo.play();
                pauseButton.setLabel("Pause");
            }
        }
    }
}
```

2. Run the project.

   After creating the pause button, you attached an event listener to the button
   to listen for the MouseEvent.CLICK event type. The event callback function
   then asks if the video is paused or not. If it is not paused, the video pauses,
   and the button updates to say "Resume," indicating that the user can click
   it again to resume playback. Alternatively, if the video is paused, the video
   will then start playing from where it was stopped, and the button label is
   updated again.

REWIND AND SEEK

To change the location of the play head of the video, you need to perform what is
called seeking. Whether you are rewinding to the beginning, or wish to seek to a
specific point, you need to tell the FLVPlayback class where you need to go.

There are two methods that are helpful for seeking video. The first is the seek
method, which accepts a parameter asking for the time index of the video you
want in seconds. As an example, for rewind, you want to seek to 0 seconds. In
some cases, you want to seek to a proportional point in the video, say the middle.
For those cases there is the seekPercent method, which accepts a percentage
amount from 0 to 100.

1. Update the Document class with the following highlighted code to create two buttons: the first to rewind to the beginning and the second to seek to the middle of the video.

```
package  {
    import flash.display.MovieClip;
    import fl.video.FLVPlayback;
    import flash.events.MouseEvent;
    public class PlayFLV extends MovieClip {
        var myVideo:FLVPlayback;
        var playButton:VideoButton;
        var pauseButton:VideoButton;
        var rewindButton:VideoButton;
        var seekToMiddle:VideoButton;
        public function PlayFLV() {
            _setupVideo();
        }
        private function _setupVideo():void
        {
            myVideo = new FLVPlayback();
            myVideo.autoPlay = false;
            myVideo.x = myVideo.y = 10;
            addChild(myVideo);
            myVideo.source = "http://www.helpexamples.com/
              ⟶ flash/video/water.flv";
            playButton = new VideoButton("Play");
            playButton.x = 400;
            playButton.y = 50;
            addChild(playButton);
            pauseButton = new VideoButton("Pause");
```

```
            pauseButton.x = 400;

            pauseButton.y = 100;

            addChild(pauseButton);

            rewindButton = new VideoButton("Rewind");

            rewindButton.x = 400;

            rewindButton.y = 150;

            addChild(rewindButton);

            seekToMiddle = new VideoButton("50%");

            seekToMiddle.x = 400;

            seekToMiddle.y = 200;

            addChild(seekToMiddle);

            playButton.addEventListener
        →     (MouseEvent.CLICK, playVideo);

            pauseButton.addEventListener
        →     (MouseEvent.CLICK, pauseVideo);

            rewindButton.addEventListener
        →     (MouseEvent.CLICK, rewindVideo);

            seekToMiddle.addEventListener
        →     (MouseEvent.CLICK, seekVideo);

    }
    public function playVideo(e:MouseEvent):void
    {
        myVideo.play();
    }
    public function pauseVideo(e:MouseEvent):void
    {
        if (!myVideo.paused)
        {
            myVideo.pause();
            pauseButton.setLabel("Resume");
```

FIGURE 18.5 Rewind and seek buttons added to the project

```
            } else {
                myVideo.play();
                pauseButton.setLabel("Pause");

            }
        }
        public function rewindVideo(e:MouseEvent):void
        {
            myVideo.seek(0);
        }
        public function seekVideo(e:MouseEvent):void
        {
            myVideo.seekPercent(50);
        }
    }
}
```

These two new buttons and the event callback functions they trigger use the seek and seekPercent methods to control the location of the play head.

2. Run the project. Notice that seek will continue playback if the video was already playing (**Figure 18.5**).

Good job! As you can see, the `FLVPlayback` component offers a lot of capabilities for you to play back and control video. The example here is using a simple FLV file that is stored on a server. Flash video has the ability to stream from a server to optimize the playback experience if you have heavy video requirements in your project. For more information on streaming video vendors, Adobe provides a list of partners: www.adobe.com/products/flashmediaserver/fvss/.

WRAPPING **UP**

In this chapter, you learned how to work with external web media in your projects with ActionScript. Through the use of a few new methods and classes, you can add references to external assets that are downloaded from the web in your project.

Here are some helpful tips for working with external media using ActionScript:

- When working with external images or SWFs, use the ProLoader class to access them and display them in your project.

- Audio loaded from an external location uses the Sound class, and requires your project to explicitly play the content using the play method.

- The FLVPlayback component is the easiest way to work with external video in your project.

- To use the FLVPlayback component, remember to add it to your Library before attempting to work with it.

- When working with functions that toggle, like pausing a video, it is recommended to provide your user with indications about what the user controls will do.

PART 5

CREATING
MULTI-SCREEN
PROJECTS

19

DESKTOP **APPLICATIONS** WITH **ADOBE AIR**

Projects you create in Flash Professional CS5.5 and ActionScript 3.0 aren't limited to the browser. With the Adobe AIR runtime that users can install on their computers, you can make projects that users can run on Windows and Mac OS X as desktop applications.

This chapter will introduce you to some of the basics of Adobe AIR so you can explore this platform. In the next chapter, you'll go even further with AIR and learn how to make mobile applications for the iOS and Andorid mobile platforms.

GETTING **STARTED**

Adobe AIR is a runtime that you can install on Windows and Mac OS X operating systems. To get the Adobe AIR runtime, download it at http://get.adobe.com/air/. When installed, applications that are based on the runtime can be in installed easily from the web. Using AIR, you can also create native installers that don't require that the users install the runtime first. You can build native installers for Windows and Mac OS X. Native installers also allow AIR applications to access deeper levels within the operating system, but these capabilities are beyond the scope of this book.

Adobe updates AIR on a regular basis, adding new capabilities and deeper integration into the desktop operating system to give you more performance, power, and control over your applications.

Desktop applications have a number of different interactive controls compared with browser-based projects. The next section will introduce you to some of these controls and how to use them to build desktop applications using AIR.

Creating an AIR project is similar to creating a browser-based project. Follow these steps to create the project in Flash Professional CS5.5:

1. Select New form the File menu.

2. Select AIR as the type of project.

3. Click OK.

4. Save your project as **MyFirstAIRApp**.

    In **Figure 19.1**, you'll see that the project properties show that AIR 2.6 is the player that will run the project. If you already started a project as a regular ActionScript 3.0 browser-based project, you can switch to AIR by selecting it in the Player drop-down list as shown in Figure 19.1.

    You have more options available that you can set by accessing the AIR settings.

FIGURE 19.1 Publish properties for an AIR 2.6 application

FIGURE 19.2 AIR Settings Window

5. Click the wrench icon next to AIR 2.6 in the Properties panel.

    You'll see the AIR Settings window as shown in **Figure 19.2**.

    In this window, you can define a number of parameters. For this project, you will make some configuration updates here.

6. In the Description field, enter **This is my first Adobe AIR desktop application!**

    When the application is installed, users will see the message listed as the Description.

7. For the Window style, click the drop-down list and choose System Chrome.

    AIR lets you select if you want to use the native window controls, called chrome, for your application, or if you want to create your own custom chrome using Flash and ActionScript. When making your own chrome you have the option of creating an opaque application that will show the background of the project, or a transparent application that will remove that background. If you make a project where you create your own chrome, you will create it in Flash Professional and add controls for common window controls like resize, minimize, close, and so on.

8. Click OK.

9. Create a new ActionScript 3.0 class named **MyButton**.

10. Add the following code to your new class and save it with your FLA file:

```
package {
    import flash.display.MovieClip;
    public class MyButton extends MovieClip {
        public function MyButton(buttonColor:Number=0x000000,
            buttonW:Number=50,buttonH:Number=50) {
            graphics.beginFill(buttonColor);
            graphics.drawRect(0,0,buttonW,buttonH);
        }
    }
}
```

This is a (very) simple button created entirely with ActionScript. In the constructor, a color, width, and height are optionally accepted, and are then used to create a rectangle using the drawing API that "designs" the button.

Not amazing looking—but it will work for now. Off to the Document class.

11. Create a Document class for your project, and enter the following code:

```
package  {
    import flash.display.MovieClip;
    public class MyFirstAIRApp extends MovieClip {
        public function MyFirstAIRApp() {
            _init()
        }
        private function _init():void
        {
            //
        }
    }
}
```

Again, nothing new here—but now your project is all set and ready to go.

WORKING WITH DESKTOP EVENTS

The most obvious difference between browser and desktop projects are the window controls that are part of the application's chrome. When you are working with the native chrome, you don't need to worry about these controls as much. But if you want to design your own, then working with the window controls becomes pretty important.

MINIMIZE

Let's start with the minimize control. When you do a lot of work with AIR window controls or events, you'll be working with the nativeWindow property of the Stage. This special property is part of any AIR application, contains valuable information about the configuration of the window, and gives you the ability to control window behavior.

1. Modify the Document class with the following highlighted code to add a minimize action to the button:

```
package {
    import flash.display.MovieClip;
    import flash.events.MouseEvent;
    public class MyFirstAIRApp extends MovieClip {
        public var myMinButton:MyButton;
        public function MyFirstAIRApp() {
            _init()
        }
        private function _init():void
        {
            myMinButton = new MyButton();
            addChild(myMinButton);
            myMinButton.addEventListener
            ➞ (MouseEvent.CLICK, minWindow);
        }
        public function minWindow(e:MouseEvent):void
        {
```

```
                    stage.nativeWindow.minimize();
            }
        }
    }
```

2. Run the project, and click on the black square. You will see the window minimize to the task bar or dock. Clicking the minimized icon will restore the window.

You needed very little new ActionScript to use the minimize control. You created the button based on the MyButton class. You added an event listener that executed a callback function. The event callback was triggered when the MouseEvent.CLICK event was fired.

Inside the callback function, you accessed the nativeWindow property of the Stage object and executed the minimize method. That's really all it takes.

Pretty simple, don'tcha think?

MAXIMIZE

Maximize is similar to minimize, but it offers an interesting twist.

1. Modify the code with the following highlighted code:

```
package  {
    import flash.display.MovieClip;
    import flash.events.MouseEvent;
    public class MyFirstAIRApp extends MovieClip {
        public var myMinButton:MyButton;
        public var myMaxButton:MyButton;
        public function MyFirstAIRApp() {
            _init();
        }
        private function _init():void
        {
```

```
        myMinButton = new MyButton();
        addChild(myMinButton);

        myMaxButton = new MyButton(0xFF0000);
        myMaxButton.x = 75;
        addChild(myMaxButton);
        myMinButton.addEventListener
          (MouseEvent.CLICK, minWindow);
        myMaxButton.addEventListener
          (MouseEvent.CLICK, maxWindow);
    }
    public function minWindow(e:MouseEvent):void
    {
        stage.nativeWindow.minimize();
    }
    public function maxWindow(e:MouseEvent):void
    {
        stage.nativeWindow.maximize();
    }
  }
}
```

2. Run the project. You'll see a clickable red button.

3. Click the button. The window maximizes.

The issue that exists now is that the maximize and restore from maximize button is usually the same button. How do we know when the window is already maximized to switch the behavior?

Luckily for you, Adobe already thought of that.

They're so smart.

4. Update the code as shown to add restore behavior to the button:

```
package {
    import flash.display.MovieClip;
    import flash.events.MouseEvent;
    import flash.display.NativeWindowDisplayState;
    public class MyFirstAIRApp extends MovieClip {
        public var myMinButton:MyButton;
        public var myMaxButton:MyButton;
        public function MyFirstAIRApp() {
            _init();
        }
        private function _init():void
        {
            myMinButton = new MyButton();
            addChild(myMinButton);
            myMaxButton = new MyButton(0xFF0000);
            myMaxButton.x = 75;
            addChild(myMaxButton);
            myMinButton.addEventListener
                (MouseEvent.CLICK, minWindow);
            myMaxButton.addEventListener
                (MouseEvent.CLICK, maxWindow);
        }
        public function minWindow(e:MouseEvent):void
        {
            stage.nativeWindow.minimize();
        }
        public function maxWindow(e:MouseEvent):void
        {
```

```
            if (stage.nativeWindow.displayState ==
             ⇒ NativeWindowDisplayState.MAXIMIZED)
            {
                stage.nativeWindow.restore();
            } else {
                stage.nativeWindow.maximize();
            }
        }
    }
}
```

Using the displayState property, you can use a conditional to test the current state. The NativeWindowDisplayState (very succinct name, don't you think?) is a class that contains three properties: MAXIMIZED, MINIMIZED, or NORMAL. If the displayState is MAXIMIZED, then the window should be restored using the restore method. If it isn't, it needs to use the maximize method.

OK, that was too easy—time to do something a bit more challenging.

DRAG

When you use native system chrome, dragging the window around is easy. Users just click and drag the title bar around the screen. Without the chrome, users will need a way to move the window around the screen.

Using AIR, there is an API to do exactly that.

1. Update the project with the following highlighted code to add this new behavior—and heads up, it won't work the way you expect (I'll explain in a bit):

```
package {
    import flash.display.MovieClip;
    import flash.events.MouseEvent;
    import flash.display.NativeWindowDisplayState;
    public class MyFirstAIRApp extends MovieClip {
        public var myMinButton:MyButton;
```

```
public var myMaxButton:MyButton;
public var myDragButton:MyButton;
public function MyFirstAIRApp() {
    _init();
}
private function _init():void
{
    myMinButton = new MyButton();
    addChild(myMinButton);
    myMaxButton = new MyButton(0xFF0000);
    myMaxButton.x = 75;
    addChild(myMaxButton);
    myDragButton = new MyButton(0x00FF00);
    myDragButton.x = 150;
    addChild(myDragButton);
    myMinButton.addEventListener
        (MouseEvent.CLICK, minWindow);
    myMaxButton.addEventListener
        (MouseEvent.CLICK, maxWindow);
    myDragButton.addEventListener
        (MouseEvent.CLICK, dragWindow);
}
public function minWindow(e:MouseEvent):void
{
    stage.nativeWindow.minimize();
}
public function maxWindow(e:MouseEvent):void
{
```

```
        if (stage.nativeWindow.displayState ==
        →  NativeWindowDisplayState.MAXIMIZED)
        {
            stage.nativeWindow.restore();
        } else {
            stage.nativeWindow.maximize();
        }
    }
    public function dragWindow(e:MouseEvent):void
    {
        stage.nativeWindow.startMove();
    }
    }
}
```

In this new code, you added a new button, and then created a basic MouseEvent listener for the CLICK event. The handler for that listener activates the startMove method of the nativeWindow object, which should move the window.

2. Run the project.

It isn't working as you expected. Time for your troubleshooting hat. Think about what you are doing with the mouse when you are dragging the window.

That's right, you aren't clicking the mouse, you are pushing the mouse button down—which is the MOUSE_DOWN event type, not CLICK.

3. Update the event listener with the right event type:

```
myDragButton.addEventListener
    →  (MouseEvent.MOUSE_DOWN, dragWindow);
```

4. Run the project again; you'll be able to drag the window around.

CLOSE

The last basic window control is close. This exits out of the running application using the close method.

1. Update the project with the following highlighted code:

```
package  {
    import flash.display.MovieClip;
    import flash.events.MouseEvent;
    import flash.display.NativeWindowDisplayState;
    public class MyFirstAIRApp extends MovieClip {
        public var myMinButton:MyButton;
        public var myMaxButton:MyButton;
        public var myDragButton:MyButton;
        public var myCloseButton:MyButton;
        public function MyFirstAIRApp() {
            _init();
        }
        private function _init():void
        {
            myMinButton = new MyButton();
            addChild(myMinButton);
            myMaxButton = new MyButton(0xFF0000);
            myMaxButton.x = 75;
            addChild(myMaxButton);
            myDragButton = new MyButton(0x00FF00);
            myDragButton.x = 150;
            addChild(myDragButton);
            myCloseButton = new MyButton(0x0000FF);
            myCloseButton.x = 225;
```

```
        addChild(myCloseButton);

    myMinButton.addEventListener
        (MouseEvent.CLICK, minWindow);

    myMaxButton.addEventListener
        (MouseEvent.CLICK, maxWindow);

    myDragButton.addEventListener
        (MouseEvent.MOUSE_DOWN, dragWindow);

    myCloseButton.addEventListener
        (MouseEvent.CLICK, closeWindow);

}
public function minWindow(e:MouseEvent):void

{

    stage.nativeWindow.minimize();

}
public function maxWindow(e:MouseEvent):void

{

    if (stage.nativeWindow.displayState ==
        NativeWindowDisplayState.MAXIMIZED)

    {

        stage.nativeWindow.restore();

    } else {

        stage.nativeWindow.maximize();

    }

}
public function dragWindow(e:MouseEvent):void

{

    stage.nativeWindow.startMove();

}
public function closeWindow(e:MouseEvent):void
```

```
            {
                stage.nativeWindow.close();
            }
        }
    }
```

2. Run the project.

3. Click the blue close button that you just created. You will see your AIR application quit.

Pretty easy stuff—the next section gets a little more crazy.

RESIZE

If you have played with the window you have created, you'll notice that the window can resize, and the contents of the window scale and get larger with it. Sometimes this is a desirable behavior, but often you don't want the control to work that way.

Window resizing is very application specific, and you'll need to decide which type of resizing is appropriate for your application. For this example, you'll update the application to allow the user to resize the window, but constrain the buttons to different sides of the window, which will change their location as you resize the window.

Using ActionScript, you can define the mode of scaling you want the application to use. You control this using the scaleMode property of the Stage. By default, the scaleMode property is set to StageScaleMode.EXACT_FIT. If you want the Stage to get bigger with the window, you'll need to change the scaleMode property setting. You also need to tell the Stage where to scale from. By default, it scales somewhat from the center of the window. To get the right effect, the Stage needs to align to the upper-left corner of the window, which is done setting the align property of the stage object to TOP_LEFT.

The other piece to this puzzle is to listen to when the window resizes and reposition the objects on the screen as needed. Let's not tackle that quite yet—but let's get the rest of the items mentioned in place.

To help manage the code a little better, you are going to refactor some portions of it as well.

1. Update the project with the following highlighted code:

```
package  {
    import flash.display.MovieClip;
    import flash.events.MouseEvent;
    import flash.display.NativeWindowDisplayState;
    import flash.display.StageScaleMode;
    import flash.display.StageAlign;
    import flash.events.Event;
    public class MyFirstAIRApp extends MovieClip {
        public var myMinButton:MyButton;
        public var myMaxButton:MyButton;
        public var myDragButton:MyButton;
        public var myCloseButton:MyButton;
        public function MyFirstAIRApp() {
            _init();
        }
        private function _init():void
        {
            _configureWindow();
            _setupObjects();
        }
        private function _configureWindow():void
        {
            stage.scaleMode = StageScaleMode.NO_SCALE;
            stage.align = StageAlign.TOP_LEFT;
        }
        private function _setupObjects():void
        {
```

```
            myMinButton = new MyButton();

            myMaxButton = new MyButton(0xFF0000);

            myDragButton = new MyButton(0x00FF00);

            myCloseButton = new MyButton(0x0000FF);

            _positionControls();

            addChild(myMinButton);

            addChild(myMaxButton);

            addChild(myDragButton);

            addChild(myCloseButton);

            myMinButton.addEventListener
              → (MouseEvent.CLICK, minWindow);

            myMaxButton.addEventListener
              → (MouseEvent.CLICK, maxWindow);

            myDragButton.addEventListener
              → (MouseEvent.MOUSE_DOWN, dragWindow);

            myCloseButton.addEventListener
              → (MouseEvent.CLICK, closeWindow);

            stage.addEventListener
              → (Event.RESIZE, handleResize);

        }

        private function _positionControls():void

        {


        }

        public function minWindow(e:MouseEvent):void

        {

            stage.nativeWindow.minimize();

        }

        public function maxWindow(e:MouseEvent):void
```

```
        {
            if (stage.nativeWindow.displayState ==
            →   NativeWindowDisplayState.MAXIMIZED)
            {
                stage.nativeWindow.restore();
            } else {
                stage.nativeWindow.maximize();
            }
        }
        public function dragWindow(e:MouseEvent):void
        {
            stage.nativeWindow.startMove();
        }
        public function closeWindow(e:MouseEvent):void
        {
            stage.nativeWindow.close();
        }
        public function handleResize(e:Event):void
        {
            _positionControls();
        }
    }
}
```

The new _configureWindow method defines the scale mode of the window and specifies where the Stage will align with the outer container, in this case, the native window.

2. Run the project. You'll see that the window, when resized, doesn't scale up the contents within it, and the position of the items stay in the same place.

OK, back in the code, in addition to creating the new _configureWindow method, you refactored the _init method and broke that out into separate private methods. The first change was to move the button creation to _setupObjects. Within this method, you removed the positioning of the objects, but created a reference to a new, but empty, _positionControls method.

After the event handlers for the buttons, you also created a new event listener for the Stage. This event is listening for the generic Event.RESIZE event, which is broadcast anytime the Stage is resized. The callback method for this executes the empty _positionControls method.

Whew! Quite a few changes, but with the help of your friend arithmetic, you can create a layout for your buttons that will update as the window resizes.

CREATING A RESIZABLE LAYOUT

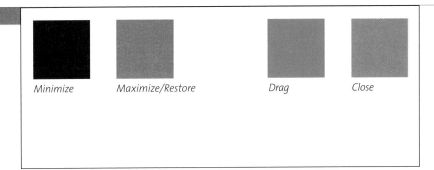

FIGURE 19.3 Diagram of button layout

FIGURE 19.4 Position of minimize button

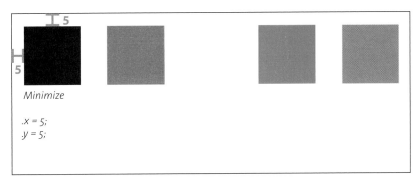

Let's start with a diagram of the button layout to discover how this will work (**Figure 19.3**).

The four buttons are divided into two groups. The left group will have the black and red buttons appear "stuck" to the left edge of the window. The right two buttons will be "stuck" to the right edge of the window. Between the two buttons in each group is a 25-pixel gap. There is a 5-pixel gap from the top of the window, and 5 pixels between the left and right edges to the left-most and right-most buttons.

Now, you need to define the locations of each button. When you do this with ActionScript, you'll use a combination of the location and widths of the buttons to calculate the location of the buttons. Before you create the code, it is always a good idea to sketch on paper exactly how this will work. So, let's do that now.

The first button is easy, the location of the minimize button (**Figure 19.4**) can be determined through simple x and y property values because it needs to be positioned 5 pixels from the top and 5 pixels from the left. Since the StageAlign property was set to TOP_LEFT, you can do this with no problems.

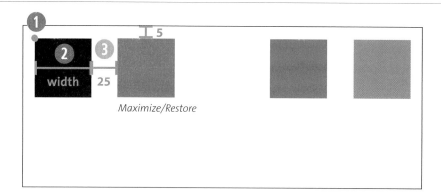

Maximize/Restore

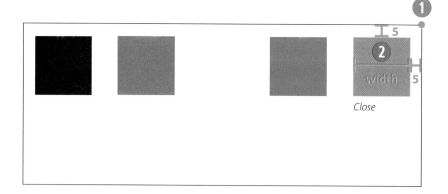

Close

Let's look at the maximize button next. Although you could specifically define the location of the button using the x and y properties, you can also position it relative to the location of the minimize button, which is what is shown in **Figure 19.5**.

You can calculate the maximize button's location using a few factors. You can calculate the location of the x property by taking the location of the first button ❶, adding the width of the button using its `width` property ❷, and then adding 25 ❸, which is the fixed button spacing distance. By adding these together, you can determine the location of the button on the x coordinate. The y coordinate is the same as before, 5, another fixed distance.

With the right side finished, it is time to move to the other group of buttons. Starting from the outside and moving inward, defining the close button is next (**Figure 19.6**).

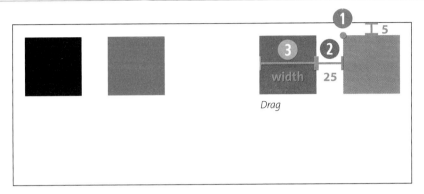

FIGURE 19.7 Layout of the drag button

You want to position this group of buttons relative to the right side of the Stage. When the user resizes the window, it will adjust the width of the Stage, and you can use the Stage width to determine the various objects that will be positioned along its edge.

You can position the close button in this way. First, you calculate the width of the entire Stage using the width property of the stage object ❶, then subtract the width of the button, which gives you the correct point. Again, the y property is the same as the other buttons, 5.

Finally, you must position the drag button, which is the most complex of all (**Figure 19.7**).

Like the maximize button, you want to position the drag button relative to the button that is outside of it. You need to take the x coordinate of the close button, and subtract the 25-pixel space that is used for spacing of the buttons, and then subtract the width of the drag button itself. Again, the y property is the same as the others, 5 pixels.

Great! With this layout sketched out, you can start creating the ActionScript to make the layout rules work. Before you do that though, there are a couple of things to point out.

In this exercise, you established two constant values. The first is the padding around the group of buttons on the top, left, and right edge of the buttons. This is 5 pixels. The second constant value is the space between the buttons. In ActionScript, there is a special variable type called a constant that you can use to store values that don't change. To create these, you'll use the const statement in place of var to establish these values. To differentiate constant value names from variables, the best practice is to name them in all caps.

1. Update the project with the following highlighted code:

```
package  {
    import flash.display.MovieClip;
    import flash.events.MouseEvent;
    import flash.display.NativeWindowDisplayState;
    import flash.display.StageScaleMode;
    import flash.display.StageAlign;
    import flash.events.Event;
    public class MyFirstAIRApp extends MovieClip {
        public var myMinButton:MyButton;
        public var myMaxButton:MyButton;
        public var myDragButton:MyButton;
        public var myCloseButton:MyButton;
        public const BUTTONPADDING:uint = 5;
        public const BUTTONSPACING:uint = 25;
        public function MyFirstAIRApp() {
            _init();
        }
        private function _init():void
        {
            _configureWindow();
            _setupObjects();
        }
        private function _configureWindow():void
        {
            stage.scaleMode = StageScaleMode.NO_SCALE;
            stage.align = StageAlign.TOP_LEFT;
        }
```

```
private function _setupObjects():void
{
    myMinButton = new MyButton();
    myMaxButton = new MyButton(0xFF0000);
    myDragButton = new MyButton(0x00FF00);
    myCloseButton = new MyButton(0x0000FF);
    _positionControls();
    addChild(myMinButton);
    addChild(myMaxButton);
    addChild(myDragButton);
    addChild(myCloseButton);
    myMinButton.addEventListener
      ➝ (MouseEvent.CLICK, minWindow);
    myMaxButton.addEventListener
      ➝ (MouseEvent.CLICK, maxWindow);
    myDragButton.addEventListener
      ➝ (MouseEvent.MOUSE_DOWN, dragWindow);
    myCloseButton.addEventListener
      ➝ (MouseEvent.CLICK, closeWindow);
    stage.addEventListener
      ➝ (Event.RESIZE, handleResize);
}
private function _positionControls():void
{
    myMinButton.x = BUTTONPADDING;
    myMaxButton.x = myMinButton.x +
      ➝ myMinButton.width + BUTTONSPACING;
    myCloseButton.x = stage.stageWidth -
      ➝ myCloseButton.width - BUTTONPADDING;
```

```
            myDragButton.x = myCloseButton.x -
            ➡ myDragButton.width - BUTTONSPACING;


        myMinButton.y = myMaxButton.y = myCloseButton.y =
        ➡ myDragButton.y = BUTTONPADDING;
    }
    public function minWindow(e:MouseEvent):void
    {
        stage.nativeWindow.minimize();
    }
    public function maxWindow(e:MouseEvent):void
    {
        if (stage.nativeWindow.displayState ==
        ➡ NativeWindowDisplayState.MAXIMIZED)
        {
            stage.nativeWindow.restore();
        } else {
            stage.nativeWindow.maximize();
        }
    }
    public function dragWindow(e:MouseEvent):void
    {
        stage.nativeWindow.startMove();
    }
    public function closeWindow(e:MouseEvent):void
    {
        stage.nativeWindow.close();
```

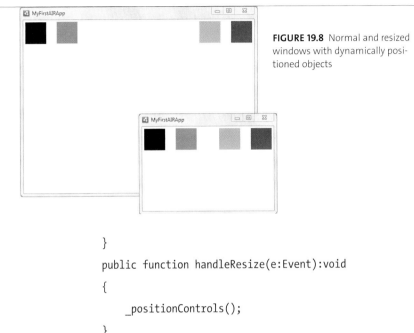

FIGURE 19.8 Normal and resized windows with dynamically positioned objects

```
        }
        public function handleResize(e:Event):void
        {
            _positionControls();
        }
    }
}
```

The constants are defined in the top of the class definition and are immediately assigned values. If you attempt to change the values of these constants later in the project, you'll get an error in Flash Professional:

`1049: Illegal assignment to a variable specified as constant.`

In the _positionControls method, you created the rules for the layout of the buttons, defining the location of the x and y properties based on the objects or properties of other objects and the Stage. Spacing values were then defined using the constants at the top of the class.

2. Run the project.

You can resize the window and see the buttons on the right stay "stuck" to the edge. The event listener that listens for when the Stage resizes executes the _positionControls method and repositions the buttons based on the new Stage size (**Figure 19.8**).

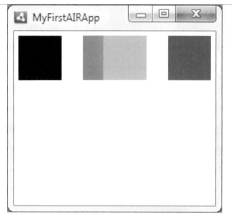

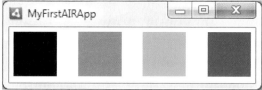

FIGURE 19.9 Resizing the window too small

FIGURE 19.10 Resizing the window to the minimum size

There is one final thing you need to learn about resizing, and that is to establish the minimum size of the window. If you resize the window too small, the buttons will start to overlap (**Figure 19.9**).

You need to define the minimum window size of the project. You can define this in the AIR Settings dialog box.

3. Open or select the tab for the project FLA.

4. Select AIR 2.6 Settings from the File menu.

5. Open the Advanced tab.

   In this panel, you can define the minimum and maximum window size of the project.

6. Set the Minimum width to **300**.

7. Set the Minimum height to **100**.

8. Save and run the project again.

   Now when you attempt to resize the window, the window will prevent resizing below the defined minimum width and height (**Figure 19.10**).

With a little planning, creating a resizable layout is not extremely complicated—just remember to sketch your layout and resizing rules ahead of time. It will save you a lot of time and aggravation.

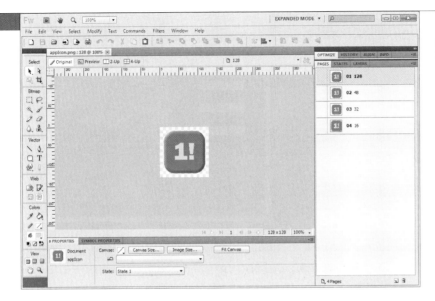

FIGURE 19.11 Creating an icon in Adobe Fireworks

When you have finished your Adobe AIR project, you need to configure and build it for testing and eventually to release to your users. The AIR Settings window handles most of the configuration options for you.

ICONS

When you build your project, you can give your application a custom icon that displays in the task bar or dock of the operating system and other areas where the icon is displayed.

For desktop AIR applications, there are four icon sizes that you need to create. Using a product like Adobe Fireworks, you can create an icon design (**Figure 19.11**).

In Fireworks, you can create multiple pages that represent the icon at various sizes. Adobe AIR requires that you provide graphic files for the following icon sizes:

- 128x128

- 48x48

- 32x32

- 16x16

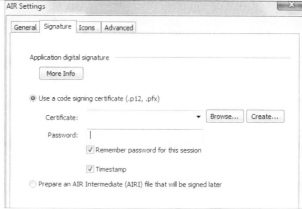

FIGURE 19.12 Setting icons in the AIR Settings window

FIGURE 19.13 Certificate Signature Settings window

Using Fireworks, you can create unique document sizes for individual pages in the design, and then export these as unique graphics for use in your AIR project. For more information on Fireworks, visit the Adobe Fireworks web page at www.adobe.com/go/fireworks.

To associate these graphics with the application icons, use the AIR Settings window. In the Icons tab, you can select the files you want to have for each of the sizes (**Figure 19.12**).

With these icons created and associated with the project, when it is published, it will display these icons when you see the application in the Applications folder in Mac OS X, or the Start Menu in Windows.

CERTIFICATE

To ensure your application is being installed from a trusted source, AIR applications require a signature to protect the security of the application user. While creating an app, you can create what is known as a *self-signed certificate* that you can use to test and install the application on your own machine.

To create the self-signed certificate, you can use the AIR Settings window (helpful little window, isn't it?).

1. Open the AIR Settings window for the FLA project (**Figure 19.13**).

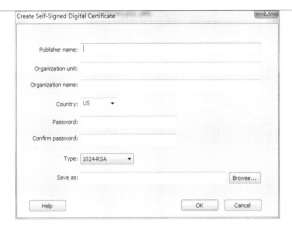

Create Self-Signed Digital Certificate

Publisher name:

Organization unit:

Organization name:

Country: US

Password:

Confirm password:

Type: 1024-RSA

Save as: Browse...

Help   OK   Cancel

FIGURE 19.14 Self-Signed Certificate window

2. Click Create, the Create Self-Signed Digital Certificate window will appear (**Figure 19.14**).

3. Enter your name as the Publisher name.

4. Enter your name (or your company name if you wish) as Organization unit.

5. Enter your name (or your company name if you wish) as Organization name.

6. Enter a password.

7. Reenter the password in Confirm password.

8. Enter **MyFirstAIRApp** in the Save as field, and click Browse to save it to the same directory as your FLA project.

9. Click OK.

   The certificate file will be populated in the Certificate field.

10. Enter the password for the certificate you just created in the Password field.

11. Select the Remember password for this session [check box?]. This will alleviate you from entering the password each time you try to publish the project during your session in Flash Professional.

12. Click OK.

   The project is now configured with a self-signed certificate that you can use to publish and test the application.

FIGURE 19.15 Publishing the project as an Adobe AIR application

FIGURE 19.16 The AIR application installer

FIGURE 19.15 Publishing the project as an Adobe AIR application

FIGURE 19.16 The AIR application installer

When you need to create a public version of your application that you distribute to others, you can purchase a commercial code-signing certificate from a vendor, such as VeriSign from Symantec. For more information, see www.verisign.com/code-signing/adobe-air/index.html.

If you are releasing the application internally, you can use the self-signed certificate. When the user attempts to install it, AIR will notify them that it may not be secure since it doesn't have a commercial certificate—(this can be acceptable in some situations, but all applications that are released publicly should have a commercial certificate).

PUBLISH AND INSTALL

With the certificate signed, it is time to publish the project.

1. Select Publish from the File menu, you will see the confirmation message display **Figure 19.15**.

   If you look at the location of your FLA, you'll see a couple new files. The first is MyFirstAIRApp.air. This is the file that will install your AIR application. The second is MyFirstAIRApp-app.xml, this is a configuration file containing setup and configuration information. The XML file contents are beyond the scope of this book.

2. To install the application, double click the MyFirstAIRApp.air file.

   You'll see an installer display and prompt you to begin the installation of the application on your computer (**Figure 19.16**).

FIGURE 19.17 AIR application installer options

As you can see, since you are using a self-signed certificate, the installer warns the user that they are installing an application from an unknown publisher, with unrestricted access to the system, potentially putting their system at risk. When you use a commercial certificate, the icons will appear as green and will give the user more confidence about the security level of the application.

For you as an app creator though, the self-signed certificate is an easy way to test your application as an installed application on your computer.

3. Click the Install button.

   The installer displays the install options for the application (**Figure 19.17**).

   You can opt to change the installation preferences here or change the installation location if you wish. If your system doesn't have the AIR runtime installed, it will be downloaded from Adobe before it installs the application.

MORE ABOUT PUBLISHING AIR APPLICATIONS

Publishing AIR applications offers a lot of configuration and publishing options for you as an application creator. The book *Flash Platform from Start to Finish* is a great resource on the overall build and release workflow for publishing AIR applications using the Flash Platform.

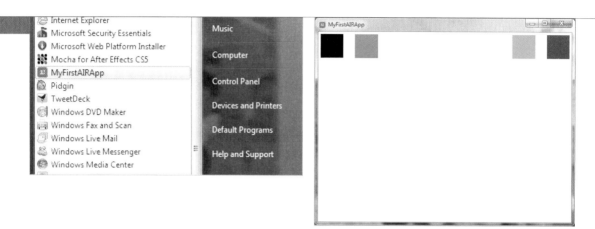

FIGURE 19.18 Your application in the Start Menu in Windows 7

FIGURE 19.19 The installed application running, with custom icon in Windows 7

4. Click Continue.

You'll see some progress indicators showing the installation process. When the install finishes, the application will launch, and you'll now see it in the Start Menu or Applications folder in your operating system (**Figure 19.18** and **Figure 19.19**).

Congratulations! You have created your first AIR application using Flash Professional CS5.5 and are on your way to creating desktop applications for Windows and Mac OS X operating systems, all with the skills you have learned in ActionScript. Great job!

WRAPPING **UP**

In this chapter, you learned the basics of creating desktop applications using Flash Professional CS5.5 and the Adobe AIR runtime. Creating cross-platform applications using tools and languages you already know is one of the biggest advantages to working with Flash. This chapter only scratched the surface of the power of AIR. You can find additional information on Adobe's website at www.adobe.com/go/air.

Here are some tips to help you work with Flash Professional, ActionScript, and the AIR runtime:

- To create an AIR project, remember to define the publishing options correctly and either select AIR as your project type when you start the project, or switch the Player type in the project Properties panel to AIR 2.6.

- AIR applications can use the native operating system chrome, or you can create your own custom chrome by modifying the AIR Settings for the project.

- When creating desktop applications, consider the different types of interactions that come along with desktop apps. The AIR API gives you control over some of these interactions to work with the window controls and to manage resizing.

- When resizing your application, remember to configure your application window properly to get the right effect when the user resizes the app.

- To create a resizable layout that will adapt to various window sizes, draft on paper or sketch the layout rules you want to add to your application before you jump into creating code.

- Create event listeners for the resize event to capture when the window size changes, and then reposition the objects in your project based on your layout rules.

- Configure your project with icons and a certificate before publishing your project.

- When publishing your project for general use, acquire a commercial certificate to reassure your users that your application is secure and their systems are protected.

20

MOBILE
APPLICATIONS
WITH **ADOBE AIR**

In this final chapter, you'll learn one of the biggest advantages of the Adobe Flash Platform— the ability to take all of your skills in Flash and ActionScript and create cross-platform mobile applications for a growing set of mobile handsets, tablets, and other screens. Using the Adobe AIR runtime, you can create applications for the popular iOS and Android operating systems, targeting the iPhone and iPad from Apple, or the dozens of Android 2.2 (Froyo) and later handsets, and Android 3.x (Honeycomb) and later tablets.

This chapter will cover some of the more common user interactions for mobile applications, and give an overview on how to provision and test an application on a device tethered to your computer.

GETTING **STARTED**

As of the writing of this book, there are two mobile app platforms that are supported out-of-the-box. The first is the iOS platform that is used by the iPhone, iPod touch, and iPad devices from Apple. Using Flash Professional CS5.5, you can create applications for these devices, which convert your project into an Apple Device Application file (.IPA) that can be uploaded to the iTunes app store to sell and distribute to users.

The second platform is the Google Android platform, which is used by a number of handset and tablet manufacturers including HTC, Dell, Samsung, Motorola, and many others. For this platform, Flash Professional CS5.5 projects are converted into Android Package file (.APK) applications that run on devices with version 2.2 or later of the Android operating system.

The main difference between the two platforms is the way that the AIR runtime works. For iOS, the AIR runtime is part of the IPA or application file, resulting in a larger download footprint for the application. For Android, the AIR runtime is installed alongside the application, reducing the file size of the application.

Adobe is working to bring Flash Professional CS5.5 projects to other platforms, including RIM for their new line of handhelds and tablets. As of this writing, the RIM platform is not part of Flash Professional CS5.5; however, check Adobe's website for more information on availability.

The gestures and other app-creation techniques in this chapter will work for both platforms; however, configuring your testing devices is unique for iOS and Android. The next section will cover how to get your devices set up for you to use with this chapter.

SETTING UP YOUR TESTING DEVICES

To get the best testing experience for your projects, it is best to invest in actual hardware for your own personal "testing lab." In my environment (**Figure 20.1**), I have the following devices:

- Samsung Captivate, Android 2.2 (Phone)

- Dell Streak 7, Android 2.2 (Tablet)

- Motorola Droid X, Android 2.2 (Phone)

- Nexus One, Android 2.3 (Phone)

- iPod touch, iOS (Phone)

- iPad, iOS (Tablet)

It is important to have a cross section of devices on which to test your content, including devices that might be a little slower than the current new available models. If you want to test the performance of your application, you need to consider the newer phones that are available today, as well as the phones that are already in customers' hands. Remember, most cell or data contracts are for two years, meaning that customers cannot upgrade to newer models without incurring additional fees or early upgrade charges.

You can use emulators for some testing; however, they can be misleading since you are not using the genuine gestures with the physical hardware, and the emulators cannot accommodate for performance limitations that come with some older hardware models. In this chapter, you'll learn how to test on tethered physical devices. For more information on how to work with emulators, refer to the mobile operating system software development kit.

Configuring your devices for first-time use requires a number of steps for both Android and iOS-based devices. For help on how to configure these devices, the appendix for this book contains information available at the time of the publication of this book. For the latest information, please visit these links:

- Publishing AIR for Android applications:
  http://help.adobe.com/en_US/flash/cs/using/
  WSb03e830bd6f770ee317e94381294c702634-8000.html

- Packaging applications for AIR for iOS:
  http://help.adobe.com/en_US/flash/cs/using/
  WSb03e830bd6f770ee-29e1e072124c0d552aa-8000.html

When you have your devices configured, it is a good idea to build a test application to make sure that everything is up and running correctly. You'll do that in the next section.

CREATING A MOBILE PROJECT

Just as with AIR desktop applications, there is a unique project type when working with iOS and Android devices. To verify that everything is up and running correctly on your system, it is best to create a simple project when you first test your devices to verify that everything works.

YOUR FIRST ANDROID APPLICATION

All Android targeted AIR applications are created the same way, so let's create one now.

1. Open Flash Professional CS5.5.

2. Select New from the File menu.

3. Select AIR for Android from the Type column.

    The default size for an Android project is the same resolution as a Nexus One and other similar devices. You can create specific layouts for various screen sizes, scale a project across screens, or create an adaptive layout based on layout and positioning rules, similarly to what you did in the previous chapter.

4. Click OK.

5. Save your project as **testAndroid.fla**.

6. Draw some shapes on the Stage with the drawing tool.

7. Save and run (not publish) the project. You should see the project run.

    When you run a project, Flash Professional uses AIR to preview the application on your computer. You can use this for quick verification of the application before you test it on an actual device.

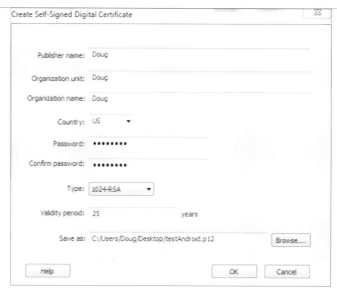

FIGURE 20.2 AIR for Android
Settings window

FIGURE 20.3 A completed self-
signed certificate form

8. From the File menu, select AIR for Android Settings.

   This panel (**Figure 20.2**) allows you to configure your application for deployment onto an Android device.

9. Select the Deployment tab.

10. In the Certificate row in the dialog box, click Create.

    This will be identical to what you did in the previous chapter to create a
    self-signed certificate that you can use with your application.

11. Enter your name (or company name) for Publisher name, Organization unit,
    and Organization name.

12. Enter a password and re-enter it in the Confirm password field in the dialog box.

13. Select a location to save the certificate by clicking Browse.

    You should have a form that looks similar to **Figure 20.3**.

14. Click OK.

15. Enter the password for the certificate if it is empty.

16. Select the Remember password for this session check box. This will alleviate you from having to enter the password for your certificate each time you publish your application during a session.

17. Make sure that "Install application on the connected Android device" and "Launch application on the connected Android device" check boxes are selected.

18. Click OK.

19. From the File menu, select Publish.

    If you don't have AIR already installed on your device, the phone will prompt you to install (**Figure 20.4**). If you need to download and install AIR, you can find the application in the Applications drawer on your device (**Figure 20.5**).

20. Click Install.

    If AIR is already installed, your application will launch automatically.

21. If the application didn't start automatically, locate it in the list of applications and run it.

    You'll see that the application runs and displays your lovely artwork on your device (**Figure 20.6**).

FIGURE 20.4 A notification to install AIR

FIGURE 20.5 The installed application ready to launch

FIGURE 20.6 Your app, in all of its glory

There you go. You have created your first Android application using Flash Professional CS5.5 and Adobe AIR.

YOUR FIRST IOS APPLICATION

Now that your provisioning is all finished, creating and building an iOS app is much easier from this point on.

1. Open Flash Professional CS5.5.

2. Select New from the File menu.

3. Select AIR for iOS from the Type column.

    You have three main resolutions available for iOS as of the writing of this book:

    - iPhone 3GS: 320x480

    - iPhone 4 and current model iPod touch: 640x960

    - iPad and iPad 2: 768x1024 (Portrait Mode)

4. Pick a resolution that is right for your target device.

5. Click OK.

6. Save your project as **myTestApp.fla**.

    Remember that app ID you worked with before? It is best practice to replicate that as your project filename as well.

7. Draw some shapes on the Stage with the drawing tool.

8. Save and run (not publish) the project. You should see the project run.

    Just as with Android, you can preview your apps before going to the physical hardware using AIR.

9. From the File menu, choose AIR for iOS settings.

10. Select the Deployment tab.

    Unlike Android, you don't create a self-signed certificate. Instead, you'll use the .p12 file you exported from Keychain Access to populate the Certificate field.

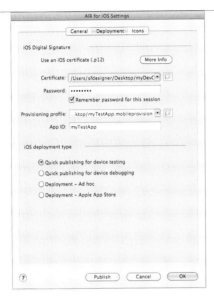

FIGURE 20.7 iOS Deployment Settings

11. Click the folder icon beside the Certificate field and navigate to and select your .p12 certificate file.

12. Enter the password for the certificate.

13. Select the "Remember password for this session" check box.

    Remember that provisioning profile you downloaded earlier? Here is where you'll need that.

14. Click the folder icon beside the Provisioning profile field and navigate to and select your provisioning profile for this application.

15. Select Quick publishing for device testing in the iOS deployment type section.

    Your window should look something similar to **Figure 20.7**.

16. Click OK.

17. From the File menu, select Publish.

    The publish process will create an IPA file for you to use to install on the physical device. The process for publishing on iOS takes a bit longer than Android, but should be finished within 15 seconds or so.

FIGURE 20.8 iTunes listing the new application for the target device

18. Locate the IPA file on your computer.

19. Double-click the IPA file to launch iTunes.

20. Select the Apps tab of your device; you should see the application listed (**Figure 20.8**).

21. Sync your device with iTunes.

22. Find the application on your device and run it.

Just like with Android, you'll see the application launch and display your awesome design handiwork (**Figure 20.9**).

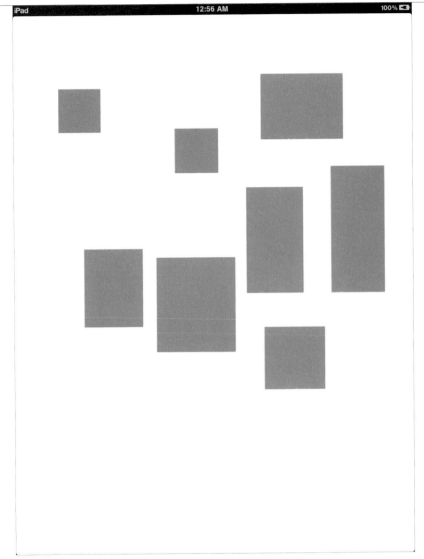

FIGURE 20.9 Your first app using Flash Professional CS5.5 and iOS.

ADOBE AIR 2.7 AND IOS MOBILE DEVELOPMENT (ADVANCED)

At the time of publication, Adobe AIR 2.7 was still in development and was not available when Flash Professional CS5.5 shipped. AIR 2.7 includes dramatic performance improvements for applications deployed onto iOS devices—near native speed improvements.

Since AIR 2.7 is shipping after Flash Professional CS5.5, to update to the new version of AIR, you need to manually update Flash Professional CS5.5. These instructions require that you make changes to your Flash Professional CS5.5 installation, so be sure to back up your system in case you have any issues:

- Browse to C:\Program Files\Adobe\Adobe Flash CS5.5 (Win) or Applications/Adobe Flash CS5.5/ (Mac) and locate the AIR2.6 folder.

- Change the folder name AIR2.6 to **AIR2.6OLD** or delete it if you don't need to save a copy of it.

- Download the latest AIR SDK from www.adobe.com/products/air/sdk, rename the folder **AIR2.6**, and place it in the Adobe Flash CS5.5 folder.

- Browse to AIR2.6/frameworks/libs/air folder in the Adobe Flash CS5.5 folder and copy airglobal.swc.

- Paste airglobal.swc in Adobe Flash CS5.5/Common/Configuration/ActionScript 3.0/AIR2.6 to replace the existing airglobal.swc.

You will now be working with the AIR 2.7 version of the runtime and as a result will get the benefits of the new optimizations made for iOS and Android platforms.

For more information on AIR 2.7 visit Adobe's website at www.adobe.com/products/air.

CREATING INTERACTIONS
FOR DEVICES

Users work with applications on handheld devices very differently than they work with applications on workstations. There is no mouse—the user's finger, through touch gestures, is what drives most interaction with mobile applications. Because of this, the AIR mobile API includes standardized behaviors for common multi-touch gestures that you'll use in your application.

For simplicity, the rest of this chapter will focus on Android applications. The same methods used in Android applications will work equally as well in iOS apps. Screenshots of the same applications will be shown, but the instructions will focus on Android applications.

TIP, TAP—BASIC TOUCH INTERACTIONS

The most basic interaction for touch gestures is the tap. Tap is similar to a mouse click, but devices broadcast a unique event type for a tap as opposed to a mouse click.

To get started, you need to create a new application to experiment with:

1. Create a new AIR for Andorid (or iOS) application in Flash Professional CS5.5.

2. Save the project as **TouchGestures.fla**.

3. Open the AIR for Andorid settings, and open the Permissions tab.

4. Select the INTERNET option.

   You don't need to enable this for all projects; however, you'll get a warning when you try to publish without this selected. Selecting the INTERNET option will avoid the warning.

5. Create a new ActionScript 3.0 class named **TouchButton**.

6. Enter the following code for the TouchButton class:

```
package {
    import flash.display.Sprite;
    public class TouchButton extends Sprite {
        public function TouchButton() {
            drawNewShape();
        }
        public function drawNewShape():void
```

```
        {
            graphics.beginFill(Math.random()*0xFFFFFF);
            graphics.drawRect(0,0,250,250);
            graphics.endFill();
        }
    }
}
```

This code creates a public method that you can use to change the color of the button when you detect a tap interaction. You now need to create an instance of the button and then add the event listener to listen for the user's tap.

7. Create a matching Document class for the project and enter the following code:

```
package   {
    import flash.display.MovieClip;
    import flash.events.TouchEvent;
    import flash.ui.Multitouch;
    import flash.ui.MultitouchInputMode;
    public class TouchGestures extends MovieClip {
        public var myTouchButton:TouchButton;
        public function TouchGestures() {
            myTouchButton = new TouchButton();
            myTouchButton.x = myTouchButton.y = 25;
            addChild(myTouchButton);
            Multitouch.inputMode =
              MultitouchInputMode.TOUCH_POINT;
            myTouchButton.addEventListener
              (TouchEvent.TOUCH_TAP, changeButton);
        }
        public function changeButton(e:TouchEvent):void
        {
```

```
                myTouchButton.drawNewShape();
            }
        }
    }
```

8. Make sure your phone is attached and publish your application (or if using iOS, publish and then use iTunes to sync the application to your device).

9. Run the application on your phone.

You'll find that when you touch the square that appears it will change color. The device is detecting the tap event and the project is broadcasting that tap event, executing the event handler that then draws a new rectangle on the screen.

Returning to the Document class, there are a few things to point out. First, you added a line that altered the `Multitouch.inputMode` property. When working with touch events, there are two modes that you can work with. The first is the `TOUCH_POINT` mode, which is used for basic touch events, like taps. The second is the `GESTURE` mode. When using this mode, you can create more advanced gesture-based interactions, and simple taps are mapped to the common mouse events.

Let's refactor this project using `GESTURE` mode.

10. Update the Document class with the following highlighted code:

```
package  {
    import flash.display.MovieClip;
    import flash.events.MouseEvent;
    import flash.ui.Multitouch;
    import flash.ui.MultitouchInputMode;
    public class TouchGestures extends MovieClip {
        public var myTouchButton:TouchButton;
        public function TouchGestures() {
            myTouchButton = new TouchButton();
```

```
            myTouchButton.x = myTouchButton.y = 25;

            addChild(myTouchButton);

            Multitouch.inputMode =
              MultitouchInputMode.GESTURE;

            myTouchButton.addEventListener
              (MouseEvent.CLICK, changeButton);

        }

        public function changeButton(e:MouseEvent):void

        {

            myTouchButton.drawNewShape();

        }

    }

}
```

When you publish the project again, the same effect will work, but this time your project is working with basic mouse events instead of tap events. Depending on your project, if you need more advanced gestures, you'll need to register tap events using this method.

Before moving to the gesture-based events, there is more that you can accomplish with the TOUCH_INPUT type—specifically, touch and drag.

SIMPLE DRAGGING WITH TOUCH

Using the TOUCH_INPUT interaction type, you can create basic drag and drop functionality in your application. You first need to define the event for starting the touch-based drag and another for the drop.

1. Update the Document class code as highlighted below, note that the Multitouch input mode has been returned to the TOUCH_INPUT type:

```
package  {

    import flash.display.MovieClip;

    import flash.events.TouchEvent;

    import flash.ui.Multitouch;

    import flash.ui.MultitouchInputMode;
```

```
public class TouchGestures extends MovieClip {
    public var myTouchButton:TouchButton;
    public function TouchGestures() {
        myTouchButton = new TouchButton();
        myTouchButton.x = myTouchButton.y = 25;
        addChild(myTouchButton);
        Multitouch.inputMode =
          MultitouchInputMode.TOUCH_POINT;
        myTouchButton.addEventListener
          (TouchEvent.TOUCH_TAP, changeButton);
myTouchButton.addEventListener
  (TouchEvent.TOUCH_BEGIN, touchDrag)
        myTouchButton.addEventListener
          (TouchEvent.TOUCH_END, touchDrop)
    }
    public function changeButton(e:TouchEvent):void
    {
        myTouchButton.drawNewShape();
    }
    public function touchDrag(e:TouchEvent):void
    {
        e.target.startTouchDrag(e.touchPointID);
    }
    public function touchDrop(e:TouchEvent):void
    {
        e.target.stopTouchDrag(e.touchPointID);
    }
}
}
```

FIGURE 20.10 Dragging using the TouchEvent.TOUCH_BEGIN and TouchEvent.TOUCH_END events

In this example, you're working with the event object that is sent to the callback methods to identify which object is currently being interacted with. The event starts by listening for the TouchEvent.TOUCH_BEGIN event type. This is broadcasted when you press your finger down on the object. When this event is "heard," the callback function receives the TouchEvent event object, which contains information you can use in the callback.

In the callback, the target of the event starts the startTouchDrag method, which is similar to the mouse-based startDrag method. Here, you need to define which touchpoint you want to work with. Remember, these are multi-touch devices, so there are multiple fingers that can be used to point and interact with objects on the device. In a single finger interaction, the touchPointID is 0.

2. Run the project.

3. Press your finger on the shape and move it around the screen.

4. Release your finger off the shape.

When you release your finger, the TouchEvent.TOUCH_END event is broadcasted. The event callback method for that event stops the drag using the stopTouchDrag method on the object (**Figure 20.10**).

TAKING YOUR TIME WITH LONG TOUCHES

The final TOUCH_POINT event you'll cover is the long press event. This is a combination of the TOUCH_BEGIN and TOUCH_END along with a Timer that you create to define how long of a delay you want to use to trigger the action.

The basis is this: First create the timer that you want to use for the event, then create the event listeners for the TOUCH_BEGIN and TOUCH_END events. Within TOUCH_BEGIN, start the timer. When the timer fires the TimerEvent.TIMER event type, make the change you want to make to the selected object. When TOUCH_END is broadcasted, you want to stop the timer, so the TimerEvent.TIMER event type isn't broadcasted anymore.

1. Update the Document class with following highlighted code to modify the drag motion to start after the user holds the object down for one second:

```
package {
    import flash.display.MovieClip;
    import flash.events.TouchEvent;
    import flash.ui.Multitouch;
    import flash.ui.MultitouchInputMode;
    import flash.utils.Timer;
    import flash.events.TimerEvent;
    public class TouchGestures extends MovieClip {
        public var myTouchButton:TouchButton;
        public var myTimer:Timer;
        public function TouchGestures() {
            myTouchButton = new TouchButton();
            myTouchButton.x = myTouchButton.y = 25;
            addChild(myTouchButton);
            myTimer = new Timer(1000);
            myTimer.addEventListener
                (TimerEvent.TIMER, touchDrag);
```

```
                         Multitouch.inputMode =
                            MultitouchInputMode.TOUCH_POINT;

                         myTouchButton.addEventListener
                            (TouchEvent.TOUCH_TAP, changeButton);


        myTouchButton.addEventListener
           (TouchEvent.TOUCH_BEGIN, startTouch)
                 myTouchButton.addEventListener
                    (TouchEvent.TOUCH_END, endTouch)
           }
           public function changeButton(e:TouchEvent):void
           {
               myTouchButton.drawNewShape();
           }
           public function startTouch(e:TouchEvent):void
           {
               myTimer.start();
           }
           public function endTouch(e:TouchEvent):void
           {
               myTimer.stop();
               myTouchButton.stopTouchDrag(0);
               myTouchButton.scaleX = 1;
               myTouchButton.scaleY = 1;
           }
           public function touchDrag(e:TimerEvent):void
           {
               myTouchButton.startTouchDrag(0);
               myTouchButton.scaleX = 1.5;
```

```
            myTouchButton.scaleY = 1.5;
        }
    }
}
```

Let's walk through this to see what is happening. First, you added a new timer to the project with an interval of 1000 milliseconds. The timer is started based on the TOUCH_BEGIN event type, and is stopped with TOUCH_END. With the timer running, when it reaches a timer interval, the TIMER event is broadcasted, activating the startTouchDrag method. To make this explicit to the myTouchButton, the event callback objects have been removed, and the touch point ID is set explicitly with the ID of 0.

To add an indication as to when you can drag and drop the object, the scaleX and scaleY properties were modified to grow the object when the drag event starts, and shrink it back to normal when it ends.

2. Publish and run the project. You'll see that when you press and hold the square for one second, it grows and you can start dragging it. When you release your finger, the object returns to the normal size.

There is one issue with this. Try this with the project and see what happens.

3. Press and hold the shape, but before the second expires, move your finger off the square.

You'll find that the square still grows and is draggable, even though your finger is not on it. This is because you aren't listening for a specific event called the TOUCH_ROLL_OUT event, which in this example should cancel the drag request. This event is broadcasted when you touch an object and then move your finger off it.

This can be easily addressed by adding a new event listener.

4. Update the code as follows:

```
package {
    import flash.display.MovieClip;
    import flash.events.TouchEvent;
```

```
import flash.ui.Multitouch;
import flash.ui.MultitouchInputMode;
import flash.utils.Timer;
import flash.events.TimerEvent;
public class TouchGestures extends MovieClip {
    public var myTouchButton:TouchButton;
    public var myTimer:Timer;
    public function TouchGestures() {
        myTouchButton = new TouchButton();
        myTouchButton.x = myTouchButton.y = 25;
        addChild(myTouchButton);
        myTimer = new Timer(1000);
        myTimer.addEventListener
            (TimerEvent.TIMER, touchDrag);

        Multitouch.inputMode =
            MultitouchInputMode.TOUCH_POINT;
        myTouchButton.addEventListener
            (TouchEvent.TOUCH_TAP, changeButton);
        myTouchButton.addEventListener
            (TouchEvent.TOUCH_BEGIN, startTouch)
        myTouchButton.addEventListener
            (TouchEvent.TOUCH_END, endTouch)
        myTouchButton.addEventListener
            (TouchEvent.TOUCH_ROLL_OUT, endTouch);
    }
    public function changeButton(e:TouchEvent):void
    {
```

```
        myTouchButton.drawNewShape();
    }
    public function startTouch(e:TouchEvent):void
    {
        myTimer.start();
    }
    public function endTouch(e:TouchEvent):void
    {
        myTimer.stop();
        myTouchButton.stopTouchDrag(0);
        myTouchButton.scaleX = 1;
        myTouchButton.scaleY = 1;
    }
    public function touchDrag(e:TimerEvent):void
    {
        myTouchButton.startTouchDrag(0);
        myTouchButton.scaleX = 1.5;
        myTouchButton.scaleY = 1.5;
    }
}
}
```

With the new event in place, if you touch and move your finger off the object, the drag action will no longer take place. Since the endTouch callback function ends the interaction, that method can be shared with the TOUCH_ROLL_OUT and TOUCH_END event listeners.

WORKING WITH GESTURE EVENTS

When working with multiple touch points or fingers, you need to switch your `Multitouch.inputMode` property to GESTURE. In this mode, common actions that involve multiple touch points can be used to create interactions in your application like zooming and rotating of objects.

PINCH TO ZOOM

One of the most common multi-touch gestures is the pinch gesture. This is when a user presses on an object with two fingers and moves their fingers farther apart or closer together.

To use this event type, you'll work with a new touch event, the `TransformGestureEvent`, which contains information about the gesture that you can apply to objects quite easily.

For this, you are going to rewrite the TouchGestures Document class.

1. Replace the code in the Document class:

```
package {
    import flash.display.MovieClip;
    public class TouchGestures extends MovieClip {
        public var myTouchButton:TouchButton;

        public function TouchGestures() {
            myTouchButton = new TouchButton();
            myTouchButton.x = stage.stageWidth / 2;
            myTouchButton.y = stage.stageHeight / 2;
            addChild(myTouchButton);
        }
    }
}
```

FIGURE 20.11 A little off-center

2. Run the project before you start adding any interactions. There is an important point here.

   You might get something unexpected (or expected, if you remember how the drawing API works) (**Figure 20.11**).

   When you draw using the API, remember that the default drawing point for a rectangle is from the top-left corner. For the next section, you'll be creating transitions that will rotate and scale an object based on pinch and rotate gestures on the device. For these to look correct, the center point of the object needs to be in the center.

3. Modify the TouchButton class as follows:

```
package  {
    import flash.display.Sprite;
    public class TouchButton extends Sprite {
        public function TouchButton() {
            drawNewShape();
        }
```

FIGURE 20.12 The object correctly positioned in the center of the screen

```
public function drawNewShape():void
{
    graphics.beginFill(Math.random()*0xFFFFFF);
    graphics.drawRect(-125,-125,250,250);
    graphics.endFill();
}
    }
}
```

4. Run the project again. You'll see that the square is now properly in the center of the screen (**Figure 20.12**).

With the object centered correctly, you can start adding the pinch to zoom interaction to your project.

5. Modify the Document class with the following highlighted code:

```
package  {
    import flash.display.MovieClip;
    import flash.ui.Multitouch;
    import flash.ui.MultitouchInputMode;
    import flash.events.TransformGestureEvent;
    public class TouchGestures extends MovieClip {
        public var myTouchButton:TouchButton;
        public function TouchGestures() {
            myTouchButton = new TouchButton();
            myTouchButton.x = stage.stageWidth / 2;
            myTouchButton.y = stage.stageHeight / 2;
            addChild(myTouchButton);
            Multitouch.inputMode =
            →  MultitouchInputMode.GESTURE;

            myTouchButton.addEventListener
            →  (TransformGestureEvent.GESTURE_ZOOM,
            →  changeScale);
        }
        public function changeScale(e:TransformGestureEvent):
        →  void
        {
            myTouchButton.scaleX *= e.scaleX;
            myTouchButton.scaleY *= e.scaleY;
        }
    }
}
```

The code starts by defining the input mode as GESTURE for the interaction. You added an event listener for the TransformGestureEvent.GESTURE_ZOOM event type (getting a little lengthy, I know). This event, when broadcasted, sends a scale parameter into the event object that you then use by proportionally modifying the object on the Stage.

6. Run the project. You'll find that you can change the object's size by pinching out or in.

However, there is an issue. You may find that when you make the object smaller, you cannot access the interaction anymore. This is because the size of the event is too small. Since the input device is a finger, you need to consider the size of a finger to complete the interaction. By making the object too small, the area in which to create the interaction can't accommodate two fingers. To adjust this, you can add a conditional that will force a minimum size.

7. Update the code as highlighted:

```
package  {
    import flash.display.MovieClip;
    import flash.ui.Multitouch;
    import flash.ui.MultitouchInputMode;
    import flash.events.TransformGestureEvent;
    public class TouchGestures extends MovieClip {
        public var myTouchButton:TouchButton;
        public function TouchGestures() {
            myTouchButton = new TouchButton();
            myTouchButton.x = stage.stageWidth / 2;
            myTouchButton.y = stage.stageHeight / 2;
            addChild(myTouchButton);
            Multitouch.inputMode =
                MultitouchInputMode.GESTURE;
```

```
myTouchButton.addEventListener
    (TransformGestureEvent.GESTURE_ZOOM,
    changeScale);
}
public function changeScale(e:TransformGestureEvent):
    void
{
    myTouchButton.scaleX *= e.scaleX;
    myTouchButton.scaleY *= e.scaleY;
    if (myTouchButton.scaleX < 1) {
        myTouchButton.scaleX =
            myTouchButton.scaleY = 1;
    }
}
}
}
```

With the conditional in place, the object will now never be smaller than its original shape, allowing the user to always have enough room to interact with it using the pinch gesture.

ROTATE

Along with pinch zoom, you can also rotate an object using two fingers. You'll use a similar event called the GESTURE_ROTATION event type.

1. Update the code as highlighted to add this new interaction:

```
package {
    import flash.display.MovieClip;
    import flash.ui.Multitouch;
    import flash.ui.MultitouchInputMode;
    import flash.events.TransformGestureEvent;
    public class TouchGestures extends MovieClip {
        public var myTouchButton:TouchButton;
```

```
public function TouchGestures() {
    myTouchButton = new TouchButton();
    myTouchButton.x = stage.stageWidth / 2;
    myTouchButton.y = stage.stageHeight / 2;
    addChild(myTouchButton);
    Multitouch.inputMode =
        MultitouchInputMode.GESTURE;

    myTouchButton.addEventListener
        (TransformGestureEvent.GESTURE_ZOOM,
        changeScale);
    myTouchButton.addEventListener
        (TransformGestureEvent.GESTURE_ROTATE,
        changeRotation);
}
public function changeScale(e:TransformGestureEvent):
    void
{
    myTouchButton.scaleX *= e.scaleX;
    myTouchButton.scaleY *= e.scaleY;
    if (myTouchButton.scaleX < 1) {
        myTouchButton.scaleX =
            myTouchButton.scaleY = 1;
    }
}
public function changeRotation
    (e:TransformGestureEvent):void
{
    myTouchButton.rotation += e.rotation;
}
}
}
```

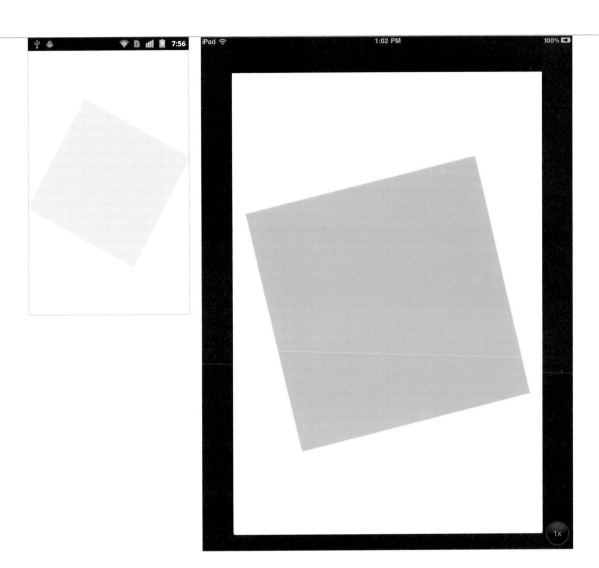

2. Publish the project. You can now zoom and rotate the object with your fingers. By pressing two fingers down on the shape and pivoting around the center of the square, you can rotate the square (**Figure 20.13** and **Figure 20.14**).

As you can see, the basic mobile interactions for touch and gestures are not that difficult to add to your project. With these interactions, plus your creativity, you can create some amazing mobile applications for the Android and iOS platforms.

FIGURE 20.13 Zooming and rotating using gesture events

FIGURE 20.14 Zooming and rotating in iOS, supporting scaling of iPhone applications on the iPad

DEBUGGING OVER USB

In the examples in this chapter, you didn't use the trace statement to send messages to the Output console. As with all projects, there will eventually (or immediately if you prefer) be a need to enable debugging with tethered devices over USB.

Luckily, using Flash Professional, you can debug your application using remote debugging. The process is a little different for Android and iOS, so they will be covered separately.

DEBUGGING ON ANDROID

To debug on Android, you need to configure the debugger to work over USB. You need to create a new project to see how this works:

1. Create a new AIR for Android application in Flash Professional CS5.5.

2. Name and save your application as **AndroidDebugger.fla**.

3. Update the matching Document class with the following code:

```
package  {
    import flash.display.MovieClip;
    public class AndroidDebugger extends MovieClip {
        public function AndroidDebugger() {
            trace("This message is brought to you by the
                letters U S and B.");
        }
    }
}
```

This is a pretty simple example, but it will demonstrate how you can send messages to the Output panel. If there are any errors in your project, they will also be sent to the Output panel.

4. Select or open the AndroidDebugger.fla tab.

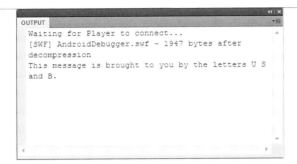

```
OUTPUT
Waiting for Player to connect...
[SWF] AndroidDebugger.swf - 1947 bytes after
decompression
This message is brought to you by the letters U S
and B.
```

FIGURE 20.15 Debugging on a tethered Android device over USB

5. From the Debug menu, select Debug Move > On Device via USB.

   This shouldn't be confused with the Test Movie > On Device menu command, which doesn't activate the debugger. You'll see an error that says that Internet permissions need to be enabled to perform device debugging. That is an easy adjustment to make.

6. Select AIR for Android Settings in the File menu.

7. Open the Permissions tab.

8. Make sure that INTERNET is selected.

9. Click OK.

10. Again, from the Debug menu, select Debug Move > On Device via USB.

   You'll see the publishing progress indicator appear, and the application will run on the device. The Output panel will open and display the message sent to it from the trace statement (**Figure 20.15**).

   That's it! Pretty easy, huh?

   When debugging over USB, you need to specifically end the Debug session.

11. Select End Debug Session from the Debug menu.

DEBUGGING ON IOS

To test on iOS, you need to perform the debugging over a WiFi network. When working in this way, your iOS device will send debugging messages over the network to your computer and the messages will appear in Flash Professional.

In the following example, you'll create a new project in Flash Professional and connect the remote application to your debugger using WiFi.

1. Create a new AIR for iOS project in Flash Professional CS5.5.

2. Name and save the project as **iOSDebugger.fla**.

3. Update the matching Document class as follows:

```
package  {
    import flash.display.MovieClip;
    public class AndroidDebugger extends MovieClip {
        public function AndroidDebugger() {
            trace("This message is brought to you by the
            ↷ letters W I F and I.");
        }
    }
}
```

4. Save your FLA and Document class and open the AIR for iOS Settings from the File menu.

5. Provision your project as you normally would and open the Deployment tab.

6. Select Quick publishing for device debugging in the iOS deployment type section of the panel (**Figure 20.16**).

7. Open the OS X System Preferences from the Apple menu or the Applications folder.

8. Open the Network panel.

9. Record the IP of your computer; you'll need this to connect the debugger.

10. Deploy the application to your iOS device.

11. In Flash Professional, from the Debug menu, select Begin Remote Debug Session > ActionScript 3.0.

12. Run the application on your iOS device.

13. Enter the IP address for your computer (**Figure 20.17**).

FIGURE 20.16 Configuring debugging in the AIR for iOS Settings window

FIGURE 20.17 Entering your computer's IP address to begin remote debugging

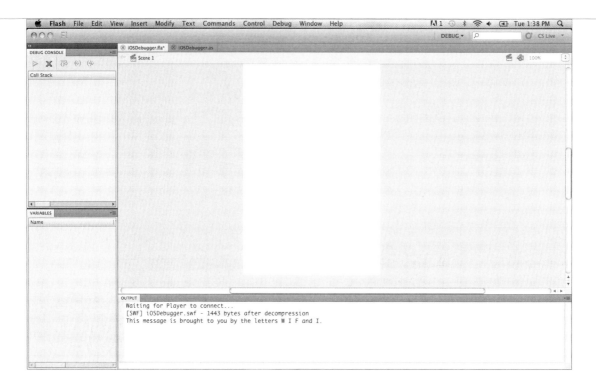

Flash File Edit View Insert Modify Text Commands Control Debug Window Help

```
Waiting for Player to connect...
[SWF] iOSDebugger.swf - 1443 bytes after decompression
This message is brought to you by the letters W I F and I.
```

FIGURE 20.18 Displaying the trace statement contents in the Flash Professional debugger over a WiFi connection

14. Click OK.

You'll see the application start, and in Flash Professional the Debugger will display the trace statement contents in the Output panel (**Figure 20.18**).

15. Select End Debug Session from the Debug menu.

Just like with Android, you need to specifically end the debugging session in Flash Professional.

Debugging with an iOS device required few more steps than working with Android, but as you can see, you can perform debugging using your iOS device.

The WiFi debugging method also works with Android devices, but USB debugging is much easier to implement, and the workflow to publish and debug is much more seamless when you use USB debugging.

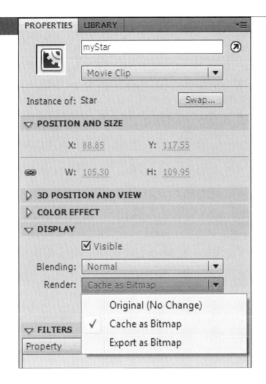

FIGURE 20.19 Setting the display properties for an object on the Stage

You have some methods available to optimize your content for mobile devices. One of these methods is to use bitmaps or bitmap caching to improve device performance. Flash is traditionally a vector graphics product, so when you work with vectors, especially complex vectors, there can be a performance impact when working with smaller devices. To help you optimize your imported vector artwork, Flash Professional CS5.5 allows you to convert your artwork to bitmaps on export or cache the object as a bitmap during runtime.

To use this optimization feature, place object instances on the Stage, select them, and open the Properties panel. From here, you can access their bitmap options in the Display section of the panel (**Figure 20.19**).

Alternatively, you can set this property with ActionScript using the cacheAsBitmap property. Setting this to true will use the bitmap optimization engine to treat the object as if it were a bitmap to give you performance gains.

There is an extensive amount of information on optimizing your content to run on mobile devices. If you are going to do more work as a mobile application creator, mastering the techniques for performance is a required skill. For more information on project optimization, there is a good overview on Ben Stucki's blog at http://blog.benstucki.net/?p=65.

WRAPPING **UP**

In this chapter, you learned the basics to start creating mobile applications using Flash Professional CS5.5 and Adobe AIR. While this chapter only scratched the surface, the ability to take your projects to mobile devices on multiple platforms is one of the biggest advantages of working with Flash. With one set of tools and one set of skills, you can create applications and content for the browser, desktop, and mobile devices. Pretty cool!

Here are some tips to help you work with the AIR runtime and Flash Professional as you embark on your new career as a mobile application creator:

- Test your projects on a variety of devices with different variations on operating systems, screen sizes, and hardware. Doing so will uncover potential issues with your project.

- Take the time to fully set up all your devices before embarking on your project, and create a simple test application to ensure that everything is working.

- When working with various touch events, determine if you need to work with TOUCH_POINT or GESTURE event types early in the process.

- Make sure your interactions can fit the fingers used to manipulate them.

- Remember to enable debugging through either USB or over WiFi to send messages and errors to your Output panel to make it easier to find issues with your project.

- Become an expert on mobile optimization. It will make your projects better and definitely more successful.

PROJECT 3

FLIPR

I'll warn you now—this project will be a difficult one and will test your knowledge of ActionScript to the limit! Since the last project, you have learned how to take your projects outside the browser and bring them to the desktop and to mobile devices.

The structure of this project is like the others—you'll review the project specs, design and kick-off meeting notes, then figure out how to complete the project on your own.

This project adds an unfortunate circumstance—your design comps are flattened files, and there are no assets you can import, meaning you have to re-create them in Flash Pro. D'oh! Although this is a situation that a good team should try to avoid at all costs, it happens, and knowing how to still meet the project requirements is critical.

Up for the challenge? I thought so.

PROJECT SPECIFICATION:
FLIPR

Flipr is a casual game for the Android platform and was designed by an external design agency.

The game is based around a grid of 16 tiles. Each tile changes color when tapped with a finger. To complete a level of the game, the user taps the tiles to display different colors until the pattern of colors matches a randomly generated pattern, taking the user to the next level. The user has 120 seconds to complete as many puzzles as possible.

The difficulty level increases as the number of colors in the patterns increase:

- Level 1: 2 colors

- Level 2 and 3: 3 colors

- Level 4 and 5: 4 colors

- Level 6 and 7: 5 colors

- Levels 8 and beyond: 6 colors

When a user starts the game, he has the option of showing the game instructions, and then starting the game, or quitting the application.

When the game timer expires, the user sees a "Game Over" screen and can either play again or quit the app.

VISUAL DESIGN REVIEW: FLIPR

A visual design agency created sample mockups of the screens. Unfortunately, they are compressed JPEGs, so you can use them only as a visual reference.

The first, a splash screen (**Figure P3.1**), should appear for a brief period when the user starts the app on their device.

After the delay, the user will see the main menu for the game (**Figure P3.2**), which gives them three options: play the game, see instructions, or quit the app.

When the user taps "Instructions," he will see the game's instructions displayed on the screen (**Figure P3.3**).

During your review of the Instructions screen, you noticed that the puzzle completion time was wrong, and there was also no way to return to the main controls screen. You note that you'll need to address this design issue in the final app.

Back on the main controls screen, when the user taps "Start Game," the game starts with a few elements in it (**Figure P3.4**).

First, you see that the game level is in the background of the window and the tile grid is in the center of the screen. At the bottom are progress bar "themometers" showing the percentage match of the secret puzzle code, and the amount of time left over.

You immediately notice that all the tiles in the comp are yellow; variations on the tile colors which display when the player taps a tile (based on the project specification) are not available, so you note that you'll have to design those yourself. In addition, the "Game Over" screen design is missing, so—sigh—you will need to make that too.

Grr!

Time to meet with the team and kick things off.

FIGURE P3.1 Flipr title screen

FIGURE P3.2 Controls for the main menu of the Flipr game

FIGURE P3.3 Instructions screen

FIGURE P3.4 The main game screen

KICK-OFF **MEETING NOTES:**
FLIPR

After documenting the lack of designs, you notify the team lead that this project will take longer than expected because of the extra work.

The logic of the game seems to make sense, but determining how to save the pattern and the pattern of the current tiles will need to be managed in an array of some sort.

Since the client is looking only for an Android app, you can save some time in the development ; no need to test iOS-based devices.

Another team member noted that when previewing a previous mobile project, the preview mode used in Flash Professional detects mouse events. A mobile project works based on touch events, so the preview mode can't decipher between mouse events and touch events. He noted that you can get around this by creating a duplicate event listener for MouseEvent.CLICK and send it to the same event callback function as the TouchEvent.TOUCH_TAP event type. The trick is to change the event object type in the callback function definition from TouchEvent to simply Event, since both of these are descendants of the generic Event class.

There was a brief discussion on how to manage the different levels of your application using event objects. Someone mentioned that at times, the object that is broadcasting a user event is at a deeper scope than expected. To resolve this, use the parent property after an instance name to change the scope to the object's container. For example, if an object called myObject is within another object called myContainer, the statement myObject.parent would refer to the myContainer object, thus giving it access to myContainer properties and methods.

Another tidbit was that you can use a property called currentCount to track the number of intervals processed of a running timer.

Finally, one team member indicated that on a previous project, she didn't realize that they could add custom properties to classes that extend MovieClip or Sprite. She suggested that it would be very helpful to provide each instance of a MovieClip or Sprite with custom information that could be used later in the project.

A challenging product—but that's why you are here, to solve challenging problems and make cool stuff.

So, give this a try.

SOLUTION AND WALKTHROUGH: FLIPR

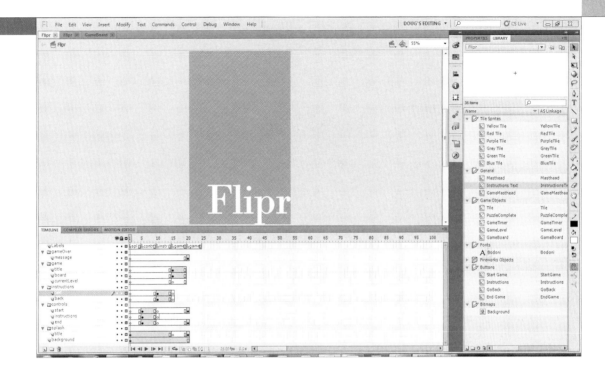

FIGURE P3.5 The splash screen

Wow...quite a challenge, wasn't it? In my personal experience, I have encountered projects like this far more often than I would like, but it is a fact of the business of interactive design, and we are all professionals, so pushing through and making it happen is what sets us apart.

Here is one way to solve this challenge. Because there are so many open-ended ways to approach this project, this is just an example—but it may introduce some solutions that you hadn't considered. The following walkthrough is how I approached the project.

REVIEW OF THE FLASH PROFESSIONAL PROJECT

Since you had to start this project from scratch, you needed to redesign the user interface. In this solution, I created parts of the design in Fireworks and imported them into Flash Professional, while others were drawn directly into Flash Professional and converted into Sprites or MovieClips (**Figure P3.5**).

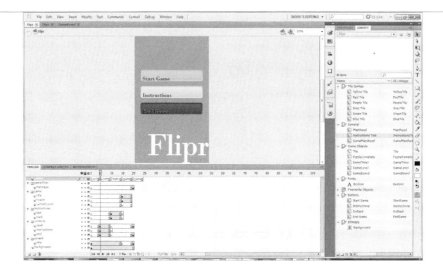

The main project contains a timeline organized into folders for the objects that are used in the game. Each game screen is denoted as a section on the timeline with frame labels to allow you to navigate from screen to screen using ActionScript.

The Library is organized into folders, with most objects saved as Sprites, since they don't need timelines.

The splash screen displays the game logo in Bodini font, which is also embedded in the project to ensure that it works correctly.

The controls screen (**Figure P3.6**) contains the same game logo (called the masthead) in the Library, and three buttons, each with a unique design. These have the instance names of startGameButton, instructionsButton, and endGameButton.

This screen displays static text for the instructions (**Figure P3.7**). Since there was no button to allow the user to return back to the main menu in the original design, it has been added with the instance name goBackButton.

The game screen is where most of the action takes place (**Figure P3.8**). Here is a single object called gameBoard, which has the gameLevelText text field, a simple drawing object for the game background, and two MovieClips.

The first MovieClip, perComplete, shows the percentage complete, the other MovieClip is the countdown timer, gameTimer.

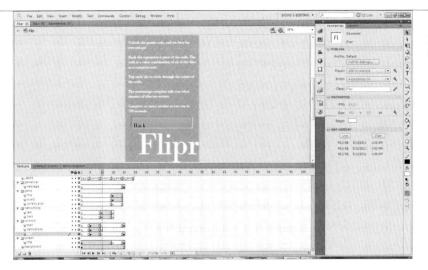

FIGURE P3.7 The instructions screen

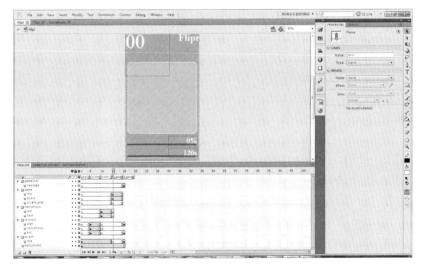

FIGURE P3.8 The main game screen

FIGURE P3.9 Construction of the percentage complete movie clip

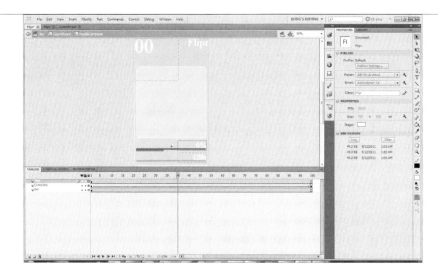

FIGURE P3.10 The missing game over screen

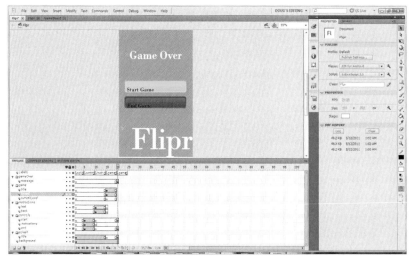

Each MovieClip has a timeline that animates the thermometer portion of the control (**Figure P3.9**).

Finally, the game over screen (**Figure P3.10**), for which there wasn't a design, contains some static text, and two buttons. The first button, startGameButton, restarts the game; the second button, endGameButton, quits the app.

All the objects that are displayed on the Stage have been set as either Export as Bitmap or Cache as Bitmap, located in the Properties panel when the object is selected to improve on-device performance.

That's the basics, let's get to the code!

REVIEW OF THE DOCUMENT CLASS

In my project, the code for the project is broken into five classes. Let's start the walkthrough by going through the flow of the app.

Here is the contents of the Document class:

```
package
{
    import flash.display.MovieClip;
    import flash.utils.Timer;
    import flash.events.TimerEvent;
    import flash.ui.Multitouch;
    import flash.ui.MultitouchInputMode;
    import flash.display.Sprite;
    import flash.events.TouchEvent;
    import flash.events.Event;
    import flash.events.MouseEvent;
    import flash.desktop.NativeApplication;
    public class Flipr extends MovieClip
    {
        public var splashTimer:Timer;
        public function Flipr()
        {
            stop();
            _init();
        }
        private function _init():void
```

```
    {
        Multitouch.inputMode = MultitouchInputMode.TOUCH_POINT;
        _displaySplash();
    }
/************************************************************

**SPLASH SCREEN
*/
    private function _displaySplash():void
    {
        splashTimer = new Timer(500);
        splashTimer.addEventListener(TimerEvent.TIMER,
        → _endSplash);
        splashTimer.start();
    }
    private function _endSplash(e:TimerEvent):void
    {
        splashTimer.stop();
        splashTimer.removeEventListener(TimerEvent.TIMER,
        → _endSplash);
        gotoAndStop("controls");
        _setupControls();
    }
/************************************************************

**MAIN CONTROLS
*/
    private function _setupControls():void
    {
        instructionsButton.addEventListener
        → (TouchEvent.TOUCH_TAP, _displayInstructions);
```

```
startGameButton.addEventListener(TouchEvent.TOUCH_TAP,
→ _startGame);
        endGameButton.addEventListener(TouchEvent.TOUCH_TAP,
        → _endGame);
        instructionsButton.addEventListener(MouseEvent.CLICK,
        → _displayInstructions);
        startGameButton.addEventListener(MouseEvent.CLICK,
        → _startGame);
        endGameButton.addEventListener(MouseEvent.CLICK, _quit);
    }
/***************************************************************

    **INSTRUCTIONS
    */
    private function _displayInstructions(e:Event):void
    {
        gotoAndStop("instructions");
        goBackButton.addEventListener(MouseEvent.CLICK,
        → _removeInstructions);
    }
    private function _removeInstructions(e:Event):void
    {
        gotoAndStop("controls");
        _setupControls();
    }
/***************************************************************

    **GAME
    */
    private function _startGame(e:Event):void
    {
        gotoAndStop("game");
```

```
        gameBoard.newGame();
        gameBoard.addEventListener("gameOver", _endGame);
    }
/*************************************************************
    **END GAME
    */
    private function _endGame(e:Event):void
    {
        gotoAndStop("gameOver");
        startGameButton.addEventListener(TouchEvent.TOUCH_TAP,
        ↪ _startGame);
        endGameButton.addEventListener(TouchEvent.TOUCH_TAP,
        ↪ _endGame);

        startGameButton.addEventListener(MouseEvent.CLICK,
        ↪ _startGame);
        endGameButton.addEventListener(MouseEvent.CLICK, _quit);
    }
/*************************************************************
    ** QUIT
    */
    private function _quit(e:Event):void
    {
        NativeApplication.nativeApplication.exit();
    }
    }
}
```

You start with all the imports for the project—there are a lot. This means you are learning a lot, so pat yourself on the back.

DISPLAY THE SPLASH SCREEN

The first element created in the class is the timer used to move from the splash screen to the main controls screen. Pretty simple opening; let's move on to the constructor:

```
public function Flipr()
{
    stop();
    _init();
}
```

Not much there. First, you need to stop the playback of the main timeline and then start an initialization method.

```
private function _init():void
{
    Multitouch.inputMode = MultitouchInputMode.TOUCH_POINT;
    _displaySplash();
}
```

Here, the input mode for the Multitouch gestures are defined, using the TOUCH_POINT method over GESTURE, since this game doesn't require any multi-point gestures to work.

There is then a method call to display the splash screen:

```
private function _displaySplash():void
{
    splashTimer = new Timer(500);
    splashTimer.addEventListener(TimerEvent.TIMER, _endSplash);
    splashTimer.start();
}
```

Here you define the timer, which displays for a half-second since the splashTimer was set with a 500 millisecond duration, and then adds the event listener for the timer. The timer is then immediately started.

DISPLAY THE MAIN CONTROLS

When the timer runs out, it executes the _endSplash callback method:

```
private function _endSplash(e:TimerEvent):void
{
    splashTimer.stop();
    splashTimer.removeEventListener(TimerEvent.TIMER, _endSplash);
    gotoAndStop("controls");
    _setupControls();
}
```

Here, the timer is stopped, and the event listener is removed. I always try to remove listeners when they aren't needed anymore as a best practice. I find that when you start creating much larger projects, having "unremoved" listeners can impact performance. The playhead is moved to the "controls" frame label, and the event listeners for the various buttons are added using the _setupControls method:

```
private function _setupControls():void
{
    instructionsButton.addEventListener(TouchEvent.TOUCH_TAP,
      _displayInstructions);
    startGameButton.addEventListener(TouchEvent.TOUCH_TAP,
      _startGame);
    endGameButton.addEventListener(TouchEvent.TOUCH_TAP, _endGame);
    instructionsButton.addEventListener(MouseEvent.CLICK,
      _displayInstructions);
    startGameButton.addEventListener(MouseEvent.CLICK, _startGame);
    endGameButton.addEventListener(MouseEvent.CLICK, _quit);
}
```

Here, the event listeners for the three buttons (instructions, start, stop) are created. Based on the recommendations from the kick-off meeting, there are two sets. This is to allow testing in preview mode with the mouse, as well as on-device tapping with touch gestures. The first is using TouchEvent.TOUCH_TAP. Then a matching set using MouseEvent.CLICK with identical callback functions is used to register the mouse event when previewing the product from Flash Professional and not a physical device.

The instructionsButton, when clicked or tapped, executes the _displayInstructions method:

```
private function _displayInstructions(e:Event):void
{
    gotoAndStop("instructions");
    goBackButton.addEventListener(MouseEvent.CLICK,
      _removeInstructions);
}
```

From there, the playhead is moved to the label "instructions" and the event listener is created for the goBackButton object. When clicked, the instructions need to go away and return to the main controls, this is done with the function _removeInstructions:

```
private function _removeInstructions(e:Event):void
{
    gotoAndStop("controls");
    _setupControls();
}
```

This sets the playhead back to "controls" and then reruns _setupControls. To display the buttons and make sure that they are set up correctly.

From the main controls screen, if the endGameButton is pressed, the _quit method runs:

```
private function _quit(e:Event):void
{
    NativeApplication.nativeApplication.exit();
}
```

Now you tell the native application to exit and return to the launcher.

If the user clicks the startGameButton, you get things going by running the _startGame method:

```
private function _startGame(e:Event):void
{
    gotoAndStop("game");
    gameBoard.newGame();
    gameBoard.addEventListener("gameOver", _endGame);
}
```

CREATE THE GAME LOGIC

This is deceptively simple, because all the game functionality has been passed to the GameBoard class. But first, you move the playhead to the "game" frame label, and then tell gameBoard to execute a public method named newGame. You also listen to a custom gameOver event that will be broadcasted from gameBoard, which then runs the _endGame method.

Let's look at the code in the GameBoard class that houses the logic and interaction for the game.

```
package
{
    import flash.display.Sprite;
    import flash.events.Event;
    import flash.events.MouseEvent;
    import flash.events.TouchEvent;
    import flash.utils.Timer;
    import flash.events.TimerEvent;

    public class GameBoard extends Sprite
    {
        // Create arrays for tile objects, values of tiles,
```

```
// and the puzzle solution
// Array of Tile MovieClips
var tileArray:Array = new Array();
// Array of the current color shown
var tileValueArray:Array = new Array();
// Array of the solution pattern
var tilePuzzleArray:Array = new Array();
// General game variables
// Current level of the game
var currentLevel:uint;
// Total correct tiles matching pattern
var totalRight:uint;
// Number of tile varieties available in the level
var tileVariety:uint;
// Create game timer
// Game timer
var gameClock:Timer;
public function GameBoard()
{
    _init();
}
// Initialize game
private function _init():void
{
    // Create the tile grid
    for (var i:uint = 0; i < 16; i++)
    {
        var newTile:Tile = new Tile();
        newTile.cacheAsBitmap = true;
```

```
                        newTile.x = (i % 4) * 110 + 10;

                        newTile.y = Math.floor(i/4) * 110 + 10;

                        newTile.idNo = i;

                        newTile.addEventListener(MouseEvent.CLICK,
                        → _clickTile);

                        newTile.addEventListener(TouchEvent.TOUCH_TAP,
                        → _clickTile);

                        addChild(newTile);

                        tileArray.push(newTile);

                        tileValueArray.push(0);

                    }

                    // General score display updater

                    addEventListener(Event.ENTER_FRAME, _updateDisplay);

                    // Configure the game clock and listeners

                    gameClock = new Timer(1000,120);

                    gameClock.addEventListener(TimerEvent.TIMER,
                    → _timerSecond);

                    gameClock.addEventListener(TimerEvent.TIMER_COMPLETE,
                    → _gameOver);

                }

                // Event callback for timer interval

                private function _timerSecond(e:TimerEvent):void

                {

                    gameTimer.setTimer(gameClock.currentCount);

                }

                // Event callback for timer completion, or game over

                private function _gameOver(e:TimerEvent):void

                {

                    // Dispatch a custom event
```

```
        this.dispatchEvent(new Event("gameOver"));
    }
    // Event callback for clicking on a tile
    private function _clickTile(e:Event):void
    {
        // Access the event object's target's parent,
        // or the MovieClip they clicked on
        var clickedTile:uint = e.target.parent.idNo;
        // Increment the tile value
        tileValueArray[clickedTile]++;
        // Determine if tile value is outside of the variety
        // range and adjust if so
        if (tileValueArray[clickedTile] >= tileVariety)
        {
            tileValueArray[clickedTile] = 0;
        }
        // Update the display of the clicked tile
        tileArray[clickedTile].displayTile
          ⇢ (tileValueArray[clickedTile]);
        // Rescore the game
        _scoreGame();
    }
    // Public function called from the main application to start
    // the game
    public function newGame():void
    {
        currentLevel = 1;
        _setupGame();
    }
```

```
// Private function that sets up a game from within the
// class, reused when reaching new levels
private function _setupGame():void
{
    // Reset the amount correct
    totalRight = 0;
    // Clear the puzzle solution array
    tilePuzzleArray = [];
    // Determine the tile variety count based on the current
    // level
    if (currentLevel < 2)
    {
        tileVariety = 2;
    }
    else if (currentLevel < 4 )
    {
        tileVariety = 3;
    }
    else if (currentLevel < 6 )
    {
        tileVariety = 4;
    }
    else if (currentLevel < 8 )
    {
        tileVariety = 5;
    }
    else
    {
        tileVariety = 6;
```

```
    }
    // Create the puzzle solution
    for (var i:uint = 0; i < 16; i++)
    {
        var newValue:uint = Math.random() * tileVariety;
        tilePuzzleArray.push(newValue);
    }
    // Create the initial random set of tiles
    for (var i:uint = 0; i < 16; i++)
    {
        var setRandomTile:uint = Math.random() *
        → tileVariety;
        tileArray[i].displayTile(setRandomTile);
        tileValueArray[i] = setRandomTile;
    }
    // Score the game with the initial set of values
    _scoreGame();
    // Start the game clock
    gameClock.start();
}
// Score the game based on the puzzle solution and currently
// displayed tiles
private function _scoreGame():void
{
    // Reset the score
    totalRight = 0;
    // Process through all the tiles and score
    for (var i:uint = 0; i < 16; i++)
    {
```

```
            if (tilePuzzleArray[i] == tileValueArray[i])
            {
                totalRight++;
            }
        }
        // Test if game is won, if so, increase level and
        // restart
        if (totalRight == 16)
        {
            gameClock.stop();
            currentLevel++;
            _setupGame();
        }
    }
    // Event callback for entering frame to update the score and
    // timer indicators
    private function _updateDisplay(e:Event):void
    {
        perComplete.setComplete(totalRight);
        gameLevelText.text = String(currentLevel);
    }
}
}
```

This code is the meat of the project. The Document class is moving the user around the various screens. Let's start with variables that are in the class:

```
// Create arrays for tile objects, values of tiles, and the puzzle
// solution
```

```
// Array of Tile MovieClips
var tileArray:Array = new Array();
// Array of the current color shown
var tileValueArray:Array = new Array();
// Array of the solution pattern
var tilePuzzleArray:Array = new Array();
// General game variables
// Current level of the game
var currentLevel:uint;
// Total correct tiles matching pattern
var totalRight:uint;
// Number of tile varieties available in the level
var tileVariety:uint;
// Create game timer
// Game timer
var gameClock:Timer;
```

Because there is so much going on here, heavy use of comments is recommended; otherwise, you will easily forget what is going on.

First there are two arrays that are created. The first is an array of MovieClips that will be created to build the game board. The second are the values of the tiles that are displayed on the game board so you know what colors are currently being displayed. The last array will hold the secret puzzle code that the user needs to match to advance to the next level.

The next set of variables holds the current level of the game, the total number of tiles that match the secret pattern, and a variable that will tell the game engine how many color variations there are in the current level that will be calculated based on the rules of the technical specification.

Finally, a timer for the game clock is created.

The constructor executes an initialization method that starts to set up the user interface of the game, the game board, the rules of the game, and the interface controls:

```
// Initialize game
private function _init():void
{
    // Create the tile grid
    for (var i:uint = 0; i < 16; i++)
    {
        var newTile:Tile = new Tile();
        newTile.cacheAsBitmap = true;
        newTile.x = (i % 4) * 110 + 10;
        newTile.y = Math.floor(i/4) * 110 + 10;
        newTile.idNo = i;
        newTile.addEventListener(MouseEvent.CLICK, _clickTile);
        newTile.addEventListener(TouchEvent.TOUCH_TAP, _clickTile);
        addChild(newTile);
        tileArray.push(newTile);
        tileValueArray.push(0);
    }
    // General score display updater
    addEventListener(Event.ENTER_FRAME, _updateDisplay);
    // Configure the game clock and listeners
    gameClock = new Timer(1000,120);
    gameClock.addEventListener(TimerEvent.TIMER, _timerSecond);
    gameClock.addEventListener(TimerEvent.TIMER_COMPLETE,
    ➝ _gameOver);
}
```

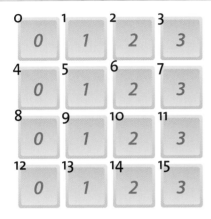

FIGURE P3.11 The game board showing index numbers and modulo calculations

CREATE THE GAME BOARD

I like to create layout mathematically if possible. I find that it leads to more adaptable layouts that can be adjusted easily with a couple tweaks rather than forcing me to go into the FLA and adjust the layout visually. The tile grid is created using a for loop that creates a new instance of the Tile class, sets the cacheAsBitmap property to true, and positions it on the screen.

The math for this is a little tricky. The x property is calculated based on a modulo operation. Since the grid is four by four, you can use that to your advantage to build the game board. For reference, look at **Figure P3.11**.

If the index number for each item was applied with a modulo operation using 4 (the number of items in a row), you can get a number you can then multiply with the width of the tile, offset based on the inset margin of the container.

For example, tile number 12, when using modulo with the value 4, returns 0 since 12 is evenly divisible by 4. 0 multiplied by the width of the tile (my design used a width of 110 pixels) becomes 0, and then you add a padding of 10 to center in the grid. Another example is tile number 10. In this case the module operation returns 2, which when multiplied by the width gives 220, plus the padding, gives an x coordinate of 230.

Pretty cool, huh? Let's look at y next.

FIGURE P3.12 The game board
showing index numbers and
results to calculate y

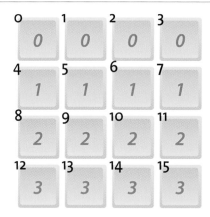

FIGURE P3.12 The game board showing index numbers and results to calculate y

For the y property, you need to do something a bit different. By using simple division, you can determine if a number, which divided by 4 and removing the decimal, sits on a specific row in the grid (**Figure P3.12**).

Let's take tile 1 as an example first. If you take the index number, divide by 4, and drop the decimal, you end up with 0. Which, you guessed it, can be multiplied with the height of the object with a padding offset. Another example is tile 14—when divided by 4 and the decimal dropped results in 3, which can then be positioned using the same calculation.

This example is obviously putting your math and layout skills to the test. An alternative here could be to position the objects on the screen and then add them to an array, which is similar to the method used in the DiceOut project, but this method offers a lot more flexibility—what if you needed to have a five by five grid instead? With just the modification of a few values, that can easily be arranged.

With the positioning finished, the tile is given a custom property called idNo. This is used to store which tile will need to be accessed when you click or tap it and which tile it is in the sequence.

User events are then listened to in the next line: one for click and the other for tap.

The tile is added to the display stack and then pushed to the array so you can loop through them easily later in the project. An initial value of 0 is assigned to the value array, just for good measure.

SET UP THE SCORE AND TIMER DISPLAYS

Next, you create an event listener that will fire with each frame. This is used to update the display of the game timer and percentage complete. Immediately following that, the game clock is configured to run for 120 seconds with a 1 second interval. Matching functions for the TIMER and TIMER_COMPLETE events are created. The first will execute _timerSecond:

```
private function _timerSecond(e:TimerEvent):void
{
    gameTimer.setTimer(gameClock.currentCount);
}
```

Here, the gameTimer MovieClip is then accessed, running a public setTimer method, sending the current interval count of the timer to the object. The game timer is another class called GameTimer:

```
package
{
    import flash.display.MovieClip;
    public class GameTimer extends MovieClip
    {
        public function GameTimer()
        {
            stop();
            resetTimer();
        }
        public function resetTimer():void
        {
            gotoAndStop(1);
        }
        public function setTimer(newTime:uint):void
        {
```

SOLUTION AND WALKTHROUGH: FLIPR **493**

```
                    var timeLeft:uint = 120 - newTime;
                    timeLeftText.text = timeLeft + "s";
                    gotoAndStop(newTime);
            }
        }
}
```

This class has a resetTimer method that sets the playhead to the first frame. setTimer takes the interval count provided and calculates the frame that the playhead should be positioned at, and then updates the text field with the total number of seconds left. Since the interval count goes up with each interval and you are displaying the timer as counting down, the number needs to be modified to create the countdown effect. For example, when the timer starts, it has an interval count of 0, but the display shows 120 seconds remain.

```
private function _gameOver(e:TimerEvent):void
{
    // Dispatch a custom event
    this.dispatchEvent(new Event("gameOver"));
}
```

When the timer is complete, the _gameOver method runs, which dispatches the custom event "gameOver" that the main Document class captures and sends the user to the game over screen.

SET UP THE PLAYER CONTROLS AND GAME RULES

Whew! Now everything is staged, but the game itself needs to be created. If you remember, this is done in the public newGame method that is called from the Document class. You are going to skip the _clickTile method for now—but you'll get to it soon.

```
// Public function called from the main application to start the
// game
public function newGame():void
```

```
{
    currentLevel = 1;
    _setupGame();
}
// Private function that sets up a game from within the class,
// reused when reaching new levels
private function _setupGame():void
{
    // Reset the amount correct
    totalRight = 0;
    // Clear the puzzle solution array
    tilePuzzleArray = [];
    // Determine the tile variety count based on the current level
    if (currentLevel < 2)
    {
        tileVariety = 2;
    }
    else if (currentLevel < 4 )
    {
        tileVariety = 3;
    }
    else if (currentLevel < 6 )
    {
        tileVariety = 4;
    }
    else if (currentLevel < 8 )
    {
        tileVariety = 5;
    }
```

```
    else
    {
        tileVariety = 6;
    }
    // Create the puzzle solution
    for (var i:uint = 0; i < 16; i++)
    {
    var newValue:uint = Math.random() * tileVariety;
        tilePuzzleArray.push(newValue);
    }
    // Create the initial random set of tiles
    for (var i:uint = 0; i < 16; i++)
    {
        var setRandomTile:uint = Math.random() * tileVariety;
        tileArray[i].displayTile(setRandomTile);
        tileValueArray[i] = setRandomTile;
    }
    // Score the game with the initial set of values
    _scoreGame();
    // Start the game clock
    gameClock.start();
}
```

The public newGame method sets the currentLevel variable to 1, and then runs the private _setupGame method. Inside of _setupGame, two variables are reset: totalRight and tilePizzleArray, which contains the puzzle solution.

The rules of the specification are used to calculate the number of the possible tile varieties for the tileVariety variable.

A for loop is used to create the puzzle solution. The value of the tile is determined using a random number multiplied by the `tileVariety` variable, providing additional variety options as the game level increases. This value is then pushed to the `tilePuzzleArray`.

To randomize the board, the same calculation is used to set the display of the tiles on the board and to then provide the `tileValueArray` with the matching number that can be used to determine the puzzle is complete.

Each tile is an instance of the `Tile` class that contains a little bit of functionality:

```
package
{
    import flash.display.MovieClip;
    public class Tile extends MovieClip
    {
        public var idNo:uint;
        public function Tile()
        {
            _init();
        }
        private function _init():void
        {
            stop();
        }
        public function displayTile(tileNo:uint):void
        {
            gotoAndStop(tileNo+1);
        }
    }
}
```

The Tile MovieClip displays a different colored tile on each frame. The displayTile method is used to take the value number created to show which tile color is displayed, which starts with 0, and convert that to an appropriate value for the frame numbers, which start at 1.

With the puzzle solution set and the initial tiles configured, the game is initially scored based on the random starting configuration using the _scoreGame method:

```
private function _scoreGame():void
{
    // Reset the score
    totalRight = 0;
    // Process through all the tiles and score
    for (var i:uint = 0; i < 16; i++)
    {
        if (tilePuzzleArray[i] == tileValueArray[i])
        {
            totalRight++;
        }
    }
    // Test if game is won, if so, increase level and restart
    if (totalRight == 16)
    {
        gameClock.stop();
        currentLevel++;
        _setupGame();
    }
}
```

Here the totalRight variable is reset, and you loop through the various arrays. First, you ask if the element of the puzzle solution is equal to that of the tile's displayed value. If it is, the totalRight variable is incremented by 1.

After the array loop finishes you ask if the total right is equal to 16, meaning that all the tiles match the secret pattern. If so, gameClock is stopped, the current level is incremented 1, and you start all over again with _setupGame.

What happens when you click or tap a tile? This is the method you skipped earlier—it is named _clickTile:

```
private function _clickTile(e:Event):void
{
    var clickedTile:uint = e.target.parent.idNo;
    // Access the event object's target's parent,
    // or the MovieClip they clicked on
    // Increment the tile value
    tileValueArray[clickedTile]++;
    // Determine if tile value is outside of the variety range and
    // adjust if so
    if (tileValueArray[clickedTile] >= tileVariety)
    {
        tileValueArray[clickedTile] = 0;
    }
    // Update the display of the clicked tile
    tileArray[clickedTile].displayTile(tileValueArray[clickedTile]);
    // Rescore the game
    _scoreGame();
}
```

You create a variable within the method that stores the value of the idNo of the item that was clicked. When using the event callback object, the target in this example is not the tile itself, but the sprite that displays the various colored variations. By using the parent property, you can access the right object and get the idNo value.

FIGURE P3.13 The fruits of your labor

When you tap the tile, you want to bump up the tile's color to the next color value, which is done by incrementing the tile value array using the `clickedTile` property to select the right element. To make sure that the color of the tile doesn't fall outside the variety of colors determined for the current level, an `if` statement is used to test the current value against the tile variety count. If it exceeds it, it is reset back to 0.

Finally, the tile itself is adjusted to display the right color, and the game is rescored (**Figure P3.13**).

Amazing to think that this game is using only the ActionScript that you have learned in this book. While there are some intermediate concepts or approaches used in this example, it illustrates how far you can take ActionScript just based on the skills you have learned so far.

But this is just the start of your adventure with ActionScript. I encourage you to dive deeper and create amazing web sites, desktop applications, or mobile apps using what you have learned in this book.

Oh, and if you ever meet me in person, say hello, or contact me on Twitter under the handle @sfdesigner and show me what you have been able to create with ActionScript. I'm always amazed by the creative projects that people build using ActionScript.

Congratulations! You have a lot to be proud of.

A

CONFIGURING
YOUR MOBILE
ENVIRONMENT

As a supplement to Chapter 20, this appendix contains configuration information on setting up your Android and iOS devices to work with Flash Professional CS5.5 to create mobile applications. This information was correct at the time of publication of this book. For the latest information on how to configure your hardware devices, please refer to these links on the Adobe documentation website:

- Publishing AIR for Android applications: http://help.adobe.com/en_US/flash/cs/using/ WSb03e830bd6f770ee317e94381294c702634-8000.html

- Packaging applications for AIR for iOS: http://help.adobe.com/en_US/flash/cs/using/ WSb03e830bd6f770ee-29e1e072124c0d552aa-8000.html

SETTING UP AN ANDROID DEVICE FOR TESTING

FIGURE A.1 Configuring USB debugging on a Nexus One running Gingerbread (Android version 2.3.x)

Android is the easiest platform to configure to work with Flash Professional CS5.5 for testing. There are a few basic steps to get everything up and running:

On each Android 2.2 and later device, there is a USB Debugging mode that can be activated from the Settings application on your device.

1. In the Settings app, select Applications, and then Development. Make sure that USB debugging is selected (**Figure A.1**).

2. Install the USB drivers for your device.

   This step is not required for computers running Mac OS X Snow Leopard; however, if you are running Windows, for each phone there are a set of USB drivers that will allow your computer to communicate with the phone. The driver for your device is available for download from the manufacturer. When you install a driver, Flash Professional will be able to find the device and send the application over USB to the device, install it, and run it for you to test with. In addition, over USB, your testing application can send messages to the Output panel in Flash Professional CS5.5.

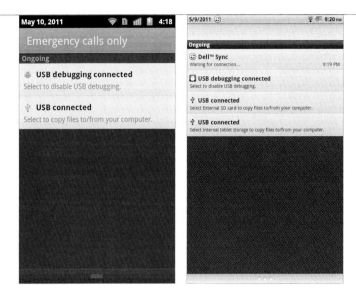

FIGURE A.2 Ready to run on Nexus One running Gingerbread (Android version 2.3.x)

FIGURE A.3 Ready to run on Dell Streak running Froyo (Android version 2.2.x)

Flash Professional CS5.5 ships with drivers for popular Android-based devices. On a typical installation, these are located in the C:\Program Files (x86)\Adobe\Adobe Flash CS5.5\AIR2.6 folder on your computer.

3. Plug in your device via USB.

The operating system should recognize your phone, and you should see "USB connected" and "USB debugging connected" in the notifications pull-down bar on your phone (**Figure A.2** and **Figure A.3**).

That's about it. Later you'll create a test application to verify that everything is up and running correctly.

NOTE: Some devices require that you are in a Charge Only mode for your device when connecting to your computer to publish applications using Flash Professional CS5.5. Refer to your device documentation for information on how to use Charge Only mode for your specific device.

SETTING UP AN IOS
DEVICE FOR TESTING

FIGURE A.4 iTunes indicating an iOS software update is available

Apple iOS devices are a little more involved to get up and running. First, you need to register with the iOS Developer Program from Apple at http://developer.apple.com. Becoming a developer costs approximately $99 per year. In addition, while it is possible to test and run using a Windows computer, it is easier to do it with a Mac with iTunes.

Here's how you set up your Mac.

1. Install the latest version of iTunes.

2. If you have a new device, configure it with iTunes. Refer to the documentation that came with your iPhone, iPad, or iPod touch on how to set up your device with iTunes.

   Make sure you are running the latest version of the iOS operating system on your device.

3. Select your device in the device list and click Update in the Summary tab of iTunes (**Figure A.4**).

4. Click the serial number on the Summary tab. It will be replaced with a longer number called the UDID. Write this down, or press Command-C to copy it to the clipboard. You'll need this later in the process.

5. Open Safari and browse to http://developer.apple.com/.

6. Log in with your Apple ID and password.

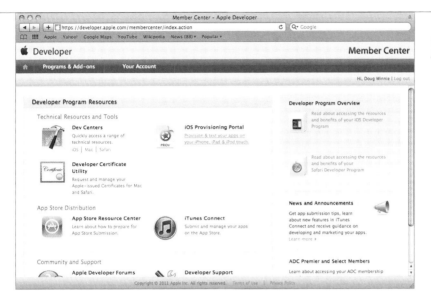

FIGURE A.5 iOS Developer Member Center

FIGURE A.6 iOS Provisioning portal

7. In the Developer portal, open the iOS Provisioning portal (**Figure A.5**).

8. Scroll down the window and click the link for the Development Provisioning Assistant to get started (**Figure A.6**).

9. Click Continue until you see Create an App ID.

    Every application you create for iOS needs to have a unique ID. When you create a new program, you need to repeat this process for each application you are going to create with Flash Professional. For now, you'll create a testing application that you'll use to test the connection to the device later in the chapter.

10. Enter **myTestApp** as the App ID Description and click Continue.

11. Select Assign a new Apple device and click Continue.

12. Enter a descriptive name for your device and re-enter or paste your UDID in the second field (**Figure A.7**).

13. Follow the instructions to generate a certificate signing request and click Continue when finished. Keep track of where you save the certificate signing request file.

    A signing certificate is required to test and deploy your application to your testing device. The Keychain Access application in Mac OS X will allow you to do this (**Figure A.8**).

14. Click Choose File, select the file that Keychain Access just saved to your machine, and click Continue (**Figure A.9**).

FIGURE A.7 Assigning a development device

FIGURE A.8 Generate a Certificate Signing Request

FIGURE A.9 Providing the signing request

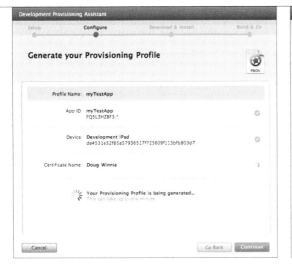

FIGURE A.10 Generating your provisioning profile

FIGURE A.11 Download your developer certificate

15. Give your provisioning profile a description and click Generate. Your profile will then be created.

The unique combination of application ID, testing device, and certificate name will allow you to deploy and test your application on your hardware.

16. Click Continue (**Figure A.10**).

17. Download the provisioning profile that was generated for you to your computer.

18. Locate the provisioning profile and drag it to iTunes.

19. Back in the Assistant, click Continue until you get to the Download & Install Your Development Certificate screen.

20. Download your certificate to a location on your computer and remember the location (**Figure A.11**).

21. Open the .cer file that you just downloaded to launch Keychain Access.

22. Select Certificates from the left side.

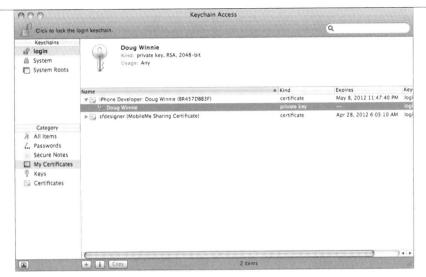

23. Locate the iPhone Developer certificate in the list of certificates and open the disclosure arrow to reveal the key within it (**Figure A.12**).

24. Right-click the key (it should be your name) and select Export.

25. Save the certificate to your computer as a .p12 file.

26. Enter a password for your certificate when asked and click OK.

27. Enter your keychain password (usually your computer login password).

The .p12 file is what you'll use to sign and prepare your project for export as an iOS IPA file using Flash Professional CS5.5. At this point, you can use a Windows machine to do the testing. You can copy the provisioning profile and the .p12 file to your Windows machine to create and compile the application.

INDEX

SYMBOLS

− operator, 50
!= statement, 195
|| operator, 218
++ operator, 59
+ operator, 44–45, 50–52
= operator, 14–15
== statement, 194
! prefix, 218
&& operator, 217–218
* operator, 53
% modulo operator

NUMBERS

1049 error, 417
1084 error, 46

A

accepting values in functions, 39–43
access
    Keychain, 434–435, 510–511
    to methods from outside classes, 153
    to objects. *See* access to objects
    passwords granting. *See* passwords
    private statement restricting, 161–162
    to values of properties, 164
access to objects
    introduction to, 3
    sending messages to output panel, 8–11
    on Stage, 5–7
    summary of, 19
Actions panel
    accepting values in functions, 39–42
    code completion assistance in, 153
    creating new objects in, 25–26
    disabled, 135
    display stacks in, 29–30
    dynamically adding objects to Stage, 26
    graphics without timelines vs., 302
    in mouse event handler creation, 71
    parameters of objects in, 15–16
    in timeline scripting with mouse
        events, 86
    writing ActionScript using,
        introduction to, 9–11
ActionScript overview. *See also* specific
    topics
    accessing and manipulating objects, 3
    Actions panel, 9–10
    ActionScript 3.0, defined, xvi
    of advanced Boolean logic, 215

of animation, 333
of building out classes, 141
of classes, generally, 131
of classes in streamlined interfaces, 157
of conditionals, 191
converting objects to MovieClips for,
    5–7
of desktop applications, 393
of drawing, 301
dynamically adding objects from
    Library, 21
of event creation, 67
of external media, 369
of frame events, 99
of functions, 35
of groups of objects, 257
instance names in, 7
interactivity for items on Stage, 3
introduction to, xiii
of keyboards, working with, 227
of mathematical operators, 49
methodology for learning, xiv
of mobile applications, 427
MovieClip properties, 14–19
new project for, 4–10
of organizing classes, 175
Output panel, 10
prerequisites for using, xiii–xvi
of random numbers, 215
of repeating actions, 257
setup, 119–121
summary of, xv
of text, working with, 227
of timeline scripting with mouse
    events, 79
of timer events, 99
versions of, 4
addChild statement, 29–30
addEventListener, 71, 75
addition operator, 50–52
Adobe AIR 2.6, defined. *See also* Adobe
    AIR for desktop applications;
    Adobe AIR for mobile applications,
    xvi
Adobe AIR 2.7, defined, 438
Adobe AIR for desktop applications
    certificates in, 420–422
    close method in, 404–406
    configuring projects in, generally, 419
    drag API in, 401–403
    events in, generally, 397
    icons in, 419–420
    installing applications in, 422–424

    introduction to, 393–394
    maximize control in, 398–401
    minimize control in, 397–398
    publishing projects in, 422
    resizable layouts in, 411–418
    resizing windows in, 406–410
    as runtime. *See* AIR runtime
    starting projects in, 394–396
    summary of, 425
Adobe AIR for mobile applications
    Android applications, creating first,
        431–434
    debugging, on Android, 458–459
    debugging, on iOS, 460–462
    debugging, over USB generally, 458
    dragging with touch in, 442–444
    gesture events, generally, 450
    interactions for devices, generally, 439
    introduction to, 427
    iOS applications, creating first, 434–438
    long press events in, 445–449
    optimizing content, 463–464
    pinch to zoom gestures, 450–455
    projects, creating new, 431–438
    projects, setup for, 428–430
    rotate gestures in, 455–457
    as runtime. *See* AIR runtime
    summary of, 465
    tap interactions in, 439–442
    testing devices in, 429–430
    touch interactions in, 439–442
Adobe Fireworks, 419–420, 471
Adobe Flash Builder 4.5, xvii
Adobe Flash Catalyst CS5.5, xvii
Adobe Flash Platform
    Adobe Flash Builder 4.5 for working
        with, xvii
    Adobe Flash Catalyst CS5.5, xvii
    Adobe Flex 4.5 for working with, xvii
    AIR for mobile applications on, 427
    defined, xvi
    resources for publishing AIR
        applications on, 423
    runtime of. *See* Flash runtime
    tools of, xvi
Adobe Flash Player
    defined, xvi
    object parameters in, 16
    Times New Roman font in, 231
    trace statements not appearing in, 10
    visible property in, 18
Adobe Flex 4.5, xvii
advanced Boolean logic. *See* Boolean logic,
    advanced

AIR runtime. *See also* Adobe AIR for
    desktop applications; Adobe AIR for
    mobile applications
    of AIR 2.7, 438
    creating desktop applications with,
        generally, 393, 425
    creating mobile applications with,
        generally, 427, 465
    downloading, 394, 423
    introduction to, xvi
    iOS vs. Android in, 428
align property, 406
alpha property
    of fills, 320
    of gradients, 321, 323
    in starfield project, 352–354, 365
    of strokes, 308
analog clock appearance, 114–115
AND operator, 217–218
Android 2.2, 427, 429
Android 3.x (Honeycomb), 427
Android devices, 430, 504–505
Android Package files (.APK), 428
Android platform
    applications for, generally, 428
    creating first application for, 431–434
    debugging on, 458–459
    Flipr game on. *See* Flipr game project
    introduction to, 427
    testing applications for, 504–505
    touch interactions in, generally, 439
    website publishing Air for, 503
animation
    adding more visual elements to,
        358–361
    brightness adjustments for, 352–355
    fluidity of, 355–358
    intervals for, 355–358
    introduction to, 333
    location on screen and rate of change
        in, 348–351
    location + time as, generally, 334–335
    of multiple objects with loops, 343–348
    random, 338–342
    rate of change of, 348–351, 355–358
    scaling size of visual elements in,
        361–365
    summary of, 366
    timer-based, 110–111, 336–338
APIs (application programming interfaces)
    drag, 401–403
    for dragging windows in AIR, 401–403
    FLVPlayback, 376–382

for graphics. *See* graphics API
    (application programming
    interface)
    for mobile applications in AIR, 439
.APK files (for Android Packages), 428
Apple Devices Application files (.IPA), 428
Apple Mac OS X
    AIR applications for, 424
    Applications folder in, 420
    desktop applications for, 394
    Snow Leopard, 504
Apple mobile devices
    introduction to, 427–429
    resolution for, 434
    testing applications on, 506
application programming interfaces (APIs).
    See APIs (application programming
    interfaces)
arithmetic functions. *See* mathematical
    operators
arrays
    animation in, 342–345
    creating groups of items with, generally,
        265–266
    creating with loops, 269–273
    defined, 257
    for game board creation, 489
    introduction to, 257
    looping through, 274–276
    loops for, 258
    modifying, 266–269
    removing items from, 268–269
    summary of, 277
    values of Flipr tiles in, 489
arrow keys, 251–253
artwork in projects. *See* drawing
.as file extension, 144, 154
assignment operator
    assigning new objects to named objects
        with, 33
    defined, 14
    on Output panel, 55
audio, 373–375
authortime, 21
auto-generated imports, 121

B

Basic Latin character range, 235
beginFill method, 318–320
beginGradientFill method, 321
bitmaps, 463, 475
Bondini font, 472
Boolean conditional tests, 258

Boolean logic, advanced. *See also* Boolean
    variables
    complex conditionals, building, 219–220
    introduction to, 215
    logic operators, using, 216–218
    NOT operator, 218
    AND operator, 217–218
    OR operator, 218
    random numbers, generating, 221–224
    summary of, 225
Boolean variables. *See also* Boolean logic,
    advanced
    adding feedback, 200–201
    defined, 18
    drag and drop for mouse, 198–200
    equality, demonstrating, 196–198
    equality, testing for, 194
    inequality, demonstrating, 196–198
    inequality, testing for, 195–196
    introduction to, 192–193
break statement, 261–262
brightness adjustments, 352–355
Brimelow, Lee, 508
broadcast-listener relationships. *See also*
    event listeners, 68
building out classes. *See* classes
buttons
    for AIR desktop applications, 395–396
    close windows, 404–406
    drag windows, 401–403
    endGameButton, 472, 474, 484
    event callback objects for, 87–88
    for Flipr, 472, 480–481
    forwardButton, 83, 90
    goBackButton, 472, 481
    graphics API and, 374, 380, 396
    hoverButton, 87–94
    instructionsButton, 472, 481
    internal timeline for special effects of,
        85–86
    labels for, 382–384
    layer of Stage, 97
    layout of, 411–418
    maximize, 398–401
    minimize, 397–398
    object type, 22
    padding around, 413
    playButton, 85–86, 87–93
    resize windows, 406–410
    start, 123
    startGameButton, 472, 474
    stopButton, 81–82, 90–93
    toggle, 382–384
    video playback, 382–384
    x and y coordinates of, 412–413

C

Cache as Bitmap object setting, 475
cacheAsBitmap property, 463
callback functions
   _endSplash, 480
   arrays and, 272–273, 276
   circleClick, 71–73
   e event callback objects, 89–95
   endTouch, 449
   hoverButton, 87–94
   introduction to, 69
   keyboardEvent handler and, 246–249
   in minimize window controls, 398
   playVideo, 381–382
   seeking to specific frames with, 83–84
   simple, 96
   for starting timers, 124–125
   stopping playback with, 83–84
   for timer events, 125–126
   TimerEvent.TIMER for, 336–338
   for touch interactions in mobile
       applications, 444
callouts, 37–38, 41
camel case, 7
capitalization, 10
Captivate, 429
ceil method, 224
cell-based animation, 334
cell phones, 429–430
centering objects, 451–452
Certificate field, 434–435
Certificate Signature Settings window, 420
Certificate Signing Requests, 509
certificates
   code-signing, 422–423
   Development, 510–511
   self-signed, 420–423, 432
character codes, 250–251
characters in fonts, 234–235
Charge Only mode, 505
chrome
   for desktop events, generally, 397
   dragging windows with, 401
   introduction to, 395–396
   native vs. custom, 425
circleClick callback function, 71–73
circles, 318
circular geometry, 325
class-based scripts, defined, 8
class constructors. *See also* classes
   button label customizing with, 146–147
   class instance creation using, 144–145

introduction to, 143
multiple properties, customizing with,
   148–149
parameters of, adding, 146–149
parameters of, generally, 146
parameters of, making optional,
   150–151
classes
   building out, generally, 141, 154
   constructor parameters in,
      generally, 146
   constructors of, generally, 143
   containers for, 133
   creating, 134–137
   customizing button labels with,
      146–147
   customizing multiple properties with,
      146–147
   definition warning, 24
   Document. *See* Document class
   extending functionality of, 305–307
   finding definitions for, 137
   flash.text.TextField, 229
   flash.text.TextFormat, 231
   fl.video class package, 378
   GameBoard, 482–488
   getter methods in, creating, 165–166
   getter methods in, generally, 164
   getter methods in, using, 166–168
   instances of, creating, 144–145
   introduction to, 131
   Math, 221–224
   methods in, accessing from outside
      classes, 153
   methods in, creating generally, 152
   optional constructor parameters in,
      150–151
   organizing, generally, 175, 187
   overview of, 132
   package folders of, creating, 176–180
   packages for, changing source paths of,
      183–186
   packages for, creating nested, 182–183
   packages for, referring to all classes in,
      180–182
   parts of, 142
   politeness of, 164
   private, best practices for naming, 163
   private, generally, 161–162
   ProLoader class, 370–371, 389
   properties of, customizing multiple,
      148–149

public, best practices, 164
public, generally, 158–160
setter methods in, creating, 165–166
setter methods in, generally, 164
setter methods in, using, 166–168
Sound class, 374–375, 389
Sprite, 302–307
in streamlining interfaces, generally,
   157, 173
summary of, 138
TextFormat, 231–232
TouchGestures Document class, 450
variables in, generally, 133
VideoButton class, 382–384
clickedTile property, 500
_clickTile method, 499
close method, 404–406
close window control, 411–413
code-signing certificates, 422–423
color
   of Flipr tiles, 468–469, 500
   hexadecimal numbers for, 231–232
   of lines, 308
combined assignment operators, 55, 57
commenting out, 29
commercial code-signing certificates,
   422–423
Compiler Errors panel, 43
complex conditionals, 219–220
complex logic patterns. *See* Boolean logic,
   advanced
complex vectors, 463
Components panel, 376
concatenation, 44–45, 51–52
conditionals
   adding feedback with, 200–201
   for animation, 345–348
   Boolean variables as, generally, 192–193
   drag and drop with, 198–200
   equality, demonstrating, 196–198
   equality, testing for, 194
   if statements, 204–206
   if.else if statements, 209–212
   if.else statements, 206–208
   inequality, demonstrating, 196–198
   inequality, testing for, 195–196
   introduction to, 191
   summary of, 213
   testing conditions with, generally,
      202–204
conditions, testing. *See* testing conditions

confirmation messages
   AIR application publication, 422
   in array creation, 273
   trace statement generating, 170
const statement, 413–417
constant values, 413–417
constructor parameters. *See also* class
   constructors
   customizing button labels with,
     146–147
   customizing multiple properties with,
     148–149
   making optional, 150–151
constructors. *See* class constructors
containers
   for classes, 133, 138
   for objects, 470
   variables as, 13
continue statement, 261–262
controls
   close window, 404–406, 411–413
   drag window, 401–403, 411, 413
   Flipr main, 480–482
   Flipr player, 494–500
   location of buttons for window, 411–413
   maximize window, 398–401, 411–412
   minimize window, 397–398, 411, 418
   native window, 395–397, 401, 409
   resizable layout of window, 415–417
   resize window, 406–410
   values in window, 413–417
   y coordinate of window, 412–413
Convert to Symbol dialog box, 5, 23
countdown clock project
   ActionScript setup in, 119–121
   auto-generated imports in, 121
   display objects in, 122–123
   event listeners for start buttons in, 123
   Flash Professional, setup in, 117–118
   kick-off meeting notes for, 116
   solution and walkthrough of, 117–126
   specifications for, 114
   summary of, 127
   timers, callback functions for events
     in, 125–126
   timers, callback functions for starting,
     124–125
   timers, timer event listeners for, 124
   visual design review of, 115
createGradientBox method, 324
curly brace locations, 38, 46
currentCount property, 470
curves, 312–315
curveTo method, 312–317

D

data types, 40
debugging
   on Android, 458–459
   on iOS, 460–462
   over USB, generally, 458
decimals, 221–225
decrement operators, 58
defaultTextFormat property, 233
defining variables, 159
degrees, 325
Dell mobile devices
   applications for, generally, 428
   testing applications with, 429, 505
Deployment Settings, for iOS, 434–435
desktop applications
   AIR for, introduction to, 393–394
   certificates for, 420–422
   close method in, 404–406
   configuring projects for, generally, 419
   desktop events in, generally, 397
   drag API in, 401–403
   icons in, 419–420
   installing, 422–424
   maximize control in, 398–401
   minimize control in, 397–398
   publishing projects in, 422
   resizable layouts in, 411–418
   resizing windows in, 406–410
   starting projects in, 394–396
   summary of, 425
desktop events. *See also* desktop
   applications
   close, 404–406
   drag, 401–403
   introduction to, 397
   maximize, 398–401
   minimize, 397–398
   resizing windows in, 406–410
Developer Member Center of iOS, 507
Developer Program for iOS, 506
Development Certificates, 510–511
DiceOut game project
   Document class overview, 284–288
   Document class walkthrough, code for
     rolling dice, 292–295
   Document class walkthrough, contents
     before constructor, 288–290
   Document class walkthrough, ending
     game, 296
   Document class walkthrough, event
     listeners, 290–292

Document class walkthrough,
     scores, 296
   introduction to, 279
   kick-off meeting notes on, 283
   solution and walkthrough,
     generally, 284
   specifications for, 280
   summary of, 297
   visual design review of, 281–282
display objects, 122–123
Display section of Properties panel, 463
display stacks
   defined, 25
   instances in, assigning properties to, 30
   objects in, creating new, 25–28
   objects in, dynamically adding to Stage,
     29–30
_displayInstructions method, 481
displayState property, 401
displayTile method, 498
division operator, 53–54
do loop, 264
Document class
   for AIR desktop applications,
     starting, 396
   for animation. *See* animation
   arrays in, 265
   Booleans, 192–193, 197–209
   creating, 169–171
   in DiceOut game project, overview,
     284–288
   in DiceOut game project, walkthrough,
     288–296
   in Flipr game project, 475–478
   for loop for, 259
   in game board creation, 488–489
   initialization methods in, 171–172
   for iOS applications, 440–449
   for minimize control, 397
   nested packages for, 182–183
   newGame method in, 494–496
   packages for, creating, 176–180
   packages for, referring to all classes in,
     180–182
   for pausing video, 382–383
   PlayAudio project and, 373–375
   for playing video from Web, 377–378
   ProLoader class and, 370–372
   RandomNumber, 221–224
   for seeking in videos, 385–387
   source path for, 183–186
   sprites. *See* sprites
   TextFields, creating, 228–230

Document class (*continued*)
  TextFields, creating KeyboardEvent
    handler in, 246
  TextFields, customizing style with,
    231–237
  TextFields, layout with, 238–245
  TouchGestures, 450–456
  for video playback alteration, 380–381
dot notation, 15
drag and drop
  for desktop applications, 401–403
  drag window control for, 411, 413
  for mobile applications, 442–444, 447
  testing for, 218
  testing location of objects, 196–198
  touch interactions for, 442–444
  using mouse, 198–200
drawCircle method, 318
drawEllipse method, 318
drawing
  circles, 318
  code for, generally, 302
  curves, 312–315
  degrees in, 325
  ellipses, 318
  fills, 318–320
  gradients, 321–326
  introduction to, 301
  lines, drawing, 307–312
  loops and, 326–329
  rectangles, 317
  rounded rectangles, 317–318
  shapes, first, 303–304
  shapes, generally, 315–317
  Sprite class, extending, 305–307
  Sprite class, generally, 302–303
  strokes for, 307–312
  summary of, 330
drawRect method, 317
drawRoundRect method, 317
Droid, 429
drop and drag. *See* drag and drop
dropDrag method, 200
dynamic text labels, 146
dynamically adding objects to Stage
  comments, creating, 31–32
  display stacks, assigning properties to
    instances, 30
  display stacks, creating new objects
    for, 25–28
  display stacks, defined, 25
  display stacks, working with, 29–30
  introduction to, 21
  named library assets in, 22–25
  spaces for, 32
  summary of, 31
dynamically created instances, 30
dynamically created instances, assigning
    properties to, 30
dynamically loading images, 370

E

e event object, 73, 89–95
editing-in-place, 85
ellipses, 318
embedded fonts, 234–237
embedded video, 376
emulators, 430
endFill method, 320
endGameButton, 472, 474
_endSplash callback method, 480
endTouch callback function, 449
ENTER_FRAME event, 104–107
equality, 194, 196–198
errors
  1049 error, 417
  1084 error, 46
  class definition warning, 24
  required parameter, 42–43
  type mismatch, 43
e.target, 92–94
event callback objects
  finished example of, 92–94
  introduction to, 87–88
  using, 89–92
event handlers. *See also* interfaces
  for desktop application buttons, 410
  dynamic, 85, 94–95
  function definitions as, 96
  for keyboard events, 246–253
  for mouse events, 69, 70–73
  for seeking to specific frames, 84
  for sprites, 302
event listeners
  addEventListener, 71, 75
  in countdown clock project, 123
  for dragging windows, 403
  for Flipr main controls, 480–481
  for Flipr score and timer displays, 493
  introduction to, 69
  in keyboardEvent handlers, 246–249
  in MouseEvent handlers, 69–73
  parentheses in, 71
  removing, 106–107
  for resizable layout of window controls,
    415–417
  for resizing windows, 408–410, 425
  seeking to specific frames with, 83–84
  simple callback functions in, 96
  for splash screen timers, 479–480
  for start buttons, 123
  stopping playback using, 82–84
  in timers, 124
  for touch interactions in mobile
    applications, 444
event objects
  e, 73, 89–95
  in mobile applications, 470
event target data example, 94–95
event types, 73, 75
Event.RESIZE event, 410
events
  adding, 75
  close, 404–406
  desktop. *See* desktop events
  drag, 401–403
  frame. *See* frame events
  gesture, 450–457
  handlers for. *See* event handlers
  introduction to, 68–69
  listeners for. *See* event listeners
  maximize, 398–401
  minimize, 397–398
  mouse. *See* mouse events
  objects for. *See* event objects
  resizing window, 406–410
  summary of, 76
  timer. *See* timer events
Export as Bitmap object setting, 475
external media
  audio from Web, playing, 373–375
  images, 370–372
  introduction to working with, 369
  summary of, 389
  video from Web, playing, 376–378
  video playback, altering, 379–382
  video playback, pausing, 382–384
  video playback, rewinding and seeking,
    384–388

F

false value
  for loop testing for, 258
  introduction to, 17
  NOT operator testing for, 218
  AND operator testing for, 217–218
feedback, 200–201
fills, 318–320

Fireworks, 419–420, 471
FLA project files. *See also* Flash
    Professional CS5.5
    classes in packages, referring to,
        180–182
    Document class in, creating, 169–171
    Document class linking to, 302
    equality and inequality in, 196–198
    fonts in, 234
    getName method for, 160
    nested packages for, 182–183
    package folders for, 176–180
    publishing AIR applications and, 422
    resizing windows in, 418
    self-signed certificates in, 420–421
    source path for, 183–186
Flash Platform. *See* Adobe Flash Platform
Flash Platform from Start to Finish, 423
Flash Player 10.2, defined. *See also* Adobe
    Flash Player, xvi
Flash Professional CS5.5. *See also* Adobe
    Flash Platform
    Actions panel in, generally, 9–11
    AIR projects in, creating, 394–396
    AIR projects in, using, 424–425, 438
    Android applications in, debugging,
        458–459
    Android applications in, generally,
        431–434
    Android applications in, testing, 504
    Boolean variables in. *See* Boolean
        variables
    Components panel in, 376
    Convert to Symbol dialog box in, 5
    countdown clock project in, 117–118
    creating classes in, generally, 158–160
    creating Document classes in,
        169–171, 173
    defined, xvi
    drawing with ActionScript and, 302
    FLA files for. *See* FLA project files
    Format Embedding dialog box, 234
    frame rate property in, 108–110
    iOS applications in, creating generally,
        434, 437
    iOS applications in, debugging, 460
    looping with drawing API in, 326–328
    mobile device applications in. *See*
        mobile applications
    nested packages in, 182–183
    New Project dialog box in, 4
    preview mode in, 470
    project review in, 471–475
    random number generator in, 221–224

runtime of. *See* Flash runtime
text fields in, 228
timeline scripting in, generally, 80
video delivery in, 376
Flash runtime. *See also* Flash
    Professional CS5.5
    animation in, 333
    API for artwork in, 302
    default location of objects in, 16
    display stack contents in, 28
    displaying object locations, 16
    evaluating order of operations, 61–62
    introduction to, xiii, xvi
    pixel hinting in, 318
    text fields in, 228
    triggering frame events, 99, 104
flash.display.Sprite class, 303
flash.text.TextField class, 229
flash.text.TextFormat class, 231
flattened files, 506–511
Flipr game project
    Document class review in, 475–478
    Flash Professional project review in,
        471–475
    game board, creating, 491–492
    game logic, creating, 482–490
    game rules, setting up, 494–500
    introduction to, 467
    kick-off meeting notes for, 470
    main controls, displaying, 480–482
    player controls, setting up, 494–500
    score displays, setting up, 493–494
    solution and walkthrough of,
        generally, 471
    specifications for, 468
    splash screen, displaying, 479
    summary of, 501
    timer displays, setting up, 493–494
    visual design review of, 469
floor method, 222–223
fl.video class package, 378
FLVPlayback
    adding to projects, 376–378
    altering video playback with, 379–382
    rewinding video with, 384–397
    seeking video with, 384–387
    summary of, 388–389
folders. *See also* packages, 176–180, 420
Font Embedding dialog box, 235
fonts
    Bondini, 472
    changing later, 233–234
    creating custom, 234–237
    formatting, 231–232

for loop
    drawing API and, 326–328
    for Flipr game board, 491
    introduction to, 257–260
    for puzzle solutions, 497
Format Embedding dialog box, 234
formatting text, 231–232
forwardButton instance, 83, 90
FPS (frame rate property), 108–110
frame events
    ENTER_FRAME, 104–107
    introduction to, 99
    removing event listeners, 106–107
    summary of, 111
    timer events vs., 108–110
frame labels, 90
frame rate property (FPS), 108–110
frame scripts, defined, 8
frames, seeking to specific, 83–84
Froyo, 427, 505
fully qualified package names, 178
function statement, 37
functions
    accepting values in, 39–43
    errors when running, 42–43
    fundamentals of, 36–38
    introduction to, 35
    for methods, 152
    returning values from, 44–46
    summary of, 47

G

game boards. *See also* Flipr game project,
    491–492
game logic, 482–490
"Game Over" screen
    absence of, 469
    appearance of, 474
    specifications for, 468
    timer triggering, 494
game rules, 494–500
gameBoard, 472
GameBoard class, 482–488
gameLevelText text field, 472
_gameOver method, 494
gameTimer, 472, 493–494
generic objects, 159
geometry, 325, 338
gesture events. *See also* touch interactions
    introduction to working with, 450
    pinch to zoom, 450–455
    rotate, 455–457

GESTURE mode, 441, 450, 454
GESTURE_ROTATION event type, 455–456
getter methods
    creating, 165–166
    politeness of, 164
    using, 166–168
GIF files, 370
Gingerbread, 504–505
glyphs, 234–235
goBackButton, 472, 481
Google, 428
gotoAndPlay() function, 84, 90
gotoAndStop() function, 84, 90–92
gotoAndStop method call, 303
gradients, 321–326
Graphic object type, 22
graphics API (application programming
        interface)
    drawing curves with, 312–315
    drawing desktop application buttons
            with, 396
    drawing lines with, 307–312
    drawing play audio buttons with, 374
    drawing play video buttons with, 380
    drawing shapes with, 315–318
    introduction to, 301–302
    looping with, 326–329
    shape creation using, 303–304
graphics property
    extending class functionality in,
            305–307
    introduction to, 303
    lineStyle method of, 307–308
    with statement for, 311–312
groups of items. See arrays
groups of objects. See arrays

H

handling scope, 87
handsets, 428
hexadecimal numbers, 231–232, 308
Honeycomb, 427
hoverButton callback function, 87–94
HTC mobile devices, 428

I

icons, 419–420
idNo of clicked items, 499
if statements, 204–206
if.else if statements, 209–212
if.else statements, 206–208
Illegal assignment to variable
        specified as constant error, 417

images, 370–372
import flash.events.MouseEvent;, 83
import statement
    for packages, 180–182
    for sprites, 303
    for text fields, 229
increment operators, 58–59
index element selector, 266–267
index numbers, 266–268, 491–492
inequality
    demonstrating, 196–198
    equality vs. See equality
    testing for, 195–196
infinite loops, 259
infinitely running timers, 102, 111
init(), 171–172
_init, 230
initialization method
    creating, 171–172
    for Flipr user interfaces, 490
    loops running in, 272
    for splash screens, 479
    for text fields, 230
instance names
    in arrays, 273
    assigning unique, 12, 22
    on Buttons layer of Stage, 97
    camel case for, 7
    in classes, accessing, 154
    in classes, creating, 134
    in constructor parameters, adding, 146
    for creating objects, 27–28
    dot notation and, 15
    in Flipr user interfaces, 472
    of game buttons, 472
    introduction to, 3–7, 19
    mouse event handlers and, 70
    name attribute for, 95
    in objects on Stage, creating new, 28
    parent property after, 470
    prefixing playback commands with, 97
    in timeline scripts with mouse events,
            80, 95
instances
    creating, 144–145
    defined, 6
    naming. See instance names
    of objects, creating, 27
    var statement for, 133
Instructions screen for Flipr
    contents of, 472–473
    in Document class, 477
    introduction to, 469
instructionsButton, 472, 481

interactions for mobile devices. See also
        interfaces
    creating, generally, 439
    dragging with touch, 442–444
    gesture events for, generally, 450
    long press events, 445–449
    pinch to zoom gestures, 450–455
    rotate gestures, 455–457
    tap, 439–442
    touch, 439–442
interfaces. See also events
    application programming. See APIs
        (application programming
        interfaces)
    defined, 67
    Flipr user, 471–472
    for mobile devices. See interactions for
        mobile devices
    streamlining. See classes
INTERNET option, 439
intervals
    in animation, 355–358
    currentCount property for, 470
    in timers, 100–102, 111
iOS platform
    configuring devices for, 430
    creating first application for, 434–438
    debugging application for, 460–462
    testing applications for, 506–511
    touch interactions on, 439
    website packaging applications for, 503
IP addresses, 461
.IPA files (for Apple Devices Applications),
        428, 435
iPad
    introduction to, 427
    on iOS platform, 428
    resolution for, 434
    as testing device, 429
iPhone
    introduction to, 427
    on iOS platform, 428
    resolution for, 434
iPod touch
    on iOS platform, 428
    resolution for, 434
    as testing device, 429
_isCorrect, 192–194
iterators
    in controlling flow of loops, 261
    in for loop, 258–260
    in nested loops, 263
iTunes, 436, 505

J

JPEG files, 370–372, 469

K

keeping classes polite, 164
key codes
    character codes vs., 250–251
    constants containing, 253
    defined, 249
    in keyboard shortcuts, 251–253
KeyboardEvent handler
    introduction to, 246–249
    key vs. character codes in, 250–251
    special key recognition in, 251–253
keyboards, 227
Keychain Access, 434–435, 510–511
keyframes, 8, 85–86
kick-off meeting notes
    countdown clock project, 116
    on DiceOut game project, 283
    Flipr game project, 470
kuler, 308

L

layers in timeline, 8
layouts
    of buttons, 411–418
    in desktop applications, 411–418
    manually sketching, 240
    of text. See layouts for text
    of window controls in AIR, 411–418
layouts for text
    escape sequences in, 241–245
    introduction to, 238–240
    Text Layout Framework, 228
left to right evaluation, 60
length property, 274
Library
    Flipr user interfaces in, 472
    FLVPlayback, adding, 376–378, 389
    importing images into, 370
    objects in. See Library objects
Library objects
    adding dynamically, 21
    classes of, 132, 135, 137
    in countdown clock project, 117, 122
    display stacks for, 27–28
    displaying, 122
    dynamic event handlers for, 94
    ENTER_FRAME event and, 104
    equality and inequality of, 197

Font, 234–235
    introduction to, 5–6
    loops creating arrays for, 269
    on MovieClip timelines, 85
    named assets, creating, 22–25
    in Project setup of Flash
        Professional, 117
    tween-based animation of, 80
    values in functions of, accepting, 39–40
lines, drawing, 307–312
lineStyle method
    for curves, 313–314
    for extending Sprite class, 305
    for gradients, 321–322
    for lines, 307–311
    for looping, 326–328
    for rectangles, 317–319
    for shapes, 304, 315–316
    with statement and, 312
    for strokes, 307–311
lineTo method, 310–311, 315–317
Linkage class names, 137–138
listeners. See event listeners
_loadImage method, 371–372
location
    of curly braces, 38, 46
    of objects, testing, 46, 196–198
    rate of change and, 348–351
    time and, 334–335
    of window control buttons, 411–413, 418
    x coordinates for. See x coordinates
    y coordinates for. See y coordinates
logic operators, 216–218
logos, 472
long division with remainders, 53–54
long press events, 445–449
loops
    animation of multiple objects with,
        343–348
    arrays and, generally, 265–266
    break statement controlling, 261–262
    continue statement controlling,
        261–262
    creating arrays with, 269–273
    do loop, 264
    in drawing with ActionScript, 326–329
    for. See for loop
    introduction to, 257–258
    modifying arrays and, 266–269
    nesting, 262–263
    for objects already in arrays, 274–276
    summary of, 277

M

Mac OS X
    AIR applications for, 424
    Applications folder in, 420
    desktop applications for, 394
    Snow Leopard, 504
    testing mobile applications for, 506
main controls in Flipr, 480–482
manipulating objects. See also objects
    introduction to, 3
    parameters for, 8–18
    summary of, 19
manually sketching layouts. See also
    layouts, 240, 411–413
mastheads, 472
Math class, 221–224
mathematical operators
    addition, 50–52
    combined assignment, 55, 57
    concatenation, 51–52
    decrement, 58
    division, 53–54
    increment, 58–59
    introduction to, 49–50
    left to right evaluation by, 60
    long division with remainders, 53–54
    modulo, 53
    multiplication, 53
    order of operations by, evaluating, 61
    order of operations by, forcing, 62–63
    order of operations by, generally, 60
    parentheses forcing order of, 62–63
    subtraction, 50
    summary of, 64–65
    variables and, 55–57
Math.random method
    in animation, 340–341
    in drawing with ActionScript, 328
    generating random numbers with,
        221–225
matrix parameter, 324
maximize window control, 398–401,
    411–412
Menu commands, 11
menu for Flipr, 469
messages
    broadcasting mouse events, 68–69
    buttons displaying, 70
    "Click!" 75
    confirmation, in array creation, 273
    confirmation, of AIR application
        publication, 422

messages (*continued*)
    confirmation, trace statement
        generating, 170
    debugging, on Android, 458–459
    debugging, on iOS, 460
    error, in named library asset creation, 24
    functions generating, 44–46
    greeting, functions generating, 44–45
    MOUSE_OVER, 68–69
    object instances broadcasting, 68
    sending to Output panel, 8–11
    testing application, 504
    for timeline playback, 82, 95
methods
    _clickTile, 499
    _displayInstructions, 481
    _endSplash callback, 480
    _gameOver, 494
    _loadImage, 371–372
    _positionControls, 410, 417
    _quit, 481
    _scoreGame, 498
    _setupControls, 480–481
    accessing from outside classes, 153
    beginFill, 318–320
    beginGradientFill, 321
    ceil, 224
    close, 404–406
    createGradientBox, 324
    creating, 152
    curveTo, 312–317
    displayTile, 498
    drawCircle, 318
    drawEllipse, 318
    drawRect, 317
    drawRoundRect, 317
    dropDrag, 200
    endFill, 320
    floor, 222–223
    getter, 164–168
    gotoAndStop method call, 303
    of graphics property, 307–308
    initialization. *See* initialization method
    introduction to, 131
    lineStyle. *See* lineStyle method
    lineTo, 310–311, 315–317
    Math.random, 221–225, 328, 340–341
    moveTo, 310–311
    new_configureWindow, 409–410
    newGame, 494–496
    play method of FLVPlayback,
        381–382, 389

    private _setupGame, 496
    public newGame, 496
    public statement for, 152
    push( ), 267–268, 272
    resetTimer, 494
    round, 224
    seekPercent, 384–385
    setLabel, 382–384
    setter, 164–168
    setTextFormat, 233–234
    setTimer, 494
    splice( ), 268–269
    startDrag, 198, 200, 213
    startMove, 403
    startTouchDrag, 444, 447
    stopDrag, 198, 213
    stopTouchDrag, 444
    for TOUCH_POINT, 479
minimize window control
    for desktop applications, 397–398
    location of, 418
    in resizable layouts, 411
mobile applications
    on Android, creating first, 431–434
    configuring environment for.
        See mobile environment
        configuration
    debugging, on Android, 458–459
    debugging, on iOS, 460–462
    debugging, over USB generally, 458
    dragging with touch, 442–444
    gesture events for, generally, 450
    interactions for, generally, 439
    introduction to, 427
    on iOS, creating first, 434–438
    long press events in, 445–449
    optimizing, 463–464
    pinch to zoom gestures in, 450–455
    rotate gestures for, 455–457
    summary of, 465
    tap interactions in, 439–442
    test project for, 431–438
    testing devices for, 429–430
    touch interactions for, 439–442
mobile environment configuration. *See*
    also mobile applications
    Android devices, setting up for testing,
        504–505
    introduction to, 503
    iOS devices, setting up for testing,
        506–511

modulo operator
    %, 53–54
    defined, 53
    for Flipr game board, 491–492
motion. *See* animation
Motorola mobile devices, 428–429
mouse event handlers, 70–73
mouse events
    adding to existing timeline scripts,
        generally, 80
    callback objects, 87–94
    common, 75
    controlling timeline playback with, 81
    drag and drop, 198–200
    event target data example and, 94–95
    gotoAndStop( ), 92
    for handling scope, 87
    hovering, 74–75
    in mobile applications, 442
    MOUSE_OVER, 75
    for MovieClips, generally, 85–86
    for playback, stopping at specific
        frames, 83–84
    for playback, stopping generally, 81–83
    simple callback functions and, 96
    timeline scripting with, generally, 79, 97
    touch events vs., 470
MouseEvent.CLICK, 481
MouseEvent.CLICK event, 398
MouseEvent.CLICK event type, 381, 384
MOUSE_OVER events, 68–69
moveTo method, 310–311
MovieClips
    accepting values in functions in, 39–42
    Boolean variables in. *See* Boolean
        variables
    class constructors for, 143–151
    class statement for, 143
    classes in, creating generally, 134–137
    complex conditionals for, 219
    converting visual objects to, 5–7
    in countdown clock project, 118
    customizing button labels for, 146–147
    customizing multiple properties in, 148
    Document class in, creating, 169–171
    drag and drop for, 213
    ENTER_FRAME and, 104–107
    Flipr user interfaces in, 471
    for loop for, 259
    flow of loops in, 261
    frame scripts for, 8–11
    game board creation in, 489

gameTimer, 472, 493–494
graphics property in, 303–304
graphics vs., 22
import statement for, 142
looping through arrays for, 274
loops creating arrays for, 269–271
in mobile applications, 470
mouse event handlers for, 69–73
naming instances in, 7
object parameters in, 12–18
packages for. *See* packages
perComplete, 472–474
properties of, 17
random number generator for, 221–224
sprites for, 302–303
symbol properties for, 134–137
Tile, 498
in timeline scripting with mouse
    events, 85–86
TimerExpired, 118
TimerStart, 118
without timelines, 302–303
MP3 files, 373–374
multi-screen projects on desktops. *See*
    Adobe AIR for desktop applications
multi-screen projects on mobile
    devices. *See* Adobe AIR for mobile
    applications
multiplication operator, 53
Multitouch.inputMode property, 441,
    450–456

N

named Library assets. *See also* Library
    objects, 22–25
names
    fully qualified package, 178
    instance. *See* instance names
    Linkage class, 137–138
native installers, 394
native window controls
    in AIR, generally, 395–398
    drag, 401–403
    resize, 409–410
nativeWindow object, 403
nativeWindow property of Stage, 397–398
NativeWindowDisplayState, 401, 407–409
nesting
    condition statements, 216–217
    loops, 262–263
    packages, 182–183
New Project dialog box, 4

new statement, 28–30, 33
new_configureWindow method, 409–410
newGame method, 494–496
nextFrame(), 92–93
Nexus One
    configuring devices, 431
    testing Android applications on,
      504–505
    as testing devices, 429
NOT operator, 218
number of intervals in timers, 100, 111
:Number statement, 43
numbers
    hexadecimal, 308
    index, 266–268, 491–492
    random, 215, 221–224
    var statement for, 133

O

Object-Oriented Programming (OOP). *See
    also* interfaces, 131, 157
objects
    accessing. *See* access to objects
    already in arrays, loops for, 274–276
    animating multiple, loops for, 343–348
    bitmap settings for, 475
    centering, 451–452
    containers for, 470
    countdown clock, 117, 122
    creating new, 25–28
    dynamically adding. *See* dynamically
      adding objects to Stage
    event, 73, 89–95, 470
    event callback, 87–94
    generic, 159
    Graphic object type, 22
    groups of. *See* arrays
    manipulating. *See* manipulating objects
    moving with timers, 336–338
    nativeWindow, 403
    in new project creation, 4
    parameters for, 12–18
    sending messages to Output panel, 8–11
    on Stage, 5–7
    testing location of, 46, 196–198
    width property of, 413
OOP (Object-Oriented Programming). *See
    also* interfaces, 131, 157
optimization of mobile applications,
    463–464
OR operator, 218

order of operations
    evaluating, 61
    forcing, 62–63
    introduction to, 60
Output panel
    _getCodes method in, 250
    1084: Syntax error in, 46
    addition operator on, 50–52
    array modification in, 268–269
    assignment operator on, 55
    class display screen on, 144–145
    combined assignment operators in, 55
    concatenation operator on, 51–52
    decrement operator on, 58
    display stacks and, 28–29
    division operator on, 53
    from for loop, 260
    "The function runMe was executed," 36
    getter method display in, 166, 170
    if statement results on, 206
    increment operator on, 58
    loop code sending iterator values to, 260
    looping through arrays in, 276
    mathematical operators in, 50–53
    mouse click events in, 72–73, 75
    multiplication operator on, 53
    nesting loops in, 263
    AND operator in, 217
    OR operation in, 218
    playback, stopping, 82
    random numbers in, 221
    returning values from functions in,
      44–46
    sending messages to, 8–11
    setter method display in, 166, 170
    subtraction operator in, 50–52
    "Tick!" displays on, 101–103
    timers in, 101–103
    trace statement and, 28–29, 177, 180
    true value and equality statement
      on, 194
    x coordinate on, 12–13, 16, 200
    y coordinate on, 12–13, 16, 200

P

.p12 files, 434–435, 511
packages
    folders for, creating, 176–180
    nested, 182–183
    referring to all classes in, 180–182
    source paths of, 183–186

padding around buttons, 413
parameters
  of class constructors, 146–151
  of objects, 12–18
  of timer events, 100
parent property, 470, 499
parentheses
  in event listeners, 71
  forcing order of operations, 62–63
  location of, 46
passwords
  for AIR applications, 421
  AIR for Android, 432–433
  AIR for iOS, 435
  for keychain access, 511
pausing video, 382–384
pen, virtual, 310–315
perComplete, 472–474
phones. See also iPhone, 429–430,
    504–505
pinch to zoom gestures, 450–455
pipes, 218
pixel hinting, 318
play method of FLVPlayback, 381–382, 389
playback
  controlling, generally, 81
  FLVPlayback. See FLVPlayback
  messages, 95
  stopping, 81–83
  stopping at specific frames, 83–84
playButton, 85–93
player controls, 494–500
Player drop-down list, 394–395
PNG files, 370
polite classes, 164
_positionControls method, 410, 417
prevFrame(), 92–94
preview mode, 470
private
  best practices for, 163
  classes, 160, 173
  introduction to, 161–162
  restricting access with, 161–162
private _setupGame method, 496
private variables, 192–199
progressive video, 376
ProLoader class, 370–371, 389
properties
  accessing values of, 164
  align, 406
  alpha. See alpha property
  assigning to instances, 30
  cacheAsBitmap, 463

clickedTile, 500
currentCount, 470
customizing multiple, 148–149
defaultTextFormat, 233
displayState, 401
frame rate, 108–110
graphics. See graphics property
length, 274
of MovieClips, 14–19
Multitouch.inputMode, 441, 450–456
nativeWindow, 397–398
parent, 470, 499
scaleMode, 406–409
scaleX and scaleY, 447
StageAlign, 411
stageWidth and stageHeight, 328, 349
symbol, 135–136, 138
target, 89–92
of text, 231–237
values of, 17, 217–218, 258
width of objects, 413
Properties panel
  in AIR, 395
  Display section of, 463
  frame rate property (FPS) in, 108–110
  introduction to, 12–14
Provisioning portal of iOS, 507–510
public
  best practices for, 164
  classes, 143
  for classes, 158
  introduction to, 158–160
  methods, 152
public newGame method, 496
Publish preview, 11
Publish Settings window, 185
publishing AIR applications, 395, 422
push() method, 267–268, 272

Q

_quit method, 481
quiz project
  escape sequences for responses in,
    241–245
  keyboardEvent handler in, 246
  questions, creating text fields for,
    228–230
  questions, properties of text for,
    231–237
  responses in layout of, 238–240
  text fields for answers in, 242–245
quotation marks

in conditionals, 213
indicating text, 10, 19
in private variables, 193

R

radial gradients, 326
random animation, 338–342
random number generator, 340–341, 349
random numbers, 215, 221–224
rate of change, 348–351, 355–358
"ready to run," 505
rectangles, 317
remote debugging, 458, 460–461
_removeInstructions, 481
repeating actions. See loops
reposition() function, 39–43
required parameter error, 42–43
resetTimer method, 494
resizable layouts of window controls,
    411–418
resize window controls, 406–410
resuming video playback, 384
return statement, 44–46
returning values from functions, 44–46
rewinding video, 384–388
RIM platform, 425
rise over run, 338
rotate gestures, 455–457
rotating gradient boxes, 325–326
round method, 224
rounded rectangles, 317–318

S

Safari, 506
Samsung mobile devices, 428–429
scaleMode property, 406–409
scaleX and scaleY properties, 365, 447
scaling size of visual elements, 361–365
scope of code, 87–88
score displays, 493–494, 498
_scoreGame method, 498
seeking to specific frames, 83–84
seeking video, 384–388
seekPercent method, 384–385
self-signed certificates, 420–423, 432
semicolons, 15, 46
setLabel method, 382–384
setter methods
  classes, 164
  creating, 165–166
  using, 166–168
setTextFormat method, 233–234

setTimer method, 494
Settings Window in AIR
    configuring projects in, 395–396
    Create Self-Signed Digital Certificate
        window in, 421
    Icons tab in, 419–420
    introduction to, 419
    for iOS, 461
    self-signed certificates and, 432
_setupControls method, 480–481
@sfdesigner, 501
shapes, 303–304, 315–317
ShockWave Flash (SWF), 370–372, 389
shortcuts on keyboards, 251–253
simple callback functions, 96
single quotes, 96
size of images, 370
sketching layouts manually, 240, 411–413
slope of animation
    rise over run in, 338
    stageWidth and stageHeight in, 349
    summary of, 366
solutions and walkthroughs
    ActionScript setup for countdown
        clock, 119–121
    auto-generated imports for countdown
        clock, 121
    contents before constructor in DiceOut,
        288–290
    for countdown clock, generally, 117
    of countdown clock, generally, 127
    for DiceOut game project, generally,
        284, 297
    display objects of countdown clock,
        122–123
    Document class in DiceOut, generally,
        284–288
    Document class in Flipr, 475–478
    ending game in DiceOut, 296
    event listeners in DiceOut, 290–292
    Flash project review in Flipr, 471–475
    for Flipr game project, generally, 471
    game board in Flipr, 491–492
    game logic in Flipr, 482–490
    game rules in Flipr, 494–500
    main controls in Flipr, 480–482
    player controls in Flipr, 494–500
    Project setup for countdown clock,
        117–118
    rolldie method in DiceOut Document
        class, 292–295
    score displays in Flipr, 493–494
    scores in DiceOut Document class, 296

splash screen in Flipr, 479
start button event listeners in
    countdown clock, 123
starting timer in countdown clock,
    124–125
timer and timer event listeners in
    countdown clock, 124
timer displays in Flipr, 493–494
timer events in countdown clock,
    125–126
Sound class, 374–375, 389
speaker-listener relationships. See also
    event listeners, 68
special key recognition, 251–253
specifications
    for countdown clock project, 114
    for DiceOut game project, 280
    for Flipr game project, 468
speed of startup, 370
splash screens
    displaying, 479
    in Document class, 476
    game logos on, 472
    introduction to, 469, 471
splice() method, 268–269
Sprite class, 302–307
sprites
    class of, generally, 302–303
    defined, 302
    extending classes of, 305–307
    in Flipr user interfaces, 471–472
stacks in Library. See also display stacks;
    Library objects, 23
Stage
    accepting values in functions on, 39–40
    accessing objects on, 5–7
    animation on. See animation
    comments on, creating, 31–32
    countdown clock on, 122–123
    display objects on, 122
    display properties of mobile
        applications on, 463
    display stacks, assigning properties to
        instances, 30
    display stacks, creating new objects
        for, 25–28
    display stacks, defined, 25
    display stacks, working with, 29–30
    dynamic event handlers for objects
        on, 85
    dynamically adding objects to. See
        dynamically adding objects
        to Stage

editing-in-place on, 85
    mouse event handlers on, 70
    named library assets in, 22–25
    parameters of objects on, 12–18
    playButton instance on, 85–86
    scaleMode property of, 406–409
    spaces, working with, 32
    summary of, 31
    tween-based animation on, 80
StageAlign property, 411
StageScaleMode, 406–409
stageWidth and stageHeight properties,
    328, 349
starfield project. See animation
startDrag method
    Boolean variables and, 198, 200
    summary of, 213
startGameButton, 472–474, 482
startMove method, 403
startTouchDrag method, 444, 447
startup times, 370
stop()
    in timeline playback, 82
    in timeline scripting, 97
    in timer intervals, 111
    for timers, 102–103
stopButton instance, 81–82, 90–93
stopDrag method, 198, 213
stops, gradient, 321
stopTouchDrag method, 444
Streak, 429, 505
streaming video, 376, 388
string concatenation, 44–45, 51–52
strings
    constructor parameters optional
        with, 150
    customizing multiple properties
        with, 148
    defined, 10
    defining variables for, 164
    getter method for, 165–167
    of lines, 310–311
    in method creation, 152
    private, 161, 163
    setter method for, 165–167
    text as, 10
    text field labels with, defining, 146
    var statement for, 133
    variables for, defining, 159
strokes, 307–312
Stucki, Ben, 464
style of lines, 307–308

style of text
  changing later, 233–234
  customizing, generally, 231–232
  fonts, creating custom, 234–237
subtraction operator, 50
SWF (ShockWave Flash), 370–372, 389
Symantec, 422
Symbol properties window, 135–136, 138
syntax errors, 46
System Chrome
  custom vs., 425
  dragging windows with, 401
  introduction to, 395–396

T

t operator, 53
tablets, 428–429
tap interactions. *See also* touch
  interactions, 439–442
target property, 89–92
testing
  Android applications, 504–505
  Boolean conditional, 258
  conditions. *See* testing conditions
  drag and drop, 218
  for equality, 194
  for false value, 217–218, 258
  for loop for, 258
  for inequality, 195–196
  iOS applications, 506–511
  location of objects, 46, 196–198
  mobile applications, 431–438, 465
  mobile devices for, 429–430
  NOT operator for, 218
  AND operator for, 217–220
  OR operator for, 218
  trace statement for, 202
  for true value, 217–218, 258
  x coordinate locations. *See* x coordinates
  y coordinate locations. *See* y coordinates
testing conditions. *See also* Boolean logic,
  advanced
  generally, 202–204
  if statements, 204–206
  if.else if statements, 209–212
  if.else statements, 206–208
  loops for, 258
text
  in button labels, 146
  fields of, 228–230, 242–245
  KeyboardEvent handler in TextFields,
    246–253

layout of, escape sequences in, 241–245
layout of, generally, 238–240
style of, changing later, 233–234
style of, creating custom fonts, 234–237
style of, customizing generally, 231–232
summary of, 251–253
working with, generally, 227
Text Layout Framework (TLF), 228
TextFormat class, 231–232
thermometers, 469, 474
ticking
  example of, 101–102
  generally, 100, 111
  stopping timers and, 102–103
Tile MovieClip, 498
tilePuzzleArray, 496–497
tiles
  arrays for values of, 489
  grid for, 469, 490–491
  specifications for, 468
tileVariety variable, 496–497
time-based animation
  introduction to, 334
  summary of, 366
  TimerEvent.TIMER for, 336–338
time + location, 334–335
timeline
  accepting values in functions on, 39
  animating thermometers with, 474
  class instances in, 144
  constructor parameters optional on, 150
  ENTER_FRAME event in, 104
  Flipr user interfaces on, 472
  frame scripts on, 8–10
  functions on, 36
  introduction to, 5
  layers of, 8
  mathematical operators in, 50, 53
  mouse event handlers in, 71
  in multiple property customizing,
    148–149
  new scripts, 25–26
  playback, 82
  scripting. *See* timeline scripting with
    mouse events
Timeline panel, 8, 26
timeline scripting with mouse events
  event callback objects in, finished
    example of, 92–94
  event callback objects in, generally,
    87–88
  event callback objects in, using, 89–92
  event target data example, 94–95

gotoAndStop() shortcuts for, 92
handling scope in, 87
introduction to, 79
in MovieClips, 85–86
playback, controlling generally, 81
playback, stopping, 81–83
playback, stopping at specific frames,
  83–84
project for (ball moving across screen),
  introducing, 80
simple callback functions in, 96
summary of, 97
Timer, defined, 100
TIMER event, 493
timer events
  callback functions for, 125–126
  frame events vs., 108–110
  introduction to, 99
  parameters of, 100
  stopping, 102–103
  summary of, 111
  using, 100–102
TIMER_COMPLETE event, 100–102
TimerEvent, 100
TimerEvent.TIMER, 336–338, 445
timers
  _timerSecond for game displays, 493
  in animation, 336–338
  displaying, 493–494
  event listeners for, 124
  events in. *See* timer events
  "Game Over" screen triggered by, 494
  gameTimer, 493–494
  intervals in, 355–358
  in mobile applications, 470
  resetTimer method for, 494
  setTimer method for, 494
  for splash screens, 479–480
  starting with callback functions,
    124–125
  ticking of, 100–103, 111
  TIMER event for game displays, 493
  _timerSecond, 493
Times New Roman, 231
times, startup, 370
TLF (Text Layout Framework), 228
toggle buttons, 218, 382–384
totalRight variable, 496, 498–499
touch interactions. *See also* gesture events
  creating, 439–442
  mouse events vs., 470
  splash screens and, 479
TOUCH_BEGIN event type, 443–448

TOUCH_END event type, 443–449
TouchEvent.TOUCH_TAP, 481
TouchGestures Document class, 450
TOUCH_INPUT interaction type, 442
TOUCH_POINT method, 441, 479
touchPointID, 444
trace statement
    arrays and, 266
    calling functions with, 44–47
    for conditionals testing, 202
    debugging on iOS with, 462
    defined, 10–12
    in timeline scripting, 89
TransformGestureEvent, 450–456
transparency, 308, 323
true value
    for loop testing for, 258
    introduction to, 17
    AND operator testing for, 217–218
    OR operator testing for, 218
tween-based animation, 80, 334
tweens, 80, 82
Twitter, 501
type mismatch error, 43
typeof statement, 52

U

UDID, 506
uint (unsigned integer), 259
URLs, 371–372, 378
USB debugging, 458, 504
user experience, 382, 389
user interfaces, 471–472

V

values
    accepting in functions, 39–43
    Boolean. See Boolean variables
    false. See false value
    of properties, 164
    returning from functions, 44–46
    true. See true value
    in window controls, 413–417
var statement
    for class variables, generally, 133
    in for loop, 259
    for mathematical operators, 56
    text fields, creating with, 228, 230

variables
    Boolean. See Boolean variables
    of classes, generally, 133
    defining, 159
    introduction to, 12
    of mathematical operators, 55–57
    private, 192–199
    specified as constant, 417
    tileVariety, 496–497
    totalRight, 496, 498–499
    var statement for, see var statement
vectors, 463
Verdana font, 234
VeriSign, 422
video from Web, 376–378
video playback
    altering generally, 379–382
    pausing, 382–384
    rewinding, 384–388
    seeking, 384–388
VideoButton class, 382–384
virtual pen, 310–315
visibility settings, 18
visual design review
    of countdown clock project, 115
    of DiceOut game project, 281–282
    of Flipr game project, 469

W

walkthroughs. See solutions and
    walkthroughs
while statement, 264
whitespace characters, 32, 38
width property of Stage objects, 413
WiFi, 460–461
window controls
    close, 404–406
    drag, 401–403
    maximize, 398–401
    minimize, 397–398
    native, 395–397
    resizable layouts of, 411–418
    resize, 406–410
Windows
    AIR applications for, 424
    desktop applications for, 394
    Start Menu in, 420, 424
    testing Android devices in, 504
    testing iOS applications and, 508
wireframes, 114–115

with statement, 311–312, 328
workspace for ActionScript development,
    136–137

X

x coordinates
    in adding animation elements, 358–361
    in animation brightness, 352–355
    in animation fine-tuning, generally, 349
    in animation fluidity and rate of
        change, 355–358
    curveTo method and, 312–315
    feedback identifying, 200–201
    for Flipr game board, 491
    if statement testing, 204–206
    if.else if statement testing, 209–212
    if.else statement testing, 206–208
    introduction to, 12–15
    in loops animating multiple objects,
        343–348
    AND operators testing, 219–220
    in random animation, 339–342
    in scaling size of animation elements,
        361–365
    testing for, 196–200, 202–203
    window control buttons on, 412–413

Y

y coordinates
    in adding animation elements, 358–361
    in animation brightness, 352–355
    in animation fine-tuning, generally, 349
    in animation fluidity and rate of
        change, 355–358
    curveTo method and, 312–315
    feedback identifying, 200–201
    for Flipr game board, 492
    if statement testing, 204–206
    if.else if statement testing, 209–212
    if.else statement testing, 206–208
    introduction to, 12–15
    in loops animating multiple objects,
        343–348
    AND operators testing, 219–220
    in random animation, 339–342
    in scaling size of animation elements,
        361–365
    testing for, 196–200, 202–203
    window control buttons on, 412–413